FREE Study Skills DVD Offer

Dear Customer,

Thank you for your purchase from Mometrix! We consider it an honor and a privilege that you have purchased our product and we want to ensure your satisfaction.

As a way of showing our appreciation and to help us better serve you, we have developed a Study Skills DVD that we would like to give you for FREE. This DVD covers our *best practices* for getting ready for your exam, from how to use our study materials to how to best prepare for the day of the test.

All that we ask is that you email us with feedback that would describe your experience so far with our product. Good, bad, or indifferent, we want to know what you think!

To get your FREE Study Skills DVD, email freedvd@mometrix.com with *FREE STUDY SKILLS DVD* in the subject line and the following information in the body of the email:

- The name of the product you purchased.
- Your product rating on a scale of 1-5, with 5 being the highest rating.
- Your feedback. It can be long, short, or anything in between. We just want to know your impressions and experience so far with our product. (Good feedback might include how our study material met your needs and ways we might be able to make it even better. You could highlight features that you found helpful or features that you think we should add.)
- Your full name and shipping address where you would like us to send your free DVD.

If you have any questions or concerns, please don't hesitate to contact me directly.

Thanks again!

Sincerely,

Jay Willis
Vice President
jay.willis@mometrix.com
1-800-673-8175

PMP

Exam Prep 2021 & 2022

Project Management Professional Certification Secrets Study Guide

Full-Length Practice Test

Step-by-Step Review Video Tutorials

Updated for the PMBOK Guide, 6th Edition Book

Written and edited by Mometrix Test Preparation

Printed in the United States of America

This paper meets the requirements of ANSI/NISO Z39.48-1992 (Permanence of Paper).

Paperback
ISBN 13: 978-1-5167-1516-9
ISBN 10: 1-5167-1516-0

DEAR FUTURE EXAM SUCCESS STORY

First of all, **THANK YOU** for purchasing Mometrix study materials!

Second, congratulations! You are one of the few determined test-takers who are committed to doing whatever it takes to excel on your exam. **You have come to the right place.** We developed these study materials with one goal in mind: to deliver you the information you need in a format that's concise and easy to use.

In addition to optimizing your guide for the content of the test, we've outlined our recommended steps for breaking down the preparation process into small, attainable goals so you can make sure you stay on track.

We've also analyzed the entire test-taking process, identifying the most common pitfalls and showing how you can overcome them and be ready for any curveball the test throws you.

Standardized testing is one of the biggest obstacles on your road to success, which only increases the importance of doing well in the high-pressure, high-stakes environment of test day. Your results on this test could have a significant impact on your future, and this guide provides the information and practical advice to help you achieve your full potential on test day.

Your success is our success

We would love to hear from you! If you would like to share the story of your exam success or if you have any questions or comments in regard to our products, please contact us at **800-673-8175** or **support@mometrix.com**.

Thanks again for your business and we wish you continued success!

Sincerely,
The Mometrix Test Preparation Team

Need more help? Check out our flashcards at:
http://mometrixflashcards.com/PMP

Written and edited by the Mometrix Exam Secrets Test Prep Team
Printed in the United States of America

TABLE OF CONTENTS

Introduction

Thank you for purchasing this resource! You have made the choice to prepare yourself for a test that could have a huge impact on your future, and this guide is designed to help you be fully ready for test day. Obviously, it's important to have a solid understanding of the test material, but you also need to be prepared for the unique environment and stressors of the test, so that you can perform to the best of your abilities.

For this purpose, the first section that appears in this guide is the **Secret Keys**. We've devoted countless hours to meticulously researching what works and what doesn't, and we've boiled down our findings to the five most impactful steps you can take to improve your performance on the test. We start at the beginning with study planning and move through the preparation process, all the way to the testing strategies that will help you get the most out of what you know when you're finally sitting in front of the test.

We recommend that you start preparing for your test as far in advance as possible. However, if you've bought this guide as a last-minute study resource and only have a few days before your test, we recommend that you skip over the first two Secret Keys since they address a long-term study plan.

If you struggle with **test anxiety**, we strongly encourage you to check out our recommendations for how you can overcome it. Test anxiety is a formidable foe, but it can be beaten, and we want to make sure you have the tools you need to defeat it.

Secret Key #1 – Plan Big, Study Small

There's a lot riding on your performance. If you want to ace this test, you're going to need to keep your skills sharp and the material fresh in your mind. You need a plan that lets you review everything you need to know while still fitting in your schedule. We'll break this strategy down into three categories.

Information Organization

Start with the information you already have: the official test outline. From this, you can make a complete list of all the concepts you need to cover before the test. Organize these concepts into groups that can be studied together, and create a list of any related vocabulary you need to learn so you can brush up on any difficult terms. You'll want to keep this vocabulary list handy once you actually start studying since you may need to add to it along the way.

Time Management

Once you have your set of study concepts, decide how to spread them out over the time you have left before the test. Break your study plan into small, clear goals so you have a manageable task for each day and know exactly what you're doing. Then just focus on one small step at a time. When you manage your time this way, you don't need to spend hours at a time studying. Studying a small block of content for a short period each day helps you retain information better and avoid stressing over how much you have left to do. You can relax knowing that you have a plan to cover everything in time. In order for this strategy to be effective though, you have to start studying early and stick to your schedule. Avoid the exhaustion and futility that comes from last-minute cramming!

Study Environment

The environment you study in has a big impact on your learning. Studying in a coffee shop, while probably more enjoyable, is not likely to be as fruitful as studying in a quiet room. It's important to keep distractions to a minimum. You're only planning to study for a short block of time, so make the most of it. Don't pause to check your phone or get up to find a snack. It's also important to **avoid multitasking**. Research has consistently shown that multitasking will make your studying dramatically less effective. Your study area should also be comfortable and well-lit so you don't have the distraction of straining your eyes or sitting on an uncomfortable chair.

The time of day you study is also important. You want to be rested and alert. Don't wait until just before bedtime. Study when you'll be most likely to comprehend and remember. Even better, if you know what time of day your test will be, set that time aside for study. That way your brain will be used to working on that subject at that specific time and you'll have a better chance of recalling information.

Finally, it can be helpful to team up with others who are studying for the same test. Your actual studying should be done in as isolated an environment as possible, but the work of organizing the information and setting up the study plan can be divided up. In between study sessions, you can discuss with your teammates the concepts that you're all studying and quiz each other on the details. Just be sure that your teammates are as serious about the test as you are. If you find that your study time is being replaced with social time, you might need to find a new team.

Secret Key #2 – Make Your Studying Count

You're devoting a lot of time and effort to preparing for this test, so you want to be absolutely certain it will pay off. This means doing more than just reading the content and hoping you can remember it on test day. It's important to make every minute of study count. There are two main areas you can focus on to make your studying count:

Retention

It doesn't matter how much time you study if you can't remember the material. You need to make sure you are retaining the concepts. To check your retention of the information you're learning, try recalling it at later times with minimal prompting. Try carrying around flashcards and glance at one or two from time to time or ask a friend who's also studying for the test to quiz you.

To enhance your retention, look for ways to put the information into practice so that you can apply it rather than simply recalling it. If you're using the information in practical ways, it will be much easier to remember. Similarly, it helps to solidify a concept in your mind if you're not only reading it to yourself but also explaining it to someone else. Ask a friend to let you teach them about a concept you're a little shaky on (or speak aloud to an imaginary audience if necessary). As you try to summarize, define, give examples, and answer your friend's questions, you'll understand the concepts better and they will stay with you longer. Finally, step back for a big picture view and ask yourself how each piece of information fits with the whole subject. When you link the different concepts together and see them working together as a whole, it's easier to remember the individual components.

Finally, practice showing your work on any multi-step problems, even if you're just studying. Writing out each step you take to solve a problem will help solidify the process in your mind, and you'll be more likely to remember it during the test.

Modality

Modality simply refers to the means or method by which you study. Choosing a study modality that fits your own individual learning style is crucial. No two people learn best in exactly the same way, so it's important to know your strengths and use them to your advantage.

For example, if you learn best by visualization, focus on visualizing a concept in your mind and draw an image or a diagram. Try color-coding your notes, illustrating them, or creating symbols that will trigger your mind to recall a learned concept. If you learn best by hearing or discussing information, find a study partner who learns the same way or read aloud to yourself. Think about how to put the information in your own words. Imagine that you are giving a lecture on the topic and record yourself so you can listen to it later.

For any learning style, flashcards can be helpful. Organize the information so you can take advantage of spare moments to review. Underline key words or phrases. Use different colors for different categories. Mnemonic devices (such as creating a short list in which every item starts with the same letter) can also help with retention. Find what works best for you and use it to store the information in your mind most effectively and easily.

Secret Key #3 – Practice the Right Way

Your success on test day depends not only on how many hours you put into preparing, but also on whether you prepared the right way. It's good to check along the way to see if your studying is paying off. One of the most effective ways to do this is by taking practice tests to evaluate your progress. Practice tests are useful because they show exactly where you need to improve. Every time you take a practice test, pay special attention to these three groups of questions:

- The questions you got wrong
- The questions you had to guess on, even if you guessed right
- The questions you found difficult or slow to work through

This will show you exactly what your weak areas are, and where you need to devote more study time. Ask yourself why each of these questions gave you trouble. Was it because you didn't understand the material? Was it because you didn't remember the vocabulary? Do you need more repetitions on this type of question to build speed and confidence? Dig into those questions and figure out how you can strengthen your weak areas as you go back to review the material.

Additionally, many practice tests have a section explaining the answer choices. It can be tempting to read the explanation and think that you now have a good understanding of the concept. However, an explanation likely only covers part of the question's broader context. Even if the explanation makes sense, **go back and investigate** every concept related to the question until you're positive you have a thorough understanding.

As you go along, keep in mind that the practice test is just that: practice. Memorizing these questions and answers will not be very helpful on the actual test because it is unlikely to have any of the same exact questions. If you only know the right answers to the sample questions, you won't be prepared for the real thing. **Study the concepts** until you understand them fully, and then you'll be able to answer any question that shows up on the test.

It's important to wait on the practice tests until you're ready. If you take a test on your first day of study, you may be overwhelmed by the amount of material covered and how much you need to learn. Work up to it gradually.

On test day, you'll need to be prepared for answering questions, managing your time, and using the test-taking strategies you've learned. It's a lot to balance, like a mental marathon that will have a big impact on your future. Like training for a marathon, you'll need to start slowly and work your way up. When test day arrives, you'll be ready.

Start with the strategies you've read in the first two Secret Keys—plan your course and study in the way that works best for you. If you have time, consider using multiple study resources to get different approaches to the same concepts. It can be helpful to see difficult concepts from more than one angle. Then find a good source for practice tests. Many times, the test website will suggest potential study resources or provide sample tests.

Practice Test Strategy

If you're able to find at least three practice tests, we recommend this strategy:

Untimed and Open-Book Practice

Take the first test with no time constraints and with your notes and study guide handy. Take your time and focus on applying the strategies you've learned.

Timed and Open-Book Practice

Take the second practice test open-book as well, but set a timer and practice pacing yourself to finish in time.

Timed and Closed-Book Practice

Take any other practice tests as if it were test day. Set a timer and put away your study materials. Sit at a table or desk in a quiet room, imagine yourself at the testing center, and answer questions as quickly and accurately as possible.

Keep repeating timed and closed-book tests on a regular basis until you run out of practice tests or it's time for the actual test. Your mind will be ready for the schedule and stress of test day, and you'll be able to focus on recalling the material you've learned.

Secret Key #4 – Pace Yourself

Once you're fully prepared for the material on the test, your biggest challenge on test day will be managing your time. Just knowing that the clock is ticking can make you panic even if you have plenty of time left. Work on pacing yourself so you can build confidence against the time constraints of the exam. Pacing is a difficult skill to master, especially in a high-pressure environment, so **practice is vital**.

Set time expectations for your pace based on how much time is available. For example, if a section has 60 questions and the time limit is 30 minutes, you know you have to average 30 seconds or less per question in order to answer them all. Although 30 seconds is the hard limit, set 25 seconds per question as your goal, so you reserve extra time to spend on harder questions. When you budget extra time for the harder questions, you no longer have any reason to stress when those questions take longer to answer.

Don't let this time expectation distract you from working through the test at a calm, steady pace, but keep it in mind so you don't spend too much time on any one question. Recognize that taking extra time on one question you don't understand may keep you from answering two that you do understand later in the test. If your time limit for a question is up and you're still not sure of the answer, mark it and move on, and come back to it later if the time and the test format allow. If the testing format doesn't allow you to return to earlier questions, just make an educated guess; then put it out of your mind and move on.

On the easier questions, be careful not to rush. It may seem wise to hurry through them so you have more time for the challenging ones, but it's not worth missing one if you know the concept and just didn't take the time to read the question fully. Work efficiently but make sure you understand the question and have looked at all of the answer choices, since more than one may seem right at first.

Even if you're paying attention to the time, you may find yourself a little behind at some point. You should speed up to get back on track, but do so wisely. Don't panic; just take a few seconds less on each question until you're caught up. Don't guess without thinking, but do look through the answer choices and eliminate any you know are wrong. If you can get down to two choices, it is often worthwhile to guess from those. Once you've chosen an answer, move on and don't dwell on any that you skipped or had to hurry through. If a question was taking too long, chances are it was one of the harder ones, so you weren't as likely to get it right anyway.

On the other hand, if you find yourself getting ahead of schedule, it may be beneficial to slow down a little. The more quickly you work, the more likely you are to make a careless mistake that will affect your score. You've budgeted time for each question, so don't be afraid to spend that time. Practice an efficient but careful pace to get the most out of the time you have.

Secret Key #5 – Have a Plan for Guessing

When you're taking the test, you may find yourself stuck on a question. Some of the answer choices seem better than others, but you don't see the one answer choice that is obviously correct. What do you do?

The scenario described above is very common, yet most test takers have not effectively prepared for it. Developing and practicing a plan for guessing may be one of the single most effective uses of your time as you get ready for the exam.

In developing your plan for guessing, there are three questions to address:

- When should you start the guessing process?
- How should you narrow down the choices?
- Which answer should you choose?

When to Start the Guessing Process

Unless your plan for guessing is to select C every time (which, despite its merits, is not what we recommend), you need to leave yourself enough time to apply your answer elimination strategies. Since you have a limited amount of time for each question, that means that if you're going to give yourself the best shot at guessing correctly, you have to decide quickly whether or not you will guess.

Of course, the best-case scenario is that you don't have to guess at all, so first, see if you can answer the question based on your knowledge of the subject and basic reasoning skills. Focus on the key words in the question and try to jog your memory of related topics. Give yourself a chance to bring the knowledge to mind, but once you realize that you don't have (or you can't access) the knowledge you need to answer the question, it's time to start the guessing process.

It's almost always better to start the guessing process too early than too late. It only takes a few seconds to remember something and answer the question from knowledge. Carefully eliminating wrong answer choices takes longer. Plus, going through the process of eliminating answer choices can actually help jog your memory.

Summary: Start the guessing process as soon as you decide that you can't answer the question based on your knowledge.

How to Narrow Down the Choices

The next chapter in this book (**Test-Taking Strategies**) includes a wide range of strategies for how to approach questions and how to look for answer choices to eliminate. You will definitely want to read those carefully, practice them, and figure out which ones work best for you. Here though, we're going to address a mindset rather than a particular strategy.

Your chances of guessing an answer correctly depend on how many options you are choosing from.

How many choices you have	How likely you are to guess correctly
5	20%
4	25%
3	33%
2	50%
1	100%

You can see from this chart just how valuable it is to be able to eliminate incorrect answers and make an educated guess, but there are two things that many test takers do that cause them to miss out on the benefits of guessing:

- Accidentally eliminating the correct answer
- Selecting an answer based on an impression

We'll look at the first one here, and the second one in the next section.

To avoid accidentally eliminating the correct answer, we recommend a thought exercise called **the $5 challenge**. In this challenge, you only eliminate an answer choice from contention if you are willing to bet $5 on it being wrong. Why $5? Five dollars is a small but not insignificant amount of money. It's an amount you could afford to lose but wouldn't want to throw away. And while losing $5 once might not hurt too much, doing it twenty times will set you back $100. In the same way, each small decision you make—eliminating a choice here, guessing on a question there—won't by itself impact your score very much, but when you put them all together, they can make a big difference. By holding each answer choice elimination decision to a higher standard, you can reduce the risk of accidentally eliminating the correct answer.

The $5 challenge can also be applied in a positive sense: If you are willing to bet $5 that an answer choice *is* correct, go ahead and mark it as correct.

Summary: Only eliminate an answer choice if you are willing to bet $5 that it is wrong.

Which Answer to Choose

You're taking the test. You've run into a hard question and decided you'll have to guess. You've eliminated all the answer choices you're willing to bet $5 on. Now you have to pick an answer. Why do we even need to talk about this? Why can't you just pick whichever one you feel like when the time comes?

The answer to these questions is that if you don't come into the test with a plan, you'll rely on your impression to select an answer choice, and if you do that, you risk falling into a trap. The test writers know that everyone who takes their test will be guessing on some of the questions, so they intentionally write wrong answer choices to seem plausible. You still have to pick an answer though, and if the wrong answer choices are designed to look right, how can you ever be sure that you're not falling for their trap? The best solution we've found to this dilemma is to take the decision out of your hands entirely. Here is the process we recommend:

Once you've eliminated any choices that you are confident (willing to bet $5) are wrong, select the first remaining choice as your answer.

Whether you choose to select the first remaining choice, the second, or the last, the important thing is that you use some preselected standard. Using this approach guarantees that you will not be enticed into selecting an answer choice that looks right, because you are not basing your decision on how the answer choices look.

This is not meant to make you question your knowledge. Instead, it is to help you recognize the difference between your knowledge and your impressions. There's a huge difference between thinking an answer is right because of what you know, and thinking an answer is right because it looks or sounds like it should be right.

Summary: To ensure that your selection is appropriately random, make a predetermined selection from among all answer choices you have not eliminated.

Test-Taking Strategies

This section contains a list of test-taking strategies that you may find helpful as you work through the test. By taking what you know and applying logical thought, you can maximize your chances of answering any question correctly!

It is very important to realize that every question is different and every person is different: no single strategy will work on every question, and no single strategy will work for every person. That's why we've included all of them here, so you can try them out and determine which ones work best for different types of questions and which ones work best for you.

Question Strategies

Read Carefully

Read the question and answer choices carefully. Don't miss the question because you misread the terms. You have plenty of time to read each question thoroughly and make sure you understand what is being asked. Yet a happy medium must be attained, so don't waste too much time. You must read carefully, but efficiently.

Contextual Clues

Look for contextual clues. If the question includes a word you are not familiar with, look at the immediate context for some indication of what the word might mean. Contextual clues can often give you all the information you need to decipher the meaning of an unfamiliar word. Even if you can't determine the meaning, you may be able to narrow down the possibilities enough to make a solid guess at the answer to the question.

Prefixes

If you're having trouble with a word in the question or answer choices, try dissecting it. Take advantage of every clue that the word might include. Prefixes and suffixes can be a huge help. Usually they allow you to determine a basic meaning. Pre- means before, post- means after, pro - is positive, de- is negative. From prefixes and suffixes, you can get an idea of the general meaning of the word and try to put it into context.

Hedge Words

Watch out for critical hedge words, such as *likely, may, can, sometimes, often, almost, mostly, usually, generally, rarely,* and *sometimes.* Question writers insert these hedge phrases to cover every possibility. Often an answer choice will be wrong simply because it leaves no room for exception. Be on guard for answer choices that have definitive words such as *exactly* and *always.*

Switchback Words

Stay alert for *switchbacks.* These are the words and phrases frequently used to alert you to shifts in thought. The most common switchback words are *but, although,* and *however.* Others include *nevertheless, on the other hand, even though, while, in spite of, despite, regardless of.* Switchback words are important to catch because they can change the direction of the question or an answer choice.

Face Value

When in doubt, use common sense. Accept the situation in the problem at face value. Don't read too much into it. These problems will not require you to make wild assumptions. If you have to go beyond creativity and warp time or space in order to have an answer choice fit the question, then you should move on and consider the other answer choices. These are normal problems rooted in reality. The applicable relationship or explanation may not be readily apparent, but it is there for you to figure out. Use your common sense to interpret anything that isn't clear.

Answer Choice Strategies

Answer Selection

The most thorough way to pick an answer choice is to identify and eliminate wrong answers until only one is left, then confirm it is the correct answer. Sometimes an answer choice may immediately seem right, but be careful. The test writers will usually put more than one reasonable answer choice on each question, so take a second to read all of them and make sure that the other choices are not equally obvious. As long as you have time left, it is better to read every answer choice than to pick the first one that looks right without checking the others.

Answer Choice Families

An answer choice family consists of two (in rare cases, three) answer choices that are very similar in construction and cannot all be true at the same time. If you see two answer choices that are direct opposites or parallels, one of them is usually the correct answer. For instance, if one answer choice says that quantity x increases and another either says that quantity x decreases (opposite) or says that quantity y increases (parallel), then those answer choices would fall into the same family. An answer choice that doesn't match the construction of the answer choice family is more likely to be incorrect. Most questions will not have answer choice families, but when they do appear, you should be prepared to recognize them.

Eliminate Answers

Eliminate answer choices as soon as you realize they are wrong, but make sure you consider all possibilities. If you are eliminating answer choices and realize that the last one you are left with is also wrong, don't panic. Start over and consider each choice again. There may be something you missed the first time that you will realize on the second pass.

Avoid Fact Traps

Don't be distracted by an answer choice that is factually true but doesn't answer the question. You are looking for the choice that answers the question. Stay focused on what the question is asking for so you don't accidentally pick an answer that is true but incorrect. Always go back to the question and make sure the answer choice you've selected actually answers the question and is not merely a true statement.

Extreme Statements

In general, you should avoid answers that put forth extreme actions as standard practice or proclaim controversial ideas as established fact. An answer choice that states the "process should be used in certain situations, if..." is much more likely to be correct than one that states the "process should be discontinued completely." The first is a calm rational statement and doesn't even make a definitive, uncompromising stance, using a hedge word *if* to provide wiggle room, whereas the second choice is a radical idea and far more extreme.

Benchmark

As you read through the answer choices and you come across one that seems to answer the question well, mentally select that answer choice. This is not your final answer, but it's the one that will help you evaluate the other answer choices. The one that you selected is your benchmark or standard for judging each of the other answer choices. Every other answer choice must be compared to your benchmark. That choice is correct until proven otherwise by another answer choice beating it. If you find a better answer, then that one becomes your new benchmark. Once you've decided that no other choice answers the question as well as your benchmark, you have your final answer.

Predict the Answer

Before you even start looking at the answer choices, it is often best to try to predict the answer. When you come up with the answer on your own, it is easier to avoid distractions and traps because you will know exactly what to look for. The right answer choice is unlikely to be word-for-word what you came up with, but it should be a close match. Even if you are confident that you have the right answer, you should still take the time to read each option before moving on.

General Strategies

Tough Questions

If you are stumped on a problem or it appears too hard or too difficult, don't waste time. Move on! Remember though, if you can quickly check for obviously incorrect answer choices, your chances of guessing correctly are greatly improved. Before you completely give up, at least try to knock out a couple of possible answers. Eliminate what you can and then guess at the remaining answer choices before moving on.

Check Your Work

Since you will probably not know every term listed and the answer to every question, it is important that you get credit for the ones that you do know. Don't miss any questions through careless mistakes. If at all possible, try to take a second to look back over your answer selection and make sure you've selected the correct answer choice and haven't made a costly careless mistake (such as marking an answer choice that you didn't mean to mark). This quick double check should more than pay for itself in caught mistakes for the time it costs.

Pace Yourself

It's easy to be overwhelmed when you're looking at a page full of questions; your mind is confused and full of random thoughts, and the clock is ticking down faster than you would like. Calm down and maintain the pace that you have set for yourself. Especially as you get down to the last few minutes of the test, don't let the small numbers on the clock make you panic. As long as you are on track by monitoring your pace, you are guaranteed to have time for each question.

Don't Rush

It is very easy to make errors when you are in a hurry. Maintaining a fast pace in answering questions is pointless if it makes you miss questions that you would have gotten right otherwise. Test writers like to include distracting information and wrong answers that seem right. Taking a little extra time to avoid careless mistakes can make all the difference in your test score. Find a pace that allows you to be confident in the answers that you select.

Keep Moving

Panicking will not help you pass the test, so do your best to stay calm and keep moving. Taking deep breaths and going through the answer elimination steps you practiced can help to break through a stress barrier and keep your pace.

Final Notes

The combination of a solid foundation of content knowledge and the confidence that comes from practicing your plan for applying that knowledge is the key to maximizing your performance on test day. As your foundation of content knowledge is built up and strengthened, you'll find that the strategies included in this chapter become more and more effective in helping you quickly sift through the distractions and traps of the test to isolate the correct answer.

Now it's time to move on to the test content chapters of this book, but be sure to keep your goal in mind. As you read, think about how you will be able to apply this information on the test. If you've already seen sample questions for the test and you have an idea of the question format and style, try to come up with questions of your own that you can answer based on what you're reading. This will give you valuable practice applying your knowledge in the same ways you can expect to on test day.

Good luck and good studying!

Foundational Elements

Projects

PROJECT

A project is officially defined by the Project Management Institute as "a temporary endeavor undertaken to create a unique product, service, or result." A project typically consists of many phases that essentially serve to plan, procure, execute, and communicate the project. Projects, and their subcomponents called deliverables, are the events that are performed to achieve broader organizational objectives. Projects themselves may have objectives that link to the project deliverables that serve as evidence of success. Projects can be executed by individuals or small teams as well as by large improvement groups and up to complex multinational organizations. The project is temporary in the sense that a defined start date and end date are expected and essential to planning. Examples of projects include quality improvement initiatives, building construction, developing a new consumer product, launching a space satellite, field research in economics, and retooling a factory.

COMMON DELIVERABLES RESULTING FROM PROJECTS

The four most common deliverables in project management reflect the elements of the definition of a project. Unique services or the ability to perform such services may be considered a deliverable. Service projects often require data and performance indicators to provide a form of evidence of completion. Unique products as a deliverable can be a new consumer good, a part or component to another good, or the improvement upon an existing product or service. Deliverables that result from a unique results project may include finished research, gained knowledge or skill, and marketplace performance. The final form of deliverable is a combination of the three. Due to the complexity of organizations, societal needs, and business organizations, deliverable combination is widely expected.

CREATION OF BUSINESS VALUE THROUGH SUCCESSFUL EXECUTION OF PROJECTS

In business, government, and non-profit organizations, projects are not performed for isolated and non-impactful results. Projects, especially those that are tied to organizational or strategic objectives, are evidence of organizational change. Projects service to transform all or part of organizations from a lower former state to an improved, stronger, and more competitive future state. Projects can vary in how much change they create and how widely across an organization or marketplace they can influence. Nonetheless, the incremental progress of project deliverables and completion of projects serves to transform and ultimately create business value or stronger achievement of an organizations mission. For example, a for-profit company can understate an operational improvement project to reduce costs by several hundred million dollars. Business value may materialize as stronger stock performance, greater market share, higher profits, higher revenues, or brand reputation. A non-profit organization may perform a project to launch a new fundraising initiative in a new continent or country where their mission can grow. Non-profit value creation can include stronger financial security, wider influence, higher membership, lower costs, and public benefits.

Importance of Project Management

Project Management

Project management is defined as the discipline of achieving project objectives through the skillful use of communication, knowledge, tools, and resources. Effective project management facilitates organizational improvement and achievement of the desired future state of the organization. Project management is used to efficiently and effectively achieve planned project objectives. As a set of tools and behaviors, project management also allows individuals, teams and organizations to satisfy stakeholders, meet broader strategic or business goals, better use limited resources, and execute projects on-time and on-budget. Furthermore, the premise of project management can be described as valid methods used to achieve project outcomes under financial, time, and resource constraints. When executed effectively, project management is a transformative discipline for organizations seeking growth, improvement, and excellence.

Positive Results of Well Managed Projects and Negative Results of Poorly Managed Projects

When projects are well managed, positive results can include building stakeholder and shareholder value, balanced use of scarce organizational resources, improved project predictability, and the timeliness of delivering the right market needs at the right timeframe. Additional benefits of well executed project management include risk-mitigating effects, such as the prevention and mitigating responsiveness to project problems, resource constraint mitigation, and disciplined change management. Alternatively, poorly managed projects can succumb to failures, such as project delays, cost overruns, poor quality deliverables, unclear or unbounded scope expansion, rework and waste, and dissatisfied customers and stakeholders.

Relationship of Project, Portfolio, Program, and Operations Management

Projects, Portfolios, and Programs

Organizations may use a hierarchy of project management systems to achieve larger organizational change and meet objectives. At the base of the hierarchy is the project itself. Programs are defined as a collective series of interrelated projects and related supporting program administrative activities that all support a related objective or strategic goal. Programs are often used to coordinate the resources and benefits of multiple projects, though not necessarily on a wide or expansive scale. Portfolios are used by larger organizations and multinational corporations to coordinate programs and sub-projects on a larger scope. Project, program, and portfolio managers all utilize project management principles, yet must be cognizant of the resource constraints created with multiple layers of management working towards strategic accomplishment. Practices such as portfolio review, project executive oversight, and strategic alignment can all play important roles in coordinating these hierarchical project scales.

Program Management and Interdependency Management

Program management is a broader classification of the project management discipline where multiple projects within an affiliated scope or strategic focus can be grouped into a larger collective called a program. These programs of projects are often of great complexity, with multitudes more resources and communication than the typical project. Program management has a longer life-cycle, broader scope, and higher-level planning than underlying projects. The high-level planning by program managers must account for the interdependency of the components, subprojects, and shared resources within the organization between other programs and projects, not simply within one project itself. Program managers must monitor interdependencies such as continued scope alignment, risks, resource conflicts and constraints, change requests, budget overlaps, and benefits realization. Program management has a defined standard as supplement to the project management professional certification.

Portfolio Management

Portfolio management is defined as the oversight and management of an array of programs, projects, and supporting activities, but it is more closely tied to execution of overall organizational strategy and objectives. Though the projects and programs within portfolios are interdependent and interrelated, this is not necessarily always the case. The function of portfolio management includes steering programs and projects to maximize organizational return on investment, steer program and project economics, optimize project and program timing to meet organizational strategy, centralize common tasks and resources where needed, provide strategic decision-making, and influence investment decisions by the organization as it relates to strategy. Certain projects and programs that most heavily impact positive strategic outcomes must be given priority regarding schedule and resources.

Operations Management

Operations management is the planning and execution of business operations activities to meet customer demands for goods and services. Operations management is concerned with the activities that are required to transform raw materials and inputs into sellable outputs meeting customer quality expectations. Though not directly an aspect of project management, both disciplines can occur simultaneously in an organization and have to compete for shared financial, personnel, and scheduling resources. Projects may be undertaken that positively or negatively affect operations. Likewise, operational needs may influence when projects can be scheduled and completed. Projects are undertaken often to support and improve operations, as well as to build new business opportunities to increase the activity of operations. Examples of the intersection of operations management and project management include continuous improvement efforts such as lean or Six Sigma, new product development and piloting, infrastructure improvement to expand operations, and strategic maintenance activities.

Organizational Project Management

The interaction of projects, programs, and portfolios within an organization seeking to achieve strategic business objectives often requires that an organization use organizational project management (OPM) to better coordinate all such efforts efficiently. The correct allocation of resources and selection of projects that align and best achieve strategic objectives are the primary goals of OPM. Communication of the organization's strategic objectives and deliverables as they relate to the projects and programs being pursued is also a goal of OPM.

Key Project Components

Project Life Cycle and Development Life Cycle

Project life-cycle is defined by the Project Management Institute as the ordered set of phases that a project flows through from its start through its completion. The project life cycle has a common framework pattern that generally remains consistent regardless of the specific goals or outcomes being sought. Generally, life cycle phases can be summarized to include the start, preparation, execution, and closing; different models of the life cycles can have differences in how these phases are performed. Project life cycles are classified as either predictive or adaptive, depending upon when planning and adjustments are made to the cycle. Adaptive projects have a predetermined scope in the start phase but continue with increased agility in the face of changes. Predictive project models are more traditional and take a waterfall approach. Early scope, cost, and resource decisions are made and strong control is placed on the flow of the project. Development life cycles also include iterative models, where the project scope is set, but cost and resource decisions are made as the project evolves over time; and incremental models, where functionality is added over a set schedule to achieve the deliverable.

Type of life cycle	Development	Project
Models Commonly Used	**Predictive** (waterfall) – Set scope, costs, resources early; strong control on execution	
	Adaptive – Set scope early and adjust execution and resources with agility.	
	Iterative – early scope, resource decisions made as project evolves	
	Incremental – functionality added in a set timeframe to achieve deliverable.	
	Hybrid – blend of predictive and adaptive models.	

Project Phase

A project phase is defined as a group of common and logically similar activities that are performed simultaneously or sequentially in a project in order to complete a deliverable or milestone that signifies the transition into a new or next phase. Phases can be communicated as numerical, alphabetical, by duration, by the types of resources being developed, or using the key deliverable(s) that conclude the phase. Furthermore, projects may be broken down into common colloquial terms based on the typical deliverables that similar projects require. For example, a project to launch a new consumer product would likely include phases such as research and development, consumer testing, and packaging design. The phase concept to projects allows compartmentalization of the tasks and milestones, division of labor, and paced execution needed to achieve the final goals.

Phase Gate

The phase gate is a figurative point at the end of each phase where project management and/or organization decision makers determine if the phase outcome has been successful and how the project should continue. Previous performance indicators are reviewed based on what was performed in the phase to that point. Decision makers determine based on the data if they should move on to the next phase, adjust their approach to the project and move to the next phase, repeat the phase, continue working on elements of the current phase, or to end the project entirely. Decision-makers are likely to use the project management plan, the project charter, strategic objectives, and other business-related data to make their determination to either go through the gate to the next phase or not. Phase gate steps are very common in product or service development projects where feasibility and design must be proven before launch.

Stage-Gate Process Flow

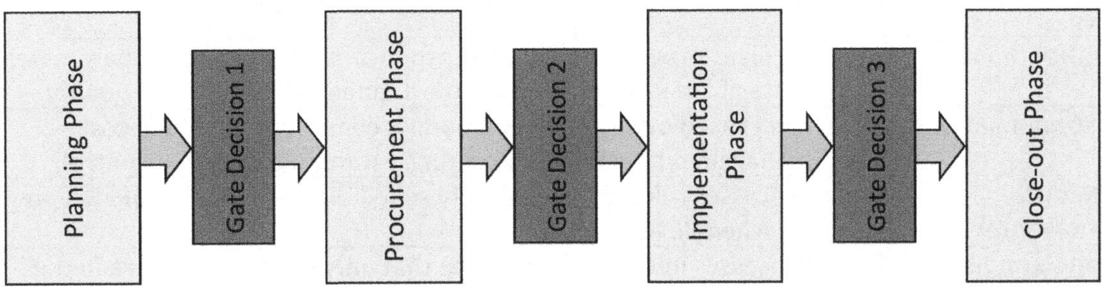

Project Management Processes and Process Categories

The execution of project management processes serves the project manager in keeping the project life-cycle on track. The concept of project management (PM) process is applicable across many industries that use project management techniques. The underlying concept of their use is that inputs entering a process become transformed using tools and techniques to create an output or outcome. That output or outcome of one process becomes either the input for a downstream process, a phase-completing deliverable, or a final project deliverable. Generally, PM processes can be categorized by their frequency of use: One-time predefined, recurring, or continuous. One-time pre-defined processes can include writing the charter or other unique actions to be taken. Recurring processes can include phase gates, resource procurements, or data analysis. Continuous processes are those that are fundamental to effective project management and can include examples such as monitoring, communication, and control activities.

Project Management Process Groups

Project management process groups are created when assessing and logically grouping related processes and activities into collective groups that support achievement of specific objectives in the project. While project phases follow a more time-based flow, process groups are not necessarily chronological and may draw from tasks in various points in the project. Process can be classified into five major groups: monitoring, planning, executing, initiating, and closing.

Process Group	Description
Initiating	Grouped activities that define the charter, team, working rules, new phases, and project authorization.
Planning	Activities that create the project scope, objectives, and project work-breakdown and schedule.
Executing	Activities that perform the planned work in the project.
Monitoring	Processes that oversee the use of time, resources, quality, and change management.
Closing	Processes used to complete phases or the project itself.

Project Management Knowledge Area

Project management knowledge areas (PMKAs) are essential disciplines within the project management professional body of knowledge. These knowledge areas are characterized by the relatively unique skill involved for the project manager to be successful in. Similar to process groups, knowledge groups are defined by their typical tasks, inputs, outputs, and tools used to transform. Each knowledge area requires different skill sets to achieve mastery, such as communication, time management, financial management, and stakeholder analysis.

Project Knowledge Area	Description
Quality management	Involves processes related to product or service quality parameters, voice of the customer, and project management process quality.
Cost management	Area based on financial and budget constraint involving cost management, financing, planning, estimating, and cost control.
Schedule management	Processes related to accurately scheduling the project and keeping it on schedule thereafter.
Scope management	Processes involved in ensuring that only the defined work in the project scope gets completed.
Integration management	Involves integrating and coordinating the activities within the project process groups.
Stakeholder management	Involves analyzing internal and external stakeholders and how the project progress and outcomes impact these important persons or organizations.
Procurement management	Processes involved in buying or obtaining the goods, services, and outcomes needed from contributors outside of the project team.
Risk management	Involves risk management studies and mitigation.
Communications management	Includes timely and accurate collection, distribution, and control of information.
Resource management	Involves the identification and attainment of the right resources for project completion.

Importance of Project Management Data and Information

An expected result of project management planning and execution is the generation of various forms of data that is analyzed, communicated, and ultimately transformed into useful information throughout the project life cycle that is further used for project decision-making. The resulting data and information can be both stored in a repository and communicated in progress reports to various stakeholders as necessary to the project team. Relevant terminology to the project management process is work performance. The term is used to refer specifically to data, information, and reports that arise from the project management process. Work performance data —such as activity completion dates, quality measurements, and completion progress—is raw data collected during the execution of the project and its knowledge areas. Work performance information is the result of data transformed through analysis to make project insights and decisions. Work performance reporting refers to relevant communications and summaries of critical data and information gained through the project management process.

Tailoring

Tailoring is defined as the appropriate application of the necessary inputs, tools, techniques, and phases to manage a given project effectively. The tailoring concept is used for project management because there is no one methodology applicable to all projects. Methodology for project management can vary based on expert insights, professional groups, third party vendors, and government agencies. Project managers are responsible for collaborating with stakeholders, the project team, organizational leadership, and persons overseeing resource allocation to tailor the project approach accordingly. Many factors must be considered, including timeframe, quality requirements, resource constraints, financial needs, internal and external stakeholders, and risk. These constraints can be competing with each other and will invariably drive tailoring decisions by the project manager.

Project Management Business Documents

Business Cases

The project business case document is used in the life cycle of the project to establish the economic feasibility and validity of the planned project. The business case justifies the start and continuation of the project. Business case files demonstrate, especially to stakeholders and public shareholders, that the undertaking of a certain project will be of benefit to the organization and be a value-added use of limited capital and human resources. The importance of such an approach is reflected in the preference for projects that align with organizational objectives and are a wise use of resources towards stated goals. The use of business cases to justify projects is common in continuous improvement initiatives such as lean or Six Sigma. The business case allows the project manager, project team, and project stakeholders to remain aligned during the execution of the project phases. After completing the project, the organization can reassess how well the project met the stated case and objectives, allowing for improvement in the alignment and strategic focus of future projects.

Business Benefits Management Plans

The business benefits management plan is a precursor document or set of documents that describe how and when the benefits of the project itself will be realized by the organization. The benefits management plan explains the specific mechanics of how the benefit is realized; business case files often serve as the input to create the benefit plan. The benefits plan serves to specifically show the financial and measurable gains that will be achieved. Thus, the benefits plan usually must begin with a baseline data analysis so that the improved state can be presented. The proposed future state is described in the early phases of the project. As the project nears completion or is fully completed, actual measurements of the improved state can be compiled and demonstrate the true benefit.

Project Charters

The project charter is an official documentation of the project's authorization—generally issued by the project sponsor or champion to a project manager—and signals the approval for the project to begin initial phases and resource procurement. The charter is a critical milestone in a project and reflects the organization's acknowledgement that the project meets strategic objectives and has a satisfactory business case and benefit to be pursued. The charter also initiates the use of the project management plan—a detailed account of how project resources will be utilized during the project life cycle. Key elements of the charter include project objectives, purpose, and deliverables needed for success. Secondary but important elements include explanation of risks, financial and time constraints, project assumptions, identification of the manager and project team, and information about key stakeholders. Under Project Management Professional criteria, a project is not authorized to start without an approved charter.

Key Success Measures in Project Management

Key success measures are established at the start of the project by the project manager and key stakeholders. The measures of success are determined as well as how success is to be measured and what aspects of the project will impact the desired success. Key success measures are likely to include traditional measurements, such as time, budget, quality, and scope. However, it is in the interest of the organization and project stakeholders that success is also measured by how well the project meets organizational objectives and achieves the planned benefit. Key success measures can be included as an element of the project charter. Common measurements include customer satisfaction, schedule attainment, return on investment, cost savings realized, payback period, meeting strategic objectives, or meeting business case objectives.

Project Operating Environment

Enterprise Environmental Factors

Internal to the Organization

Enterprise environmental factors (EEF) are circumstances that occur outside of the control of the project management team that nonetheless may influence the actions taken by the team. Internal EEFs are those factors that occur within the organization performing the project. These factors are indicative of how the organization is designed and operated. Organizations that perform many projects or rely on projects to drive strategic plan achievement will act to prevent internal factors from negatively impacting projects.

Factor	Description
Organizational design, culture, and governance	The mission and vision established for the organization, the cultural behaviors, and the levels of authority that exist.
Physical location of the operations	Where the operations and teams are located geographically.
Infrastructure	Facilities, telecommunications, information technology, operating capacity, and related equipment.
IT software	Software programs used and available, such as project management software, enterprise resource planning, and design software.
Resources	Vendors and related approval processes, subcontractors, and contractual agreements.
Employees	Human resources, skill sets, training, and competencies.

External to the Organization

Enterprise environmental factors (EEF) are influences that can impact the progress and measurements of a project, yet are outside the control of the project team. External EEFs are those factors that exist outside of the organization or firm that houses the project team. All organizations operate within an external ecosystem of influences from various markets, governments, geopolitical events, social forces, cultures, and natural phenomena. Project managers and organizational leadership must be attentive to the external factors when designing business strategies, project charters, as well as project risks and deliverables.

Factor	Description
Government regulations	Local, state, national, and international laws that determine permitted and restricted actions by an organization.
Legal business restrictions	Laws related to employees, business conduct, and purchasing.
Fiscal influences	Access to capital markets, interest rates, inflation, trade factors.
Marketplace barriers	Intellectual property, competitive forces, market share.
Social and cultural	Ethics and social norms, identity politics, public perception.
Environmental impacts	Geographic locations, weather, seasons, climate changes, working conditions.
Project management commercial databases	Compiled data regarding risks, benchmarking, and cost estimates.
Scientific research	Evidence-based studies, expert knowledge, and benchmarking.

Organizational Process Assets

Overview

Organizational process assets (OPAs) are both historical practices and the knowledge that any stakeholders or supportive elements involved in the project are able to bring to its execution to influence the project management process. Many supportive persons, organizations, vendors, and stakeholders are involved with project phases and execution. These individuals or organizations have various levels of procedures, expertise, and processes that can add value to any current project they are involved in. Project managers benefit from identifying and using these OPAs to their advantage to achieve project deliverables. Although organizations often may house a dedicated project management office that oversees project policies, procedures, and plans, organizational knowledge bases represent assets—in the form of lessons learned, adjustments, quality issues, and financial performances—that are gained during the course of the execution of the project's phases. Successful organizations using project management are apt at managing expertise assets, as well as learning from the inconsistencies as they occur.

Policies, Procedures

Project Policies and Procedures Related to Initiating, Planning, and Closing Projects

Within the context of organizational process assets (OPAs), an organization has at its disposal well defined polices and historical practices for project process groups, including the initiating, planning, and closing activities. OPAs in the initiating and planning groups include foundational approaches to organizational behavior and project quality. Policies focused on health, safety, environmental and quality standards; human resource standards; and security are common in these asset groups. Furthermore, organizational policies on tailoring, project life cycles, metrics, and management methods serve as administrative norms. Other common assets for initiating and planning include project management templates commonly used in the process. The closing assets often include evaluation methods, policies on follow-up auditing, agreement closure, and steps necessary to transfer ownership of an asset or service to another stakeholder.

Project Policies and Procedures Related to Execution, Monitoring, and Controlling Projects

Organizational process assets (OPAs) utilized in an organization's project management system would be commonly used and available to project managers as standards and guidance for actionable project process groups, such as execution and monitoring. These critical phases often contain unexpected risks and delays to the project; having well-defined procedures to manage through these difficult parts of the project inevitably improve project outcomes. Common policies and procedures in the execution process group can include change management processes, financial controls and accounting practices for projects, quality milestones and policies to be monitored throughout the project, communication policies, workflow prioritization, verification procedures, and validation methods.

Organizational Knowledge Repositories

Organizations performing multiple project management streams simultaneously and over the course of many periods benefit from the shared knowledge gained from each project itself. Databases and knowledge mines give project planning and management stakeholders the advantage of organizational learning, faster lead times in the early project phases, more rapid execution, and lower unforeseen risks in future projects. Tools such as quality management systems, shared document servers, resource planning platforms, and unified communication methods all reduce the barriers to repeat success. Project management-specific repositories often include shared project management software platforms, shared project document templates, financial databases, vendor management databases (such as enterprise resource planning specifically used for projects), and formal project final reports from past projects. Furthermore, these repositories are ideal places to store past metric performance data, past data on schedule attainment and risk analysis, and past decision-making on project tailoring and business cases.

Organizational Systems Overview

Theory of Business Organization Systems

Organizations—whether for profit or non-profit—operate under the constraints and influence of organizational behavior and dynamics. Organizations consist of people, and those people have various levels of influence, power, leadership, and capabilities that can have degrees of benefit or detriment to any project. Foremost, top leadership of an organization must be accountable to develop a well-functioning organizational design and culture that both establish the means to effective project management. The project manager and related stakeholders must be able to recognize the power, influence, relationships, and competences that they and their other stakeholders have towards the successful completion of a project. It is likewise important for project managers to understand the organizational governance and norms as they relate to individual projects and in terms of how these can impact project metrics.

Systems Thinking and Systems Dynamics

Systems thinking is defined as the ability to analyze how an organization or project's goals, elements, and interconnectivity are enjoined and become impacted as progress or change is made over the course of functioning. Project managers that use systems thinking are aware that decisions made in one part of the project may affect different parts of the project in the present or the future. The project management plan and its sub-elements are highly interrelated; project managers must be aware of and review how changes to certain project elements will alter project trajectory. Systems dynamics are defined as the behavior of complex systems in non-linear patterns charted and tracked to better understand systems behaviors; decision-making; and change in a project, process, or organization. Projects are highly interrelated and can be highly complex. A project manager with the ability to monitor complex behaviors is able to make better decisions and adjustments to the project towards expected outcomes.

Organizational Governance Frameworks

Organizational governance is defined as the interactive and structural configuration—such as hierarchical or matrix formats—of personnel within an organization that are used by management to influence the behaviors, culture, and objective outcomes of the organization itself. The oversight of organizational governance thus requires framework considerations such as roles, responsibilities, and human resources to objectively monitor effectiveness and change the governance structure as needed. How an organization is governed is often a result of the culture within its ranks. Norms such as rules, policies, SOPs, business systems, quality systems, and modes of communication can all influence how governance is executed and in turn how effective project management can be. Aligning these elements—especially as projects become more complex in size and scope—reinforces effective use of project resources. Governance frameworks can become inhibitory when organizations are performing project portfolios and programs with many active projects running at the same time. Governance frameworks must be factored into the tailoring process in early planning phases of projects.

Project Scale	Common Governance Elements
Project	Common governance domains: alignment, risk, performance, communications.
Program	Each domain with common functions: oversight, control, integration, decision-making.
Portfolio	Each function has a governance supporting process.

Management Elements

Modern management has multitudes of practices and methods to be effective in management of a system, group, or process. The organizational governance and structure will influence what general management principles are both used and effective in various parts of the organizational structure. Key principles can be grouped by common themes: standards, efficiency, top-down management, and matrix management. These principles are not all inclusive; many more principles are used and likely highly effective based on the organization's governance and the culture of the business.

Group	Common Principles
Efficiency	Division of labor and specialization
	Skills development
	Economic use of resources
Matrix	Unity of goal
	Balanced goals and objectives
	Innovation and contribution by stakeholders
	Discipline of action and rules
	Compensation and fair labor
Standards	Effective communication modes
	Quality of execution and performance
	Safety and security
	Morale and culture management
Top-down	Authorization
	Unity of command

Organizational Structure Types

Tradeoff Between Organizational Structure Types and Structure Optimization

The elements to an effective organizational structure often depend on the desired outcomes of the project or strategy sought by the organization and its stakeholders. Many organizational structures are available to use, each with different elements that can be adjusted to create permutations and flexible structure styles based on desired outcomes. The project management process benefits from well designed and planned organizational structures; often multiple organizational structures may be used within a project or portfolio. The most influential characteristics of a project include:

- Work group arrangement
- Degree of project manager authority
- Project manager's role

- Degree of resource availability
- Budget ownership
- Scope of project administrative staff

Degrees and combinations of these factors can create a continuum of organizational structures ranging from simple organic projects with little complexity to matrix and hybrid styles with various sub-structures and work arrangements.

Complexity Scale (low)	**Simple/Organic**	Flexible with little project manager (PM) authority. Limited resources and part-time focus.
	Functional	Work-group focused on job at hand, little PM authority and few resources outside of work group.
	Multidisciplined	Multiple org functions working part-time, little PM authority. Few resources overseen by functional manager.
	Matrix	PM involved; varies with strong, weak, or mixed forms of matrix teams. Increase in resources as project more complex.
	Virtual	Distributed network of colleagues and stakeholders. Limited face-to-face work. PM can be full or part time and resources depend on complexity.
	Hybrid	Mixed attributes from all styles.
Complexity Scale (high)	**PMO**	High resource needs, full-time dedicated PMs leading teams and budgets. High levels of authority for PMs.

Factors to Consider When Implementing or Changing an Organizational Structure

The task of designing and continuously adjusting an organizational structure to fit strategic and project needs requires the awareness and consideration of several factors common within organizations. These factors can be grouped into categories such as strategic, hierarchical, flexible, and functional. Strategic factors center on those that link to the overall organizational strategy and objectives. [1] How well the structure aligns with those broader objectives and [2] how accountability and responsibility are upheld against those aligned objectives. Hierarchical factors provide a structural operating norm among the organization's members. The culture of the organization must be considered against hierarchical factors. Factors include [3] clear authority and decision escalation, [4] authority to delegate, [5] clear communications, and [6] span of control. Flexible factors include [7] adaptability and simplicity of design. Lastly, functional factors focus on time and logistics: [8] performance efficiency, cost, and physical locations of the structure.

Impact of Simple, Moderate, and Complex Organizational Structures on Project Management Characteristics

Simple organizational structures include variants such as organic team projects, functional initiatives, and multidivisional work groups. These simple structures are generally characterized by minimal authority for the part-time project manager, constrained resources, a functional division overseeing the budget, and minimal administrative staff to support the ad hoc project. Simple structures differentiate based on how the work groups are arranged. Moderately complex structures center on the matrix design where work groups are arranged by job function and are increasingly multifaceted objectives, yet the project manager has minimal hierarchical authority. Rather, the matrix is coordinated by the project manager, either in a full or part-time role, and a range of resource availability based on project needs. Virtual structures over telecommunications can be grouped into moderate structures. Complex organizational structures are characterized by multiple work group types and high full-time project manager authority, with human, capital, and resource needs overseen largely by the project manager.

Project Management Office

The project management office (PMO) is an organizational division used in some organizations to provide coordination of project-related activities. Coordination performed by the PMO generally centers on providing facilitation, resources, and governance support to projects within the organization. Depending upon the scale and scope of organizational projects, the PMO will have various levels of indirect or direct involvement with projects themselves. PMOs exert little influence and control on projects in supportive styles. Supportive PMOs are not likely to directly lead projects; their role is largely advising other project managers. A controlling style of PMO involves more hands-on guidance and methodology building for co-project managers. These services aid in standardizing forms, procedures, and governance practices. Directive PMOs involve project managers from the office taking direct control of one or more projects, so the project team reports directly to the PMO.

Role of The Project Manager

Definition of a Project Manager

Project Manager's Function

The project manager functions within an organization to lead the team selected to achieve the objectives of a defined project. This management role differs from traditional jobs, such as functional manager or operations manager, in that the project manager does not directly supervise a business function, business unit, or operating efficiency within the organization. Rather, the project manager must lead the team to accomplish the project objectives using spheres of influence within the organization, clear mandates from senior management, and the stakeholder relationships available. The project manager is responsible to meet the project objectives for the outcomes of the project, for team communication and motivation, and ultimately for stakeholder satisfaction. Effective project managers are skilled at management; technical aptitude; planning; leadership; finance; and should be certified to a project management credential, such as PMP or lean Six Sigma.

Project Manager's Influence

The project manager must lead a team, project stakeholders, and other supportive colleagues through a transformative process to achieve a positive outcome for the organization with net positive financial and/or competitive advantage for the organization. Very often the project manager does not have role power over the persons that work with or impact the project. Just as much as planning and execution skills, the level of expertise and relationship strength the project manager holds can influence how results are obtained. A project manager must convince, influence, support, and lead the project team and stakeholders through to the success of the project. Influence can be achieved through awareness of organizational dynamics, well-developed communication skills, organizational leverage with key leaders as champions of the project, and the alignment of the project scope with broader organizational objectives.

Sphere of Influence

Project

Project Manager's Role and Function Within the Project

The project manager is analogous to a sports team head coach or a symphony conductor. The project manager serves to navigate the team through the project schedule while keeping stability through resource limits and challenging obstacles. They also serve to direct and empower the team members to perform their respective roles. Relationship and communication skills across the project team and stakeholder network can distinguish the top project managers from their peers. Essential elements to the role include formal communication plans, multiple communication mediums, as well as clarity and consistency in communications. Relationship skills essential to the role include formal and informal network development. Formal networks are those which are within the project manager's reporting structure. Informal networks include subject matter experts, executive champions, and other stakeholders that can provide support and solutions to the project team. Relationship management is an important way that project managers can navigate the team through the organizational complexities.

Organization

Project Manager's Role and Function Within the Broader Organization

Within the broader organization, project managers interact most commonly with senior executives, functional managers, specialized colleagues, and other project managers. Senior executive interaction occurs in the form of project chartering, stakeholder buy-in, and business case review. Project managers may often also report to a senior executive for special strategic projects. Project managers are likely to share resources with, report to, or support functional managers—such as operations managers—in order to achieve project objectives. Resource constraints and communication are critical functions for project managers and functional leaders. The project manager's role in the organization includes strengthening organizational competency in project management, improving the state of efficiency and performance of the organization as a result of successful projects, and developing relationships within the organization that will help achieve the project team's deliverables. The project manager also has a role in the organization to promote their profession and champion the project management discipline and system from within. This role can be achieved by building strong relationships with other internal project managers, by demonstrating the value-added outcomes of projects, and by supporting improvements in efficacy of the organization's project management function.

Industry, Professional Discipline & Across Disciplines

Influence on and by the Industry, Profession, and Across Other Disciplines

External influences such as technology advances, efficiency tools, economic shifts, market forces, regulatory changes, project discipline improvements, and resource availability changes may require project managers to adjust their planning and execution in projects. As many of these influences precipitate change in the project management body of knowledge or force new technologies onto industry, it is wise for project managers to perform continuing education and professional development within their profession or in related skills. Continuing certifications in project management, operations management, and related industries where projects may be initiated are also recommended. Project managers are also able to influence professionals in other industries of the value of using project management skills to enhance their own achievement. Skills that are highly developed in project managers—such as project quality, budgeting, resource management, and schedule adherence—are beneficial educational options for non-project managers.

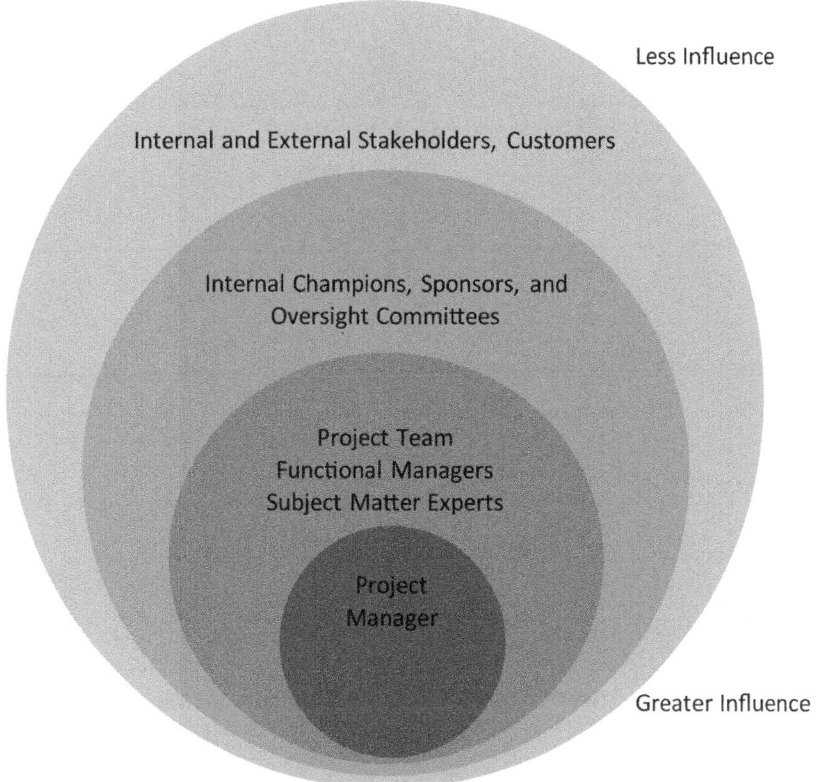

Project Manager Competencies

Skills in the PMI Talent Triangle

The Project Management Institute recognizes that competent project managers exhibit three essential skill sets: leadership, technical project management, and strategic management. The leadership skill set is evidenced by a project manager's ability to engage, motivate, and aid a project team and its stakeholders to successful achievement of organizational goals. For example, a project manager helps the project team negotiate severely constrained resources to help keep a critical project on schedule. The technical project management skill set is characterized as knowledge and behaviors represented in project, program, or portfolio management itself. For example, a project manager achieves above target schedule, budget, and quality adherence for multiple simultaneous projects. Strategic management skill sets are defined as the awareness of internal organizational and external industry knowledge and can positively impact business and project results. For example, a project manager is deeply aware of pending industry technology advancements and can adopt their use in projects to maintain a competitive advantage. While each skill upon itself can be impactful, the role of the project manager is incomplete and insufficient if all three skills are not finely developed in project managers and the project management organization.

The PMI Talent Triangle (adapted from PMI)

Technical Project Management Skills

Technical project management skills are those that are executed by the project manager and team to achieve the planned project outcomes within the project performance indicators and body of knowledge. Technical expertise is necessary for effective project management; knowing when to obtain outside assistance or subject matter support is equally important to successful project managers. Technical expertise must also be balanced with effective execution and use of the tools available to project managers. The most effective project managers can balance the competing needs of schedule adherence, financial reporting, issue resolution, focus on critical success factors of any given project, tailoring of approaches, and thorough planning.

Strategic and Business Management Skills

Strategic thinking combines awareness of the broader internal organization, external market forces, and organizational goals to make effective and innovative decisions to improve or sustain a competitive advantage. As projects tend to include elements from many different organizational disciplines (such as financial, quality, procurement, operations, engineering, and customer awareness), project managers must also be adept at multiple business management skills in order to be maximally effective. This domain knowledge allows the project manager to provide maximum benefit and value to the organization, collaborate with domain experts to meet project deliverables, and promote the benefits of projects and project management systems to the organization's strategic objectives. The project manager should be aware of and able to explain key aspects of the organization, including:

1. Organizational strategy
2. Vision and mission statement
3. Key performance indicators
4. Products and/or services
5. Competition and market forces
6. How operations function

Leadership Skills

Importance of Leadership and People Skills in Project Management

Leadership is essential to project management and is demonstrated by the ability to motivate, guide, and instruct a team or network of contributors. These abilities are achieved when project managers exhibit certain underlying talents, including conciliation, problem-solving, critical decision-making, communication skills, and relationship-building with stakeholders and team members. The people skills are a vital talent in project management that can elevate a leader's ability to achieve project outcomes consistently. All projects need people to direct, execute, and influence outcomes. Successful project managers understand the motivations, strengths, and weaknesses that their team and stakeholders exhibit and are able to adjust their own plans, communication, and influence accordingly to stay focused on the objectives.

Ideal Leadership Qualities

Emotional Intelligence and Focus

Listed and described below are ideal leadership qualities related to emotional intelligence and focus:

- **Having a vision** – Leaders fully understand and live by the mission, objectives, and values of the project or organization. They help others reach the same ideals with passion.
- **Empathy towards others** – Strong leaders have strong emotional intelligence and are able to grasp the sensitivities, needs, and concerns of others while still leading their teams and stakeholders to the goals.
- **Integrity and respect –** Leaders behave ethically, responsibly, and with integrity and respect for others.
- **Systems and critical thinking –** Strong leaders are collaborative and understanding of situations where systems thinking, critical thinking, and difficult decision-making must occur to achieve outcomes. Leaders also know that many factors influence decision-making and decisions can impact many other elements.
- **Focus on what matters most –** Strong leaders are decisive when necessary, fair when recognizing those who perform, and clear when setting expectations for others. Leaders keep their focus on priorities, revising priorities routinely, being flexible when necessary, and aware of ways to avoid distractions.

Communication and Conflict Management

Listed and described below are ideal leadership qualities related to communication and conflict management:

- **Communication** – Strong leaders are skilled at actively listening to colleagues, team members, and stakeholders. Active listening involves giving attention, comprehending, and relaying back to the presenter a verification that they are understood. Strong leaders routinely give and accept constructive feedback about performance and communication so that they and others can grow and improve. Communication is also an activity that leaders spend significant time performing.
- **Conflict and relationship management** – Leaders manage expectations and are aware when organizational behavior can lead to interpersonal conflict. Identifying, resolving, and preventing conflict is vital to a leader, especially one who leads complex and multi-disciplinary teams. Leaders build trust and actively work to prevent and resolve disagreements. Leaders are honest when dealing with conflict and relationships; they hone their skills at negotiating, persuasion and diffusion. Lastly, a strong leader actively grows their professional relationships for mutual benefit and the benefit of the organization.

Navigating Organizational Politics, Power, and Progress

Organizational politics is best described as leaders' relative influence, power, authoritative influence, and negotiation skills compared to other colleagues seeking to achieve their own goals and objectives. Politics are often competing forces within an organization and can hinder or enhance the progress of the project manager and his ability to get the job done. Careful analysis by the project manager of how the project fits within the organization's people, structure, and culture will lead to better leadership. Given the politics and the right type of power and negotiation tactics, actions taken can overcome the inertia that comes with politics. Project managers that are consistent and successful in effective execution of their project despite organizational politics will often gain or maintain levels of autonomy.

Versions of Power Within an Organization

Four groups of organizational power exist at the disposal of the project manager seeking to influence stakeholders or overcome internal politics to achieve objectives. Role-based powers rely on the organization's hierarchy and chains of command as leverage over others. Relationship-based powers rely on language, behaviors, and connections with colleagues and stakeholders to achieve results. Expertise-based powers rely on knowledge and reputation. Informational-based power uses the premise that the control of information can yield power over others. The project manager role must be aware of these forms of power, how other stakeholders may use these towards the project team, and how the managers themselves with their team can use these approaches to gain influence and achieve results.

Power` Group	Typical Styles	Example Uses
Role-based power	Positional	A formal title and role in the organization
	Punitive	Negative consequences issued by hierarchy
	Pressure	Limiting choices or freedom to get desired action
	Avoiding	Decline to participate as means to influence results
Relationship-based power	Personal	Charismatic attraction
	Connection	Building alliances and networks
	Cooperative	Finding common ground
	Guilt	Enforcing a sense of obligation
Expertise-based power	Referent	Admiration or respect gained
	Situational	Experience in unique situations
	Expert	Formal education, training, or skills
	Persuasive	Using argumentation and mental prowess
Informational-based power	Informing	Control over the collection or sharing of useful information
	Incentivization	Using monetary incentives and objectives to drive behaviors

Comparison of Leadership and Management

Leadership and Management in Projects

The terms of leadership and management are similar but, in the context of organizational achievement, are distinct in their approaches and results. Leadership in project work reflects the ability to persuade, guide, and influence team members, stakeholders, and colleagues through a project life cycle. Management is a more directed and closely enforced approach to having colleagues complete tasks towards project completion. Management often relies less on big-picture perspectives; it focuses on completing predetermined tasks and work without much use for strategic and cooperative innovation. Different phases, stakeholders, objectives, and deliverables will be achieved and motivated using a balance of both approaches from the project manager.

Furthermore, management uses role power more often while leadership focuses on relationship and expertise power. Management relies on control, administration, operations, and solving problems. Leadership is characterized by inspiring trust, innovation, vision, motivation, and doing the right things.

Leadership Styles

Styles of leadership used by project managers are likely to be adjusted based on several different characteristic groups exhibited by the project and/or team itself. The ethics, needs, values, and attitudes of the leader as well as for each team member will be variable, subject to many underlying factors and influences. The characteristics of the organization itself, such as the vision and structure, will force leadership adjustments on the project manager, especially when working on projects in differing sections of the business. Environmental characteristics occurring external to the organization, including economics, marketplace changes, and geopolitics are generally outside of the project manager's control.

Given these leadership characteristic groups, there are six leadership styles that are commonly used, solely or in combination, to stay successful in project management.

Leadership Style	Description
Charismatic	Extroverted, energetic, and inspiring style with high confidence that motivates others
Hands-off	Loose oversight and allowing team to make choices and actions themselves
Interactional	Blended approach combining charismatic, transactional, and transformational styles
Servant leadership	Service to others is primary role, team growth and learning, relationship and collaborative focus
Transactional	Goal and objective oriented; results matter and drive rewards
Transformational	Supporting team through vision and example behaviors; innovation and creativity are priorities

Importance of Personality to Effective Project Management

Complementary to technical project management skills and leadership skills, the effective project manager must also be able to implement and express different personality types in different situations in order to influence the team members and stakeholders towards achievement. The 11 most useful personality forms can be categorized into two groups: internally derived and externally derived. Internally derived are personality styles that are performed based on internal stimuli. Externally derived personality styles are those that require external stimuli from colleagues or other persons in order to be exhibited. These personalities—or the personal differences in thought and behavior patterns—are valuable tools to lead a project, portfolio, or program team.

Personality Group	Personality Style	Description
Internally derived	Courtesy	Interacting with appropriate etiquette
	Creativity	Ability to innovate
	Intellect	Aptitude over multiple disciplines
	Managerial	Administrative control and structure
	Systemic	Seeking and building systems thinking
Externally derived	Authenticity	Accepting of others and openness
	Cultural	Empathy for cultural differences
	Emotional	Interpersonal skills and sensing emotion
	Political	Ability to achieve results politically
	Service-oriented	Promoting the service towards others
	Social	Effective leadership of people

Performing Integration

Process Level

Integration in project management is defined as the coordination of the elemental parts of the project management process into a smoothly functioning system. Integration results in deliverables, including the project charter, the project plan, and the project scope. The project manager has two primary responsibilities in performing project integration. First, the project manager must work with the project champion or executive sponsor to ensure project deliverables and objectives are aligned with organizational strategy and other portfolios and programs. Second, project managers must filter out the non-essential distractions and clear a path for the team to concentrate on the objectives, scope, deliverables, plan and charter of the project facing them. The most direct form of project integration is on the underlying processes involved in project management. These processes can occur as mutually exclusive events or as overlapping, repeated, and consequential events where integration and interaction must be managed by the project leader.

Cognitive Level

Cognitive-level project integration is defined as the ability of a person to combine subject matter knowledge and expertise with qualitative skills, such as leadership, vision, and organizational acumen to form an integrated skill set in managing a project. Projects vary in many aspects, and the project manager must be able to balance and perform the necessary combination of expertise and interpersonal skills to achieve the objectives of the project or organization. Knowledge-based skill sets and interpersonal skill sets have a direct correlation with project success and achievement. Furthermore, the integration of various skill sets, both knowledge and interpersonal, requires the ability to morph from one set of behaviors to slightly different behaviors as a project manager, depending upon the progression and challenges facing the project.

Context Level

Project managers must think beyond cognitive-level integration—such as direct project and subject matter knowledge and interpersonal skills—and must be aware of broader contextual influences upon the project. Contextual influences include the project's relevance to overall business or organizational objectives, business case relevance for the project, or marketplace impacts of the project outcomes. Additional context awareness is needed towards the organization's broader strategy and objectives. Behavioral alignment with and integration of cognitive and contextual roles gives the project manager advantages in project performance and the organization's progress towards its overarching goals.

Integration and Complexity

Reconciling and Managing Project Integration with Challenges of Complexity

Complexity arises in project management when a confluence occurs between three underlying causative factors: uncertainty, human behavior, and organizational systems behavior. Though these factors are what project complexity can be attributed to, the perception of complexity is often the result of personal experiences, skills, and observations made upon a complex situation. Different project managers may perceive complexity while others may not. Uncertainty drives complexity when internal or external issues are ambiguous or unknown to the project manager and cause disruption to the execution. Complexity can also infiltrate projects due to human behaviors—the interaction between diverse teams, contributors, and stakeholders. Lastly, complexity tends to be introduced into projects from the inherent disorder and connectivity between divisions and systems within the organization (e.g., organizational design, technology systems, or communication systems). Project managers must be able to recognize elements of projects that are likely to exhibit signs of complexity, including:

- Dynamic interactions between multiple organizational or human parts
- Amount of interconnectivity between organizational parts
- Systems containing multiple parts
- Nascent behavior without simple explanations

Project Integration Management

Develop Project Charter

Overview

The project charter is a summary document that serves as valid authorization to perform the project, to use organizational resources against the project, and is a concise collection of all key details related to the deliverables, plan, scope, and resources needed to be successful. The charter serves as communication of these key details both within the project team and to relevant stakeholders. The charter links the organization's strategic objectives to the project plan and its execution. The linkage is made possible through business case files, internal and external factors, and the benefits management plan. From the charter, many supporting materials and information can be created with accuracy and validation. Materials that flow forth after the charter include the project management plan, project schedule, cost management, quality plan, resource allocation, risk management, procurement, and the appropriate project documentation. The charter also serves as a pseudo-contract within the organization to bind the assembled team and stakeholders to a committed plan and deliverables with a high likelihood for positive benefit to the organization.

Inputs

Utility of Business Documents in Creating Charters

The two most significant business documents used as inputs into the charter process include the business case and the benefits management plan. The business case documents the justification to perform the project under the analysis that the investment outlays in monetary, time, and personnel resources will benefit the organization. The business case also includes a cost-benefit analysis and has several data sources, including market research, external competitive environment studies, the state of technology in the marketplace, customer feedback, market demand, or organizational strategy. The business case is the most significant business document for charter development. In addition, the benefits management plan—a collection of analyses such as a pro forma statement that demonstrates how the benefits are likely to be obtained as the project is completed—provides a light at the end of the tunnel and is a motivator for the organization to achieve the project. Its use in the charter process is highlighted by giving validation to the cost-benefit presentation and success factors, such as rate of return and return on investment.

Use of Agreements in Developing Project Plans

Agreements are types of business documents more commonly used when a project management team is working for an external firm as a contracted service provider. Agreements serve to document terms and bind behaviors between the project team and the organization receiving the benefit of the project management services. Agreements can come in many forms, the most familiar of which for an external provider would be a contract or service agreement. Other types of agreements in lower levels of formality and more commonly used internally include memorandums of understanding, letters of intent, verbal agreements, or emailed statements. Memorandums of understanding are also common between government agencies.

Enterprise Environmental Factors and Organizational Process Assets

The project charter includes cost-benefit analysis, risk assessment, and functional validation references that require awareness of several external and internal factors. External validation ensures that the project benefits and focus are relevant to the marketplace and the organization's strategy. Internal validation ensures that the project is consistent with internal objectives and organizational culture factors. External factors may include marketplace conditions, competitive data, regulatory changes, government or industry standards such as quality and safety, and geopolitics. Internal factors include organizational culture, organizational design, growth phase of the organization, the current organizational strategy, and stakeholder expectations.

Organizational process assets support the project charter as inputs that set standards in policies, procedures, monitoring methods, reporting, governance framework, work templates, and organizational learning databases. These standards and history provide a pathway to future charter development without having to start from scratch.

Tools and Techniques

Benefit of Using Expert Judgement When Developing Project Charters

When developing the project charter, especially in new and complex projects that the organization has little to no experience performing, an external expert is beneficial to the management team. Expert judgement is the judgement of an individual or group developed through expertise, skill, training, and education to provide deliberate direction to an inexperienced project team to build confidence and increase the likelihood of good decision-making. The specialization of knowledge and skill is beneficial when complexity enters a project or is a necessary force to be overcome. Expert judgement beneficial to project managers is commonly seen in organizational optimization, risk analysis, budget and schedule management, and industry technical knowledge. External consultants are commonly used, but other sources can include government agencies, non-profits, and academia.

Project Charter Data Gathering Techniques

Project charter development requires input from various stakeholders, subject matter experts, team members, and even customers in order to align with the problem or weakness needed to be overcome. Brainstorming is a tool that involves ideation and analysis. Diverse stakeholders, experts, and team members perform facilitated, open, and collaborative idea generation to solve the problem(s) facing the project team. The ideas are analyzed and top concepts are incorporated into the project charter. Focus groups use open communication approaches and draw upon stakeholders, subject matter experts, and product (or service) end users to provide the project team with unbiased perspective on project risks, quality criteria, and success factors. Interviews are more intimate and candid ways to get high-level information about project risks, constraints, and approval criteria from stakeholders. Project managers and their teams assess the relative need for each of these techniques based on the project and situational needs.

Key Traits of Project Managers When Facilitating Project Charters

Project managers must effectively manage the human element in the charter development process and lead the team through techniques that bring positive outcomes to charter development meetings and discussions. Conflict and differing personal goals and values are common in many charter development phases. The project manager can use conflict management to bring stakeholders and team members together on differences in objectives, scope, success criteria, and milestones. The project manager must be skilled at meeting management in order to stay on track with the process and to gather information from the meeting and stakeholders. Steps such as prepared agenda, stakeholder group representation, follow-up meeting minutes, and task lists are tools for effective meeting management. Lastly, project managers must skillfully facilitate charter development meetings, much like a symphony conductor. With clear meeting goals in mind, the project manager boosts participation, communication, and buy-in from participants. The project manager also strives for mutual understanding and agreement on the final deliverables and success factors for the project. Mid-level conflict is not necessarily a bad thing in such a process; if well facilitated, mid-level conflict provides the most ideal results.

Outputs

Purpose and Elements of Project Charters

The project charter serves as a validation and authorization from the project sponsor that the project will receive resources and will be executed. The charter also provides the project manager with responsibility and authority to lead the project initiative as detailed in the charter. The charter communicates key information to internal and external stakeholders regarding the project scope and execution plan. Several elements are commonly added to the charter to maximize its effectiveness.

Charter Element	Description
Responsible parties	Lists the project manager, sponsor, and other persons responsible for carrying out or overseeing the project
Key stakeholders	Persons or organizations that impact or benefit from the project
Project description	Description is high-level and describes the project, scope, and any problems needing solved
Objectives	Listed objectives of the project, along with measurable success criteria
Purpose statement	Describes the project purpose in terms of example data and problem statements
Approval requirements	Lists how success is defined, how it is decided, and who has authority to sign off on the project
Resources allocated	Financial, human, and goods resources are defined

Problem Statement

The problem statement must clearly describe, in objective terms, the problem or challenge that the team must overcome through use of the project process. Measurable data is highly useful in validating that the problem statement actually reflects the true problem, that the objectives of the project align with resolving the problem, and that the statement does not draw premature conclusions. In lean Six Sigma projects, the statement is often written in terms of the customer's needs and benefit. The objectives, success measures, and milestones must be a skeletal support structure to achievement of problem resolution.

Develop Project Management Plan

Overview

The project management plan is a comprehensive document that provides a thorough summary of the project work and the way in which the project components will be executed. The purpose of the development of the project management plan is to perform the consolidation of the separate subcomponents into one comprehensive work. Key inputs into this process include the project charter and outputs from preliminary processes, such as business case development, enterprise environmental factors, and organizational process assets. Project management teams must be skilled at using several tools to analyze, compile, and communicate an effective project management plan. Along with professional judgement, project managers must also use team facilitation, leadership skills, and data collection methods to achieve the plan. An important feature incorporated into the plan is baselining. Baselining refers to defined reference points documented for cost, time, and scope so that performance can be measured against these reference points.

Through the course of the project, these baselines can be adjusted, but only through a formalized change management process. When a project management plan exists within a larger context of a portfolio or program, the plan should be consistent with the objectives of those overarching systems.

Inputs

Impact on Development of Project Management Plans

Enterprise Environmental Factors

Many sub-plans developed within the context of the project management plan are interdependent upon enterprise resources and systems. Two key internal enterprise factors include the organizational design and the infrastructure used to support it. The organizational design includes how hierarchies are structured, the internal culture, management behaviors, and how the organization is governed through policies and practices. The infrastructure factors include telecommunications, technology available for performing project work, and the physical assets of the organization.

Organizational Process Assets

These factors represent the norms and approved procedures used by the organization for projects or in support of project management. Core organizational policies and procedures, the project management process norms, and project tailoring procedures are such examples. Other assets of the organizational processes include policies and norms regarding change management, monitoring of sub-plans, reporting and information sharing, and how the organization learns from project progress and outcomes.

Tools and Techniques

Impact of Well-Planned Meetings on Project Management Plans

Development of the project management plan involves planned meetings—varying in duration and frequency—in order to communicate project execution strategy, objectives, and methods of monitoring and control. The development of the project management plan precedes the first team meeting and marks the transition to the implementation phase of the project. The size of the project can also determine when the kick-off meeting is held and within which project phase that meeting is held. Larger projects where the planning team is separate from the execution team will have the kick-off meeting in the implementation phase of the project. Smaller projects, where the planning team is also performing the execution, will have the kick-off meeting in the planning phase because the team memberships are the same. Generally, the kick-off meetings are intended to give team members information about their roles, responsibilities, objectives, and measurement tools for the project. The kick-off is also an opportunity to gain commitment from all team members regarding the project deliverables, objectives, and key performance indicators.

Outputs

Central Components of Project Management Plans

Subsidiary plans function within the project management plan to control key performance indicators, resources, communications, and scheduling of the plan. Common types of subsidiary plans include the schedule management plan, a cost management plan, and a communications management plan. The schedule management plan includes the criteria and monitoring steps needed for schedule management. The cost management plan describes how the team will plan and monitor project costs. The communications management plan oversees the veracity, control, and spread of the project communications. Baselines are validated and approved versions of key components of the project plan upon which team members and stakeholders may draw reference as the project elapses. Baselines are used for essential and frequently reviewed components, such as the scope, schedule, and cost plans. These approved standards are used when comparing actual performance as the project moves forward. Additional elements to the project management plan include those that focus on changes, management review, and information configuration plans. Project documents support many of the subsidiary plans within the project plan and serve as evidence and analytical tools for performance assessment and continuous improvement.

Direct and Manage Project Work

Overview

Following the completion of the project management plan, the project team must begin managing project work. Directing and managing project work is the process group of following the project management plan, its subsidiary plans, and approved changes and leading the execution of the project tasks and systems towards completion of the schedule, objectives, and deliverables. This part of the project is ongoing and is hands-on execution of tasks. Inputs of this project element include the project management plan itself, enterprise environmental factors, and organizational process assets. Accomplishment and execution are key behaviors of the project team. The project manager leads the completion of project tasks, planned activities, and achievement of deliverables in the schedule. It is equally important that the project team manage change effectively during the project work phases. Also, the project manager must ensure that work performance data is sufficiently collected, analyzed, and communicated for the subsequent control process group and for future improvements to the organization's project management processes.

Inputs

Necessary Project Input Documents

During the phase of directing and managing project work, several document sources can be used as inputs to achieve successful outcomes. These documents, commonly employed at other project steps and supplementary to the project management plan, include schedules, registers, and reports. Project schedules describe the work breakdown and timing around all tasks and milestones. The milestone list coincides with the schedule by listing dates planned for each milestone in the schedule. The requirements traceability record serves to link the project requirements for quality and performance to the project milestones. Project communications provide an obvious critical importance in the documentation process. Furthermore, the risk register and risk reporting tools serve as preventative inputs against unplanned threats to the project and quantitative assessments on overall project risks, respectively. Lastly, the project documentation change log supports documentation of updates and adjustments made during the project work.

Importance of the Change Log and Approved Change Request Processes

Project managers, often with the support of a change control board of advisors or project stakeholders, must carefully control changes to mutually agreed project plans, schedules, and deliverables. Changes to project documentation are widely communicated and can drive the decisions of many stakeholders and contributors. This control process is called the change management and approval system or perform integrated change control. When project managers approve change requests, they must schedule the change's resources and implementation and integrate it into the ongoing project. In a less formal sense, change logs document change actions taken to project documents and plans during execution.

Tools and Techniques

PMIS and Project Work Meetings

The project management information system (PMIS) is a component of the project work phase that is often overseen by the organization's information technology (IT) division. PMIS is commonly computer software that collects, analyzes, and communicates project data into useful information for the management of project work. PMIS systems can often be integrated with enterprise resource planning software tools for procurement, costing, and human resource planning. Advanced information systems can also be very positive when larger project scopes exist with more detailed deliverable performance indicators to report.

Project work meetings are highly common for the communication and execution of project work. Project manager, the project team, and relevant stakeholders are fixtures in attendance of project work meetings. Various meeting types are performed at different points in the project life cycle.

Technical meetings	Scrum daily standup meetings	Iteration meetings
Steering committee	Kick-off meetings	Technical meetings
Progress update meetings	Lessons learned meetings	Problem-solving meetings

Outputs

Deliverables

A deliverable is an outcome of a process, phase, or project itself that has a valid and supported quality, often in the form of a built capability, tangible object, process result, or product. The deliverable can be an outcome listed at the final step of the project or as several intermediary stages within the project. Deliverables may need to have change control processes applied when completed as an intermediary step and where subject to adjustments or forthcoming phases of the project that may alter the qualities of the deliverable. A deliverable may be internal or external. Internal deliverables can be a product, service, or result that is intended to satisfy the requirements or fulfill an objective of an internal stakeholder. The external deliverable serves to meet those needs of an external stakeholder. The external customer verifies that the deliverable meets the quality and performance expectations.

Use of Work Performance Data as an Output of the Project Work Phase

Work performance data is the measured and elemental result of the project activities performed in the course of executing the project phases. Work performance information is generated from the analysis of such raw performance data. Systems are used to capture raw work performance data, store it appropriately, analyze it, and transform the analysis into meaningful work performance information that can be used to report, communicate, and draw conclusions about the current project performance. Work data sources include KPIs, actual begin and end dates for tasks in the project, change requests, quality measurements, cost figures, schedule attainment, and communication records. These data sources are considered the outcomes of directing and managing the project work as scheduled.

Issue Log and Change Requests

During the course of performing project work against schedule, financial, quality, and resources constraints, the project team will often encounter issues that occur and will need to be resolved in order to meet performance objectives, deliverables, or milestones as expected. These issues can be in the form of conflicts, resource constraints, performance lags, and unforeseen errors. The issue log serves as a data source for such problems and as a location to document the corrective and preventive actions agreed upon by the project team. Data also found in the issues log include dates when issues were identified and resolved, persons finding the issues, risk or prioritization scores, and elements that define who resolves the issue and by when. Project managers and executives expect to be aware of issues and, more importantly, of the efforts being performed to resolve the issues. Future project planning can benefit from the knowledge gained from issue log accuracy. Change requests are related documents that create a formal paper trail and process around changing elements of the project plan while performing project work. These requests can alter deliverables, schedules, scope, cost, budget, resources, or quality parameters. The requests must be submitted, reviewed, and approved by the perform integrated change control process and team within the organization.

Project Document Updates Commonly Occurring During Project Work

Changes can occur at various points within a project plan. Changes to a project plan must be formally documented and submitted through the organization's change control process—often referred to as the perform integrated change control process. Several documents in the project work processes are commonly adjusted as the work is executed. The project has several supporting guidance tools used to steer decision-making during the work phases. Risk models created in early project planning phases may need to be updated or added as tasks are completed. Stakeholders are documented and defined prior to beginning project work. Tools such as RACI matrices may need updating as stakeholder relevance changes. Prior to beginning project work, assumption logs are used to inform the team of constraints. As those assumptions are tested, updates are likely needed. Requirements registered as critical to the outcome of the project may require changes and additional items based on customer needs. Furthermore, the activity list documenting the tasks needed for completion can be changed through the process due to unforeseen impactful issues. Lastly, the lessons learned register, a common source for documenting improvement opportunities, requires updating as such information is discovered.

Manage Project Knowledge

Overview

Knowledge management during the course of the project serves to better achieve the project objectives using existing knowledge from past projects and new knowledge from the current project. Both sources serve to expand and improve the organizational learning and knowledge repositories for improving the likelihood of stronger future project performance. Past history and knowledge captured and assessed benefits future project performance. Nearly all phases of the project management process serve as sources for knowledge capture. Inputs include the project management plan, various project documents, external environmental factors, and organizational assets. Tools used to transform inputs into outputs include knowledge and information management techniques as well as interpersonal and team performance skills. Outcomes are those that fall within the lessons learned register, changes approved to the project management plan, and improvements made to the organizational process asset process.

Input

In all aspects of the project knowledge management process, it is important that organizations build trust among their leaders and contributors so that the benefit of the knowledge process is maximized. As an input to the project knowledge process, the project management plan details the project's execution, monitoring, close-out, as well as the relevant details of supporting plans to the project. These essential details give insight into how the project was performed and can aid future planning efforts. Project documents such as the stakeholder register, team assignments, and the lessons learned register provide knowledge on how such influential persons were managed, how individual contributors made up the project team, and what lessons were gained from each executed project. Environmental factors within the enterprise such as positive-learning culture, working relationship strength, and blame-free employee relationships all help to reinforce the knowledge-centered organization. Lastly, the cultural routines and behaviors of the organization can support the value placed on knowledge capture and internal learning. Norms such as formal procedures for information sharing, confidentiality policies, and opportunities for informal discussions and innovations all reinforce the human element of project knowledge capture.

Tools and Techniques

Knowledge Management

Knowledge management is defined as using specific internal processes to create and apply knowledge to the benefit of the project management process. The definition can be further broadened to include the sharing of diverse knowledge and backgrounds for the benefit of projects and team members. Several tools and techniques are employed in the knowledge management process. These include social interactions, community networking, meetings, seminars, conferences, collaborative research, workshops, interactive training, and learning review meetings. The use and balance of these tools depends upon the cultural norms and acceptance of knowledge management techniques.

Information Management

Information management refers to the processes that transform data and results into useful information and the processes that allow stakeholders and project teams to access such information. Information, as a source of knowledge to be shared, can be documented and shared within a project team or within an organization through several tools: lessons learned register, project performance libraries, knowledge capture processes, information compilation, and software systems such as project management information systems (PMIS). Because people have many differences in preferred learning styles, the transfer of information and knowledge may require differing delivery approaches for different recipients. For example, project managers may benefit from face-to-face discussions of past lessons learned from those previous project managers themselves. Thus, capturing information alone does not sufficiently ensure that that information is being absorbed by those seeking the information. Furthermore, available resources, subject matter experts, and consultants with highly tuned and relevant skills can often reach answers and information sooner than the process of searching.

Expert Judgement and Interpersonal Skills

The knowledge management process can benefit from the external support by subject matter experts. Such support is preferable when coming from experts with skills specifically in project knowledge management, information management, related software and tools for managing these systems, and organizational learning. Project managers and their teams can utilize and strengthen their organization's knowledge management system by adopting interpersonal skills, such as facilitation (especially in meetings), active listening, and leadership. Facilitation would refer to the skill set of leading a team through the processes of decision-making. Active listening improves communications by infusing validation and verification behaviors to ensure understanding is certain between parties. Leadership refers to the ability to champion the organization's vision and strategy while inspiring the team and stakeholders towards peak performance. Two additional interpersonal skills desired of the project team include political awareness and networking. The former serves to discover and capture information and knowledge that may be asymmetrical based on power positions within an organization. The latter refers to the ability to gain information through formal and information connections between colleagues, acquaintances, and professionals to gain implied or unambiguous knowledge.

Outputs

Lessons Learned Register, Plan Updates, and Organizational Process Assets Updates

The lessons learned register is a transitioning tool where project leaders and team members document valuable content such as issues, problems, risks, or opportunities that were experienced. These lessons and the way in which each problem was resolved are documented as outputs of processes in the project so the register can then be used as an input in other or subsequent project phases. The life cycle of the lessons learned register is fluid throughout the project. When the project is complete, the register is added to the lessons learned repository within the organization as an organizational process asset for future project planning. Plan updates due to knowledge capture are those changes to the project management plan resulting from a formal change request and review through a change control system such as the perform integrated change control process. Template or standard content within project management plan development procedures may be updated with new knowledge as well. Organizational process assets are also components that are commonly updated as knowledge is mined or gained.

Monitor and Control Project Work

Overview

The monitor and control project work process serves to document, assess, and communicate project progress towards the achievement of the project's validated objectives. Such status reports of the project work provide stakeholders with informative progress updates and allows them to be aware when intervention or support is needed. Financial, schedule, and resource performance can also be assessed and shared. Monitoring serves to collect project data as inputs to continuous improvement opportunities. Control refers to the acts of planning, implementing, and verifying corrective and preventive actions that are taken following a deficiency or when a weakness is found. Nine essential components are considered essential to the monitor and control process.

Component	Description
Risks	Verifying the condition and impact of project risks
Key indicator performance	Actual performance versus project management plan
CAPA	Identifying and assigning corrective and preventive actions as needed
Cost and schedule	Maintaining cost and schedule forecasts and performance
Business alignment	Monitoring alignment of project against business needs
Product specification	Maintaining product or service attributes and information as developed
Data collection	Recording data on performance and forecasting
Change execution	Implementing changes from control processes
Reporting	Project progress reporting and communications

Inputs

Project Documents Used as Inputs to the Monitor and Control Project Work Process

Many project documents may be applicable as inputs to the monitor and control project work processes, however 10 project documents typically stand out as most commonly used. These documents can be grouped into forecasts, reports, and registers (or logs).

Forecasts
Schedule forecasts – Forecasting for schedule attainment is based on the projected plan, allowed tolerances to the plan, and the actual schedule attainment performance. **Cost forecasts** – The actual financial performance against planned budget is calculated and changes are implemented as necessary. **Milestone list** – Milestone lists, often also listed in the Gantt chart or project schedule, are indicated on a schedule and used to compare planned versus actual attainment.
Reports
Quality reports – Serve as a compilation of quality issues, corrective and preventive actions taken, and performance against quality parameters as set in the project planning phases. **Risk reports** – Summarizes individual as well as overall project risks into one report. **Basis of estimates report** – For estimates within the project plan, this set of information explains the basis of those estimates and guidance in the event of variances to the estimates.
Registers and Logs
Risk register – Documents the encountered threats and opportunities throughout the project. **Issue log** – The issue log tracks problems encountered during execution and who is responsible for resolving within agreed timeframes. **Assumption log** – Defines the assumptions and constraints analyzed as being impactful to the project. **Lessons learned register** – A knowledge-capturing tool used in the future improvement of project planning, variance prevention, and continuous improvement.

Work Performance Information

Work execution data generated and collected within the monitoring and control phase of the project is transferred into work performance information in order to be utilized in reporting metrics and project performance. Work execution data is collected and compared against the project management plan and the project documents in order to gauge project performance. The work performance information is stored securely for retrieval by stakeholders needing the information for reporting or variance planning. Metrics around work performance are determined within the project management plan at the early phases of the project. The information is embedded into reports and communicated among stakeholders to demonstrate how the project is being executed to plan.

Utility of Agreements in Controlling Project Work

Agreements, such as those made between a project manager acting as the buyer of services and a service provider acting as the seller of services, are methods used to control project performance when outsourced to a third party or independent entity to support the efforts of the project. It is wise for the project manager and team to design clauses, criteria, and performance metrics within any agreements or contracts made with third party providers. Such agreements most often align with the objectives and metrics of the project itself. Oversight of contractor work may also be reviewed in part by a procurement division of the organization within which the project is being performed. Procured contractors supporting a project should be aligned and following similar if not identical performance standards. In some cases, it is advised to have contractors held to tighter standards than the project itself.

Tools and Techniques

Types of Data Analysis in Monitoring Project Work

Alternatives analysis provides a project team with a selection of alternative actions to be taken as corrective actions when faced with variations or deviations from the plan. The cost-benefit analysis is a commonly used financial tool that allows the project team to financially weigh corrective action approaches based on expense and benefit or efficacy towards the problem itself. Earned value analysis tools combines the schedule, cost, and scope data into an analysis that provides a budgeted cost of work performed. Both the scope statement and the work breakdown structure (WBS) are key elements to the earned value analysis. The root cause analysis, such as a 5 Why tool, provides clarity to the true reason for a non-conformance or variance as a clear path to what the corrective and preventive actions should then be. The trend analysis tools are widely applicable and focus on collecting data and searching within that data using mathematical models for trends that provide explanations for the data behavior. Lastly, variance analysis focuses on the reasons for differences between expected results and actual results, as well as how those differences can be overcome.

Outputs

Work Performance Reports and Change Requests

Work performance reports are the result of work data as the project is executed. These reports include information that is created from the recording and analysis of project work data. Work performance reporting is intended to communicate progress and drive future decisions within the project. These reports include schedule attainment, costs incurred and variance, earned value reporting, and burnup/burndown information. These performance reports are often presented in a variety of formats, including scorecards, written reports in prose, financial charts, and schedule graphs. Key stakeholders that rely on this information receive the reports timely in order to track progress and make project or resource decisions. Change requests are used when analyzing actual project outcomes against the project plan. Where adjustments need to be made to cost, schedule, scope, quality, and procurement, the performance reporting supports those adjustment decisions. The perform integrated change control process drives the review and action upon any change requests. A change derived as an output of the project work processes can take the form of a corrective action, a preventive action, or a defect repair.

Project Documents That May Be Revised Due to Outputs of the Control Project Work Phase

As a project transitions out of the control project work processes, outputs are generated, including work performance reporting, change requests, project management plan updates, and document updates. Document updates that are commonly encountered at this transitionary point include those to forecasts or registers used within the project. As the work is executed, issues are tallied on the issues log and individual items are delegated to a responsible person to resolve by an agreed timeframe. Additionally, the risk register is updated as the project team discovers new risks to the success of the project plan. The output can also be translated into lessons learned; such information is documented into a register and used for continuous improvement for future phases or projects by the organization. Output data is very useful in assessing and changing cost and schedule forecasts. The respective cost management and schedule management processes dictate how these adjustments are made.

Perform Integrated Change Control

OVERVIEW

The perform integrated change control process (PICC) is a centralized system for the review of all project change requests, decision-making upon those requests, directing the changes to project management plans and related documents, and conveying the changes and decisions through communications with stakeholders. The controlled process by which the changes occur allow for a structured and disciplined approach to adjusting key information and tools used in project execution. An important factor considered by the centralized process is the relative risk or impact to project risks presented by the proposed change(s). The change control process is owned by the project manager, can be performed at any point within the project after baselines (initial costs, scope, and schedule) are set, and must be well documented. When baselines are impacted by the change request, the PICC process must be followed. The PICC process may sometimes be orchestrated by a change control board that performs the review, evaluation, decision-making, and communication of change dispositions. In highly customer-centric organizations, customer representatives may sit on the change control board.

INPUTS

PROJECT MANAGEMENT PLAN, PROJECT DOCUMENTS, AND CHANGE REQUESTS

Several foundational project materials serve to ensure the perform integrated change control (PICC) process is executed consistently and with validation. These inputs are either in the form of plans or baselines. Primarily, the change process relies on the project management plan as a basis for evaluating the proposed change. The PICC process and change control board, if used, employ a formal written change management plan that gives guidance and steps necessary to the organization for the change evaluation process. The related configuration management plan serves as a documented guide for the version control upon the elements of the project that keep the final product or service in a functioning state. The three baselines acting as inputs to the PICC process include scope, cost, and schedule. A baseline is an agreed and set standard against which project performance is measured. Project documents used as inputs to the PICC process include risk reports; basis of estimates reports that explain how cost, scope, and schedule estimates were determined; and the requirements traceability matrix. Change requests that get processed through the PICC may impact the project baselines and may include corrective or preventive actions or updates to formal documents and plans. Baselines are only updated after completing the PICC process via the change control board.

TOOLS AND TECHNIQUES

USE OF CHANGE CONTROL TOOLS

Configuration control is defined as the control of the features and attributes of the product or service deliverable being created by the project. Change control is defined as the control and documentation of the changes in the project, plan, baselines, and supporting documentation needed to execute the project. Change control tools, both manual and automated versions, are used to capture and govern such changes. Tools utilized will depend upon the unique needs of a project and the phases(s) where the changes are necessary. Configuration tools differ from change management tools in their scope and degree of impact towards the deliverables.

Configuration management tools include:

- **Identification of the configuration item** – A task serving to define and validate the configuration change to be made. The tool also includes verification of labeling, performance, and accountability.
- **Record and report** – Includes procedures and tools for documenting and communicating configuration changes.
- **Verification and audit** – These tools provide proof and assurance that the functional requirements are implemented in line with the configuration change documentation.

Change control tools include:

- **Analysis for need of change** – The identification of changes needed in documents or processes.
- **Change request form** – Used to document the proposal.
- **Change decision-making** – The process where supporting evidence is used to guide project leadership or the change control board (CCB).
- **Tracking changes** – Includes tools used to register documents, approval for changes, and rationale for making such changes.

Function of Data Analysis, Decision-Making, and Meetings

Commonly used tools for data analysis in the perform integrated change control (PICC) process include cost-benefit analysis and alternatives analysis. Cost-benefit uses financial assumptions to determine if the benefit of the change outweighs the expense. Risk avoidance may be an alternative means to assess benefit and should be considered by project management. Alternatives analysis weighs all competing alternatives against the proposed change to determine the optimal outcome. Decision-making tools used in the PICC process include voting, multicriteria decision-making, and autocratic decision-making. Voting provides a variety of ways to accept or reject changes by majority or plurality. Multicriteria involves a matrix approach to analyze the change against several criteria. Autocratic decision-making involves one person making the choice to accept or reject the changes. Lastly, change control board (CCB) meetings are beneficial to the PICC process as a means to review the change, assess impact to the project, and alternatives discussed. The CCB may also serve to perform configuration management reviews.

Outputs

Utility of Outputs

After the change request has been processed through the change management plan by the project manager or an appointee, the changes are implemented where necessary. The process includes steps for executing these changes. A project plan change log houses the details of all approved changes during the project life-cycle. Significant project updates may be made to the project management plan or to a variety of project documents. Changes to baselines are not retroactively effective against past data. Once approved changes are implemented, appropriate project team members or stakeholders should be notified and any retraining should be scheduled.

Close Project or Phase

Overview

Closeout and Closure

Closeout is the process where the project manager and/or team completes all remaining tasks or activities for the phase or project itself. The closure completes remaining tasks, prompts finalized reports to be archived for future learning, and the team disbands in order to pursue new or other projects in progress. Inputs include the project charter, the management plan, various documents such as the lessons learned log and milestone list, and accepted deliverables documentation. Tools include data analysis and meetings. Outputs include the lessons learned register; a final project deliverable such as a product, service, or transition; and a final report. Many actions and activities are to be reviewed during the closeout process. These can be categorized as documentation, resource allocation, waste disposition, deliverable, contractual, and summarization activities. Most importantly, the final deliverable(s) must be issued to the customer. Also, procurement and contract closure may be needed as the project or phase is completed.

Inputs

Project Documents Serving

Closeout documents may require completion, final sign-off, reporting, communication, or storage for later retrieval. The documents can be grouped into logs/registers, standards, and reports:

- Logs and registers
  - Risk register – Summarizes the risks that have been identified through the previous phases or activity.
  - Milestone list – Provides verification of the specific dates when project or phase milestones have been met.
  - Lessons learned register – All lessons learned from the phase or project are finalized before being added to the organization's central database.
  - Issue log – Closeout serves to ensure no outstanding issues are left open.
  - Change log – Any changes that were requested and executed during the project or phase are referenced here.
  - Assumption log – A pre-work summary of the project assumptions gets saved for future reference.
- Standards
  - Requirements documentation – Provides verification that the execution was within the scope of the project or phase.
  - QC measurements – Provides evidence that quality parameters were met for the phase or project deliverable(s).
  - Basis of estimates – Summarizes the performance of actual cost, duration, and resource use compared to estimated usages.
- Reports
  - Project communications – A summary of all project or phase-related communications from the project team.
  - Quality reports – Generally include quality metric summaries, suggested improvements, and all resolved quality issues.
  - Risk report – Serves to summarize risk status and verify if any risks need to be resolved before close-out.

Agreements and Procurement Documentation

Agreements are managed within the procurement management plan of the project. During close-out, contractual terms and conditions generally state what is required for agreement closure. Complexity of a project scope and its deliverables may make the agreement close-out more elaborate, especially as criteria for closure are numerous. When closing out the contractual agreements, the project team, through the procurement management plan, compiles and archives all related documentation. Examples of archived information include performance evidence on cost, scope, quality, and schedule as well as supporting specifications, manuals, inspection records, etc. The summary information for each contract closeout is beneficial to the lessons learned database for future projects or future contracts with contractors.

Tools and Techniques

Expert Judgement, Data Analysis, and Meetings

Expert judgement is beneficial in the closeout process as a means to ensure contractual agreements are fulfilled, legal language is understood during the closeout process, any final regulatory reviews are achieved through the right government agencies, and that the project results and processes receive any required closeout auditing per stakeholder requirements. Expert analysis at closeout can often identify and resolve risks that the team does not want to linger beyond closeout. Data analysis is used as a closeout tool to analyze documents and information to benefit the lessons learned repository. Furthermore, analysis techniques such as variance, trend, and regression can give reliable information on performance metric improvement, improve future planning models, and gather more confidence on the variables that drive project success, respectively. Lastly, meetings are used to primarily communicate status on the closeout process, deliverable completion, final reporting on metrics and performance to stakeholders, and ensure relevant knowledge and documentation is captured in the correct repositories.

Outputs

Final Changes Made to Project Documents and Common Organizational Process Asset Updates

Closure moves the project or phase documents into their final version and archiving for knowledge capture. The lessons learned register is finalized and used for organizational project planning improvement. The final lessons learned register is a highly important output of closure and often includes significant topics such as business case accuracy and handling risks and issues. Organizational process assets are likely to also be updated. Documents used in the closure or transfer process, such as agreements, specifications, and prior phase information, is reviewed by the project manager as a prerequisite to closure. Furthermore, organizational and operational support documents and project template documents may also be reviewed and updated as outputs of the closure process.

Issue of the Final Deliverable and Typical Elements of Final Project Reports

The final deliverable is issued to the recipient party, who is one of the stakeholders defined early in the project. The method of transfer depends upon the form in which the deliverable takes. For example, the completion of a warehouse as a deliverable has an occupancy transfer process that officially transfers responsibility when milestones are met and closeouts are verified. Alternatively, deliverable transfer may be an established process, service, or product that gets delivered verbally, physically, or electronically. Accompanying the final deliverable is a final report. This report may be provided to the stakeholder or customer receiving the deliverable, or it may remain within the project organization as reference and evidence of completion and lessons learned. Key elements of the final report include:

- Executive summary
- Scope summary and confirmation that scope was met
- Quality performance against objectives
- Performance against cost, schedule, and resource metrics
- Explanation of how project and deliverable met business needs
- Risk summary and how risks were managed

Project Scope Management

Plan Scope Management

Overview

Project scope management is the process of ensuring the project includes the required activities, and only those activities, in order to produce the deliverables within performance metrics to complete the project. Scope management is important in that it ensures clarity regarding what is in and out of the project's focus. Project scope management consists of six key elements.

Element	Description
Plan scope management	Creating a scope management plan showing how all elements will oversee the scope itself
Collect requirements	Capturing customer and stakeholder requirements to translate into scope language
Define scope	Clearly expressing the project and deliverables into a scope in objective terms
Create work breakdown structure	Parsing out each smaller activity that is needed to achieve deliverables and project work
Validate scope	Obtaining evidence that the described deliverables are sufficient
Control scope	Monitoring performance compared to the project or product scope, keeping performance aligned to the scope, and adjusting scope baseline where necessary

Scope Management Approaches in Predictive and Adaptive Project Life-Cycles

The use of predictive or adaptive scope management approaches depends on the degree of uncertainty and change inherent to the subject matter. Predictive scope management is relatively low uncertainty and the scope is well defined as a prerequisite to project start. Adaptive scope management is described as the repetitive adjustment of the scope given acquired knowledge of change, stakeholder input, and deliverable performance data. The feedback loop is used as an agile development of the deliverable and progressive reduction of requirement work backlogs. The process adjusts the deliverable and project scope several times, each time ironing out development issues important to stakeholders. Predictive scope management has well defined work breakdown, baselines, and change control processes. Agile scope management adjusts based on feedback from the iterative results of working through requirements backlogs. The status of the backlog is an indicator of forthcoming work.

Tailoring Considerations

Given that each project will have distinct characteristics, the project manager and project team must be cognizant of how the six key scope management elements may need to be tailored to fit the project. Five key tailoring considerations include:

Tailoring Approach	Description
Governance	Consideration of how the organizational design, hierarchy, and audit practices upon the scope process should proceed.
Knowledge management	Consideration of how the organization captures and uses knowledge and stakeholder requirements in scope management
Stability requirements	Does the organization gather and address unstable scope requirements? Does this impact the decision to be predictive or agile in scope management?
Development approaches	Does the organization need to use a predictive, an agile, or hybrid approach to scope management, given the stakeholder needs?
Validation and sustainability	What are the validation systems and control methods used by the project organization?

Inputs, Tools, Outputs

Plan Scope Management and Inputs

Plan scope management is a process where the project manager and team develop a plan to create the project scope using a variety of customer inputs, analysis tools, and formalized communications tools. The team must ensure that a valid, clear, and controlled scope is created to guide the project, its team, and stakeholders as the project moves forward. The plan scope management consists of a procedure or plan that will describe how the scope is to be created, how it is to be controlled, and what sources are used to give it validation. Key inputs to the scope management plan include the project charter and the project management plan. The scope must encompass the purpose, assumptions, constraints, quality parameters, and life-cycle features that are within these two input documents. Also, there may be several organizational process assets and enterprise environmental factors that are used as inputs, such as marketplace behavior, organizational norms, and past project scope lessons learned.

Transformational Tools and Resulting Outputs

Common tools such as expert judgement, meetings facilitated by the project manager, and data analysis are used to transform the scope management plan inputs into the resulting output: a clearly defined scope management plan. The **scope management plan** is an important part of the overall project management plan in that it will provide the project team with the procedures and constraints required to create the project scope. More elementally, the plan describes how the scope will be validated, monitored, controlled, created, and defined. Furthermore, the plan will describe acceptance of deliverables, defining and maintaining the scope baseline, and how the work breakdown structure will be drafted. The **requirements management plan**, also called a business analysis plan, explains as part of the project management plan how the stakeholder and customer requirements will be defined, analyzed, and controlled. The requirements management plan will also include explanations of how the requirements will be prioritized, what metrics will be monitored for performance, and how configuration activities will be performed.

Collect Requirements

Overview

Within the project scope management process, the collecting requirements sub-element refers to the process by which the project team gathers, documents, analyzes, and manages key stakeholder and customer requirements needed to meet the project objectives. An effective project scope must include feedback from stakeholders and have their concerns be met by the project as well. Project success can be heightened with active involvement from stakeholders and customers. Requirements themselves are attributes or conditions that must be found in the final product, service, or project result in order to satisfy a contractual agreement made with the customer or stakeholder. The stakeholder and customer requirements must be thoroughly captured, translated into the project scope and baseline, and controlled. The requirements are very important in the scope process because they are the foundation of the WBS and the performance measurement tools to be developed later.

Inputs

Usefulness of Inputs into the Collect Requirements

The project charter provides the project team with authority from the project sponsor to do the work and allocate resources to the project. The charter is the product of information from the business case, risks, high-level requirements and deliverables, and measurable objectives. The charter provides very key information to ensure the project scope is well defined and consistent with the chartered intent of the project. The project management plan includes several components that support the development of the project scope during the collection of requirements. The plan includes a stakeholder engagement plan that details communication modes, engagement strategies, and stakeholder participation activities. The project management plan also includes the requirements management plan and the newly created scope management plan finished prior to beginning to collect requirements for the scope itself. Key project documents used include the assumptions log, the lessons learned register, and the stakeholder register. Lastly, though not of least importance, any contracts or agreements with stakeholders, customers, or sponsors must be factored into this element of scope management.

Tools and Techniques

Techniques for Data Gathering When Collecting Stakeholder Requirements

Effective data-gathering tools used for stakeholder requirement compilations include benchmarking, focus groups, surveys, interviews, and brainstorming. Benchmarking is defined as the comparison of intended or proposed deliverables or processes to standard models or comparative existing versions from other organizations in order to obtain best practices, innovations, and performance goals. Focus groups serve to gather key demographics and potential users, stakeholders, subject matter experts, or impacted persons in an interactive group setting for data on their perspectives and advice on the proposed product, service, or process being proposed in the project. Surveys are electronic or paper-based means to collect data from a large dispersed population and provide quick statistical analysis to drive the project scope process. Interviews are one-on-one collections of stakeholder and expert data regarding the impact of the proposed project deliverable(s) and perspectives on features and deliverables themselves. Lastly, brainstorming involves grouping stakeholders to compile a multitude of relevant innovative ideas regarding product, scope, or project requirements.

Data Analysis, Decision-Making, and Data Representation

Data analysis in project scope management is largely focused on document reviews designed to find key data and draw that data into the scope defining process. A wide variety of documents may be reviewed to extract the relevant requirements. Documents commonly contained in this review include proposals, regulations, policies, procedures, process flows, business cases and processes, business plans, contracts, and agreements. The collection of requirements for scope management can also involve decision-making tools designed to narrow down choices. Similar tools such as majority voting, unanimous voting, multicriteria decision-making, and autocratic decision-making are used just as in the perform integrated change control process. Data may also be visualized and analyzed in representation formats to help effectively gather and communicate requirements. Mind mapping is a tool used to capture related brainstormed ideas and organize them into groupings. Affinity diagrams are similar mapping tools where related brainstormed topics are grouped based on common characteristics. Both tools make analysis easier than a large unsorted data set.

Interpersonal and Team Skills Used to Collect Requirements for Project Scope Management

The nominal group technique translates brainstorming event ideas into a more manageable list of choices for action based on preference from the participants in the group. Teams consisting of stakeholders, subject matter experts, and project team members will provide validation to the nominal group rankings. Observations used in project scope management refer to the physical observation by a project team member or manager upon the process or activity of a stakeholder in order to obtain a greater understanding of requirements that are not easily or readily communicated from the stakeholder. Observations are similarly referred to job shadowing, but may also include participation in the activity itself, where the participating observer would get a greater understanding of requirements. Facilitation refers to workshops where project team members serve to facilitate discussions and meetings with key stakeholders to define requirements and build trusting understandings between the two parties. This facilitation approach is especially helpful when stakeholders disagree with the priority of requirements for the project.

Quality Function Deployment

Quality function deployment (QFD) is a tool used to systematically translate stakeholder-defined requirements into technical specifications, controls, and engineering requirements. The tool uses four combined matrices to create a summary of relationships between customer requirements and resulting process parameters to create goods or services that meet those requirements. QFD also translates the customer voice into salesforce language and further into engineering and operations understanding. Cross-functional experts from the organization are important support to the project manager seeking to create a QFD successfully. To further strengthen the analysis of customer voice, the QFD matrix often includes competitive data, co-relationships of requirements, and weighted scores for communicating significance to requirements.

Context Diagram and Prototypes

The context diagram is used to model the scope in a project. The diagram provides a visual representation of how customers use the deliverable and how the business systems create and deliver the product or service. Furthermore, the diagram maps the inputs to the business transformation systems, the actors that provide the inputs, the outputs generated from the business process, and the actors receiving the process outputs. Prototypes are effective in validating stakeholder requirements by providing a testable model to obtain performance feedback. Prototypes are generally iterative versions made and adjusted in multiple cycles to confirm these requirements and validate performance to expectations. Prototypes can come in several forms, including simulations, computer models, engineered physical versions, and mock versions of the desired final product. The end of the prototype phasing results in a production-ready product with all requirements captured and performance validated.

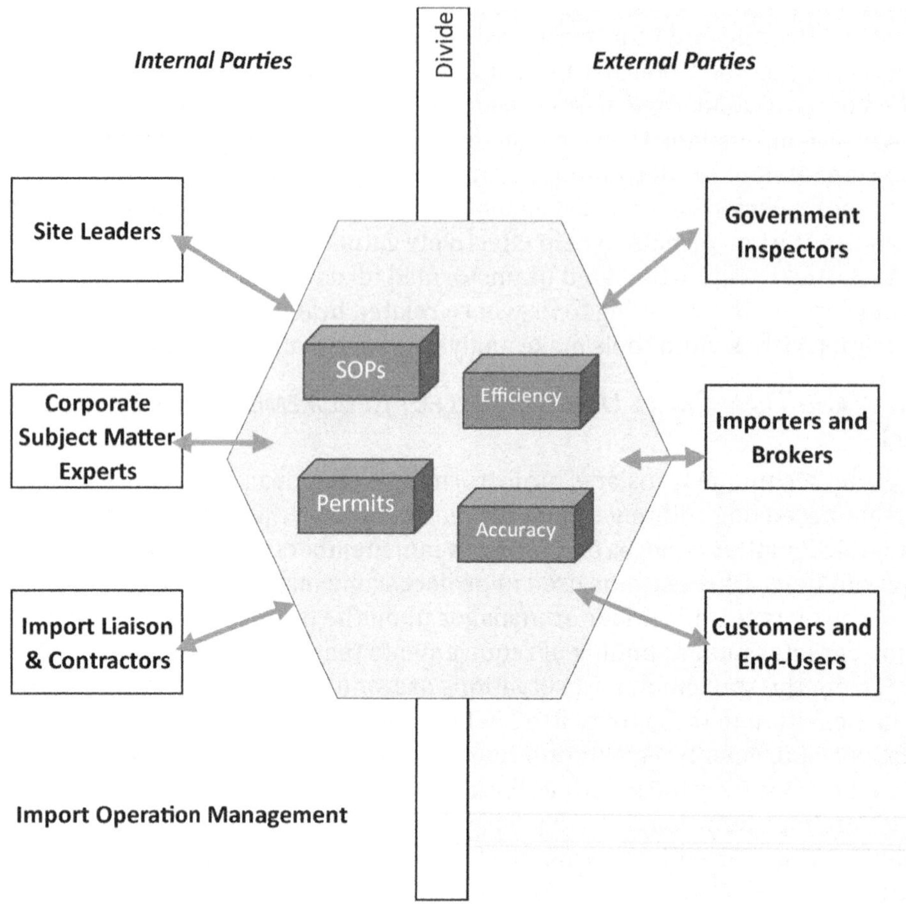

Outputs

Types of Requirements Documentation

Solutions requirements are outputs of the collection element that most completely detail the parameters, functions, and features of the service or product that will best meet the stakeholder requirements collected. Solutions requirements are divided into functional and non-functional groups based on characteristics. Functional solutions requirements are tangible features and behaviors that the product or service will exude, such as parts, actions, and processes. Non-functional solutions requirements are intangible features that are not visibly present but can be determined through statistical analysis or deeper evaluation of the product or service. Stakeholder requirements are also documented at an output. Related quality requirements detail the tests, parameters, and audits necessary to assure the project and results meet quality expectations. Project requirements detail the milestones, resource constraints, and processes needed to achieve a successful project outcome. Business requirements list the higher-level business relevance of the project. Lastly, the transition and readiness requirements describe how the project team, its stakeholders, and participants will develop the resources and systems in order to effectively begin the forthcoming project.

Requirements Traceability Matrix

The requirements traceability matrix is a tool used in scope development to bond the deliverables to the originating customer and stakeholder requirements from which they are derived. A full traceability of deliverables to requirements ensures that the project activity delivers economic value, uses resources appropriately, and meets project objectives. As performance is tracked in the project life cycle, measurement of performance against the requirements using the matrix reinforces validation. Elements of the requirements traceability matrix includes high-level validated requirements, project scope and objectives, business objectives, and work breakdown deliverables. Quality attributes are documented within the traceability matrix in sufficient detail so that each requirement can be effectively understood, measured, monitored, controlled, and compared for performance reporting needs. The requirements traceability matrix may also include final deliverable or phase acceptance criteria.

Define Scope

Overview

The core part of the project scope management process involves the activity of using relevant inputs to formally develop the scope of the project and product/service considered as the primary deliverable. The scope also delineates what is inside and what is outside the purview of the project. The process of defining the scope could potentially use any part or all of the collected requirements outputs. Iterative projects may have the scope change as the project evolves, while predictive projects have the scope well defined in the project scope management phase with no changes thereafter. The resulting output of the define scope element is a clear, detailed depiction of the project and its deliverables, including resulting products or services.

Outputs

Project Scope Statement

The project scope statement serves to describe the project scope as well as the product/service scope. It also contains highly important details, including the constraints, the deliverables, and any assumptions relevant to the project. The scope statement is written for stakeholders as the primary audience. The scope statement provides a baseline perimeter from which the project team and the PICC or change control board can base their decisions when confronted with change requests. After the scope statement is completed, the project team has more guidance and a path forward for creating more detailed plans and executing the project work. The four main features of the scope statement are acceptance criteria, deliverables, scope description, and exclusions. The acceptance criteria explain key features, parameters, or requirements that must be met before the deliverable(s) can be considered accepted. The deliverables are any type of product, service, or phase transition that meet the compiled requirements. The description of deliverables is included in the scope statement with sufficient detail to ensure it is clearly communicated. Lastly, the scope description defines the expected project deliverables using the referenced and compiled requirements as well as the project charter. Exclusions to this scope description are also defined in the exclusion section to ensure added clarity about what is in scope in the project.

Project Scope Statement vs. Project Charter

The project charter represents the authorization for the project manager and team to begin procuring resources and performing activities for the assigned project. The charter also signals that the project meets organizational strategic objectives and the business case exemplifies an endeavor that makes financial sense to pursue. The charter also lists project objectives, purpose, deliverables, and the resources needed to complete the project.

In contrast, the project scope statement reflects the input of customer and stakeholder requirements in order to ensure the project is focused on what matters most to the client and not focused on irrelevant details. In some projects, the scope statement is a critical element to the project charter. For example, it is common in lean Six Sigma projects to have a scope statement within the project charter. Furthermore, the charter describes purpose; high-level requirements and deliverables; and summary details for the project, such as schedule and objectives. The scope statement details the deliverables, acceptance criteria, and any scope exclusions.

Create WBS

Overview

Work breakdown structures (WBS) divide a project into smaller manageable activities to help the team make sense of the steps necessary to complete the project. The WBS can provide the team with the actions necessary to enact the vision and deliverables in the project within schedule and budget. The structure is an element of the project scope management process. The WBS deconstructs the entire scope of the project. The defined goals or objectives are important parts of the WBS, with all tasks and subtasks being derived from the goals. WBS plans create a hierarchy of the project by creating layers, including work packages, tasks, and subtasks. Details such as precursory and subsequent tasks, costs, and performance expectations are all included in each level of the WBS. Work within the WBS is not the individual tasks, but as deliverables that result from elemental tasks.

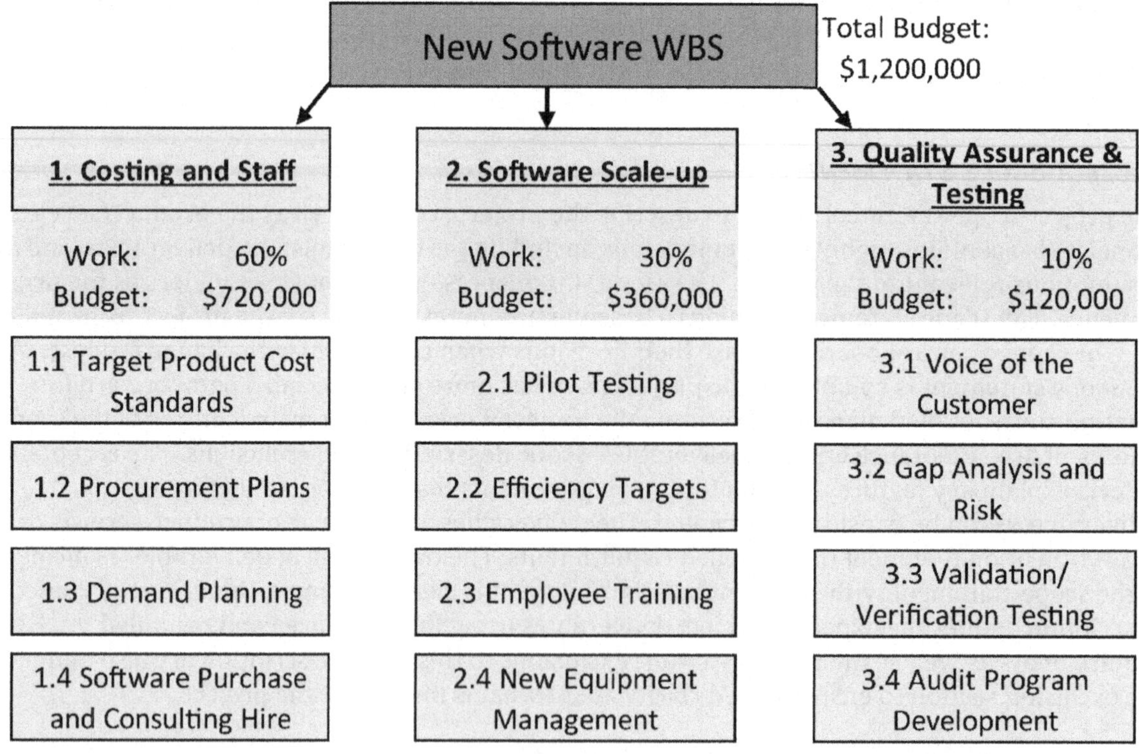

Tools and Techniques

Decomposition

Decomposition is defined as the division of the project scope and deliverables into smaller and more manageable subcomponents. Specificity is indicated in the decomposition as more detailed breakdowns reflect the degree of control desired by the project team. The smallest elements resulting from the decomposition process are work packages. Work packages themselves are not simple activities or tasks; the packages consist of several highly related tasks to be completed. Decomposition includes five key steps: deliverables analysis, WBS organization, upper-level WBS decomposition into subsidiary workings, tagging WBS steps with identification codes, and verification of effective and accurate decomposition.

OUTPUTS

SCOPE BASELINE

The purpose of the scope baseline as a work breakdown structure (WBS) output and a key part of the project management plan is a validated scope statement combined with the WBS and its associated WBS dictionary. The baseline is a controlled comparison that requires a formal change process in order to be revised. The five key components of the scope baseline include the WBS itself, the WBS dictionary, the project scope statement, the work package, and the planning package. The WBS is a detailed breakdown of the total work forthcoming in the project. The WBS dictionary provides further detailed information about deliverable, schedule, and activity for each WBS constituent. Other information provided in the dictionary includes work descriptions, milestones, resource requirements, and responsibilities. The project scope statement lists the scope itself, listings of the deliverables, constraints, and key assumptions for the project. The work package represents identified, elemental level tasks within the WBS. Each package has a unique identifier and includes related cost, schedule, and resource data linked to that identifier. Multiple work packages form a control account. The planning package is an intermediary part of the WBS without schedule details but with relevant work content included.

Validate Scope

OVERVIEW

The validate scope process involves the project manager and team obtaining objective validation for the project scope and deliverables. Such validation of each deliverable supports the allocation of resources towards the final outcomes of the project—such as a product, service, or transition—and makes commitment towards a high-quality project outcome more likely. Customers are a primary source of validation in this element; deliverables from the project control quality process are reviewed for acceptance by project customers. Inputs to the validate scope element include the scope baseline, requirements documentation, and work execution data.

INPUTS

The validate scope element to the project scope management phase includes the project management plan itself, several key project documents, deliverables, and work execution data. The subcomponents of the project management plan used as inputs include the scope baseline, the requirements management plan, and the scope management plan. Several common but important documents used as inputs include the stakeholder requirements documentation and the related requirements traceability matrix; the lessons learned register; and any quality reports generated in the project to date, such as quality assurance issues or corrective actions. Deliverables used in the scope validation process must be those that have supporting proof reflecting their alignment with customer expectations in the control quality phase. Lastly, work execution data represents an input that demonstrates the validation performance amassed in the project. These records may include measurements showing compliance to requirements, non-conformances issued, and the results of previous validation activities.

Tools and Techniques and Outputs

Inspection and Decision-Making

Decision-making is a common leadership trait in project management. Decision-making is important in the scope validation process because of the amount and impact of the information collected to derive an effective scope statement and project scope management planning. An element of the decision-making technique includes voting. Voting is utilized when the stakeholders develop the validation material. Inspection is a common approach to validate and verify systems. In the project scope management process, inspections are used to verify deliverables and customer relevance of the scope. The inspections, also referred to commonly in project management as reviews or walkthroughs, verify if work and deliverables meet the acceptance criteria and are in line with expectations. Inspections often include several facets, such as observations, record reviews, data analysis, measuring processes or workflows, and even destructive testing of finished outputs.

Control Scope

Overview

The control scope element serves to sustain the project's central scope and monitor progress in relation to that scope. The scope baseline is a very key component to this element. The baseline is the validated model against which progress is monitored. Deviation from the scope baseline would prompt reporting and communication to relay those deviations to key stakeholders and project leadership. The control scope process also ensures that the perform integrated change control (PICC) unit is utilized for any recommended baseline or scope changes and corrective actions. Limited resources committed to the project are at risk to be overused or deviate from plan in a situation called scope creep. The control scope element also serves to ensure that the defined scope is met and that creep is minimized or prevented entirely. When change is a necessity for valid reasons, the control scope process ensures that those changes are well managed and communicated. The control scope process flow begins with inputs of the project management plan, project documents such as the requirements traceability matrix, and work performance data. Through the element, outputs include work performance information, activity for the PICC unit, potentially revised project management plans, and updated project documents.

Inputs

Project Management Plan Components and Project Documents That Serve as Inputs

The process to control the scope must include critical validation documents, including the project management plan and its sub-components. Sub-components include primarily the scope management plan and the scope baseline. To control the scope against creep and uncontrolled changes, project managers and stakeholders must closely monitor performance against the scope baseline. The scope management plan serves as a standard operating procedure defining how the organization will execute the control functions upon the project scope and product scope. The baseline is the calibration model against which performance is monitored. Additional project plan components include the configuration management process, the performance measurement baseline, and the customer/stakeholder requirements management plan. These plans serve as guides of validation when monitoring scope. Project documents used as inputs include the requirements traceability matrix, all related requirements documentation, and the lessons learned register. These components and documents are also supplemented by work performance data and various associated organizational process assets.

Project Schedule Management

Plan Schedule Management

Overview

Process	Description
Plan schedule management	The encompassing policies and procedures that describe how the project schedule is to be created, managed, performed, and verified by the project team.
Define activities	The project team determines the specific activities and tasks needed to accomplish the defined deliverables of the project. This component includes the use of decomposition and rolling wave planning techniques.
Sequence activities	The process by which the project team constructs sequential and relational order to the defined activities and tasks. The schedule begins taking a rough format during this step.
Estimate activity durations	Using validation material, history, and expert opinion (among other resources) to affix time durations or work periods to each task in the body of defined activities needed to deliverable completion.
Develop schedule	This part of the schedule management process involves the analysis of the define, sequence, and duration estimate work and develops a project schedule to be followed for execution and control.
Control schedule	Procedures that serve to monitor and verify the adherence to the project schedule and use formal processes to adapt or prevent change from impacting performance against baseline.

Emerging Trends in Project Schedule Management

Alternative scheduling is a change-friendly option that uses adaptive life-cycles and is similar to rolling wave planning and agile product development schemes. Information is collected and translated into product features within sequential timeframes. During the course of each of these timeframes, value is added to the deliverable and the project in an incremental manner. On-demand scheduling relies on downstream demand or pull for intermediary inputs or signal to progress through the sequenced activity of the project schedule. The organization's throughput capacity and its ability to forecast demand are often weaknesses for on-demand schedule performance. On-demand scheduling is similarly used in lean manufacturing principles, such as Kanban and Goldratt's theory of constraints.

Inputs

The plan schedule management process is similar to that of the scope development in that it involves the development of policies and standard operating procedures regarding planning, implementing, and controlling the project schedule. Just as with the scope management plan, the schedule management planning process documents procedures, policies, and metrics that will be used to ensure that schedule development, monitoring, and sustainability is achieved. Key inputs used when developing the schedule management plan include the project charter, the project management plan, the scope management plan, and enterprise environmental factors.

Tools and Techniques

Expert Judgement, Meetings, and Data Analysis

Expert judgement focused on effective project schedule development provides the project leadership with experience and insight into optimizing the schedule early. Experts may be selected from within the organization or as an exterior consultant or stakeholder. Expertise most valuable to supporting plan schedule management can include adaptive life-cycle or predictive methods, scheduling software implementation and interpretation, scheduling basics such as creation and control, and advanced considerations within specific industries. Meetings are important approaches to collect stakeholders that impact or influence the schedule and develop the project schedule and its supporting activities. Data analysis is a common tool used when there are alternatives that need to be weighed by the project team before selecting a life-cycle model. Data analysis tools are also supportive when calculations must be made regarding rolling wave planning, lead and lag times, and related resource planning.

Outputs

Schedule Management Plan

The schedule management plan is a key component of the project management plan and serves to communicate how the schedule will be created, monitored, and controlled by the project team and relevant stakeholders and experts as needed. The level of complexity of the schedule management plan is determined by the scope of the project. The schedule management plan, as an output, will provide the team with several standards and instructions needed for the schedule life-cycle.

Results of the Schedule Management Plan	Description
Control thresholds	Acceptable schedule variation levels to be monitored.
Level of accuracy	Ranges acceptable in the estimation of activity durations.
Organizational procedure linkage	Linkage to the work breakdown structure (WBS).
Project schedule model development	The chosen scheduling development tools are defined.
Project schedule model maintenance	The procedures for updating schedule execution status.
Release and iteration length	Commonly occurs when using time-boxing in adaptive life cycle scheduling.
Reporting formats	Specific controls on schedule performance reporting.
Rules of performance measurement	Performance measurement rules such as earned value management are set.
Units of measure	Elemental units of measure are defined for consistency.

Define Activities

Overview

The define activities element is a process where work activities are defined as necessary to accomplish the project deliverables. The work breakdown structure results in work packages—small breakdowns of the project but not in the most elemental task level. The define activities process hashes out the specific tasks and activities needed to fulfill these packages. Inputs into the define activities process include the project management plan, the schedule management plan, the scope baseline, enterprise environmental factors, and various organizational process assets.

Tools and Techniques

Decomposition

Decomposition is defined as the creation of manageable pieces and activities from the scope and deliverables. The analogy used is that of organic matter decomposing into elemental nutrients that are the building blocks of the organic material itself. Fittingly, decomposition is a collaborative tool used in the creation of elemental activities needed to complete work packages. Distinct from the work breakdown process, decomposition takes deliverables a step further by breaking them into manageable tasks. The work breakdown structure packages are each decomposed into the activities or tasks needed to complete each deliverable. The WBS dictionary is also essential to creating the activity breakdown.

Rolling Wave Planning

Rolling wave planning is a technique for focusing on planning the finite details on near-term activities with increased importance while looking at more distant planning activities from a broader perspective. The rolling wave plan is repeated routinely as near-term activities are planned and executed and future activities come due. Longer-term work is kept in work packages and near-term planning is broken down into activities and details through decomposition. The technique is highly useful in agile and waterfall project life-cycles.

Outputs

Change Requests, Milestone List, Activity Attributes, and Activities List

Change requests that arise in the context of the define activities process often occur as work packages are broken down into activities and new information was obtained that exposed a weakness in the initial baselines. As with other change requests, such endeavors are routed through the perform integrated change control group in the organization. The milestone list functions within the activity schedule as markers, with no technical duration, that collections of activities had been completed and/or deliverables have been achieved during the project schedule execution. Milestones are often indicated as contractually mandatory or strongly recommended based on organizational lessons learned. Activity attributes are collections of more detailed information for each activity decomposed from work packages. These attributes provide key stakeholders and activity executors added details such as lead and lag times, assumptions, constraints, activity relationships, and resource requirements. The additional information provides support for leadership analysis of the schedule and greater clarity and context to each task. The activities list delineates, by ordered activity ID, the tasks in the schedule. A work description is also included in the list to give additional context. Iterative life cycle approaches to project schedule planning expand the activities list and activity attributes in sequential batches as the project progresses.

Sequence Activities

Overview

Sequencing activities is the act of linking project activities based upon their relationships with each other. Relationship mapping and sequencing can be based on individual linkage or grouping using related features. The intent of the sequencing activities is to give added efficiency in the execution of the schedule and lead/lag time as necessary for certain activities. Inputs to the sequencing process include activity attributes, activity lists, the milestone list, and assumptions. Transformation of the inputs results in the creation of project schedule network diagrams and updates to the input documents as necessary. Sequencing involves the use of predecessor and successor linkage, lead and lag time estimations, and duration calculations to make a visual map of the various work activity streams in parallel or sequence through every milestone and deliverable in the schedule.

Inputs

Function of Key Inputs

Input	Use in Sequencing
Activity attributes	Added detail within the activity attributes often provides unambiguous durations, sequences, predecessor relationships, and duration uncertainty (in the form of lead and lag times). These details provide straightforward sequencing input.
Activity lists	The activity list provides a summary of all activities that must be sequenced in the sequencing phase.
Milestone list	The milestone list describes the collective activities that must be completed before each milestone is considered as achieved. Similarly, the milestone list may also have defined dates or elapsed days that dictate how activities are to be scheduled.
Assumptions	The assumptions and constraints documentation provide influence upon the sequencing activities, given the lists contain information on uncertainty in lag and lead times, risks, and relationships among activities. These variables impose the need to plan for uncertainties in the sequence.
Schedule management plan	The plan gives validated guidance and requirements for how the schedule management and sequencing must be performed.
Scope baseline	The scope baseline gives boundaries regarding assumptions, constraints, work breakdown structure (WBS), and deliverables necessary to sequencing.

Tools and Techniques

Precedence Diagramming Method

The precedence diagramming method (PDM) is a tool used to visually depict the activities in the compiled sequence schedule using nodes and logical relationships. Activities will have one of four distinct relationships—or dependencies—between themselves and other activities. These dependencies can be predecessor-type or successor-type. Predecessor dependencies imply an activity that comes prior to a dependent activity. Successor dependencies imply a dependent activity that comes following a prior activity. The PDM also categorizes four types of relationships based on the possible dependency permutations. The available relationships are based on sequential, parallel, complementary, and overlapping uses.

Relationship Types

Start to finish (SF)	An overlapping relationship where the successor activity does not begin until the predecessor activity finishes.
Start to start (SS)	A complementary relationship where the successor activity does not start until the predecessor activity also starts.
Finish to start (FS)	The most common relationship where sequentially the successor activity does not start until the preceding activity finishes.
Finish to finish (FF)	The successor activity is not considered finished until the predecessor activity finishes.

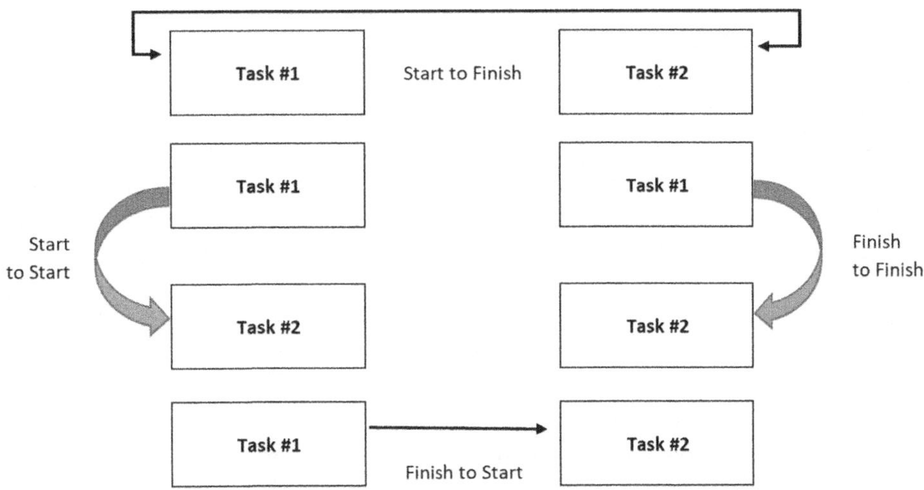

Activity Relationships in Precedence Diagramming Method

Dependency Determination

Dependency relationships are determined in the sequencing process by first categorizing relationships as internal or external and as mandatory or optional. The classification of each dependency influences the prioritization each activity receives in the sequencing process. These two dimensions of dependency focus on the degree of control the project team has over the implied dependencies. For example, internal dependencies are generally more controllable than external dependencies. Likewise, discretionary dependencies are more flexible and can be variable based on the needs of other activities and resource constraints. However, mandatory dependencies are generally non-negotiable and must be completed before downstream activities begin. Internal dependencies are based on internal limitations and precedence. External dependencies are outside the direct control of the project team, such as a government agency. Mandatory dependencies can include contractual obligations, legal requirements, or are influenced by mathematical or physical limitations. Discretionary dependencies are those where flexibility is available, and sequencing can take advantage of that trait. These soft logic dependencies expose the project to schedule attainment variance if not tightly controlled.

Lag and Lead Times

Lead occurs in activity scheduling in finish-to-start dependencies and provides the opportunity to hasten the successor activity given the predecessor. Alternatively, lag occurs commonly, but not exclusively, as start-to-start dependencies. In lag situations, a downstream successor activity is delayed pending the completion of a predecessor. Lead is denoted in project schedule network diagrams or in planning software with the type of relationship, the numerical lead duration, and a negative sign. Similarly, lag is denoted with the relationship type, the numerical duration, and a positive sign. The process of sequencing activities must factor in the dependencies that need lead and lag times. The calculations and mapping of sequencing activities and schedule network diagrams is commonly performed with project management information systems. Such software is able to perform mapping and document leads, lags, dependencies, and help arrange logical relationships for the project team.

Outputs

Project Schedule Network Diagram

The project schedule network diagram is a visual depiction of the sequenced activities and their dependencies. The diagram is created as an output of the sequence activities step of the project schedule management process. The diagram shows logical relationships, indicates lead or lag durations as appropriate, and displays any divergence or convergence routes of the activity flow. Network diagram divergence occurs when a predecessor activity has multiple successors. Convergence occurs when a successor activity has multiple predecessors. Regardless of whether the diagram is created manually or through project management information systems (PMIS), the diagrams provide a roadmap of the sequenced schedule. Diagrams often may include descriptions of the process used to create the map—a summary narrative—and unique clusters of activities may have supporting detail added for clarity.

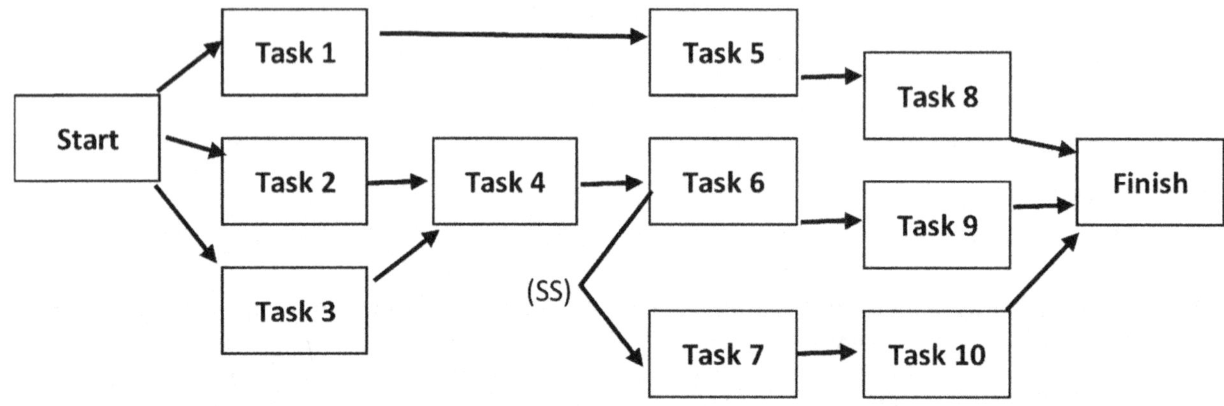

Project Schedule Network Diagram

Estimate Activity Durations

Overview

The process of estimating activity durations involves using valid project data and information inputs to attach an estimated numerical number of work cycles to each activity in the schedule. This process adds a layer of mathematical and temporal utility to the schedule and sequence. A very significant amount of input information—such as the project management plan and project documents—is needed to perform the estimations. Several of these inputs involve data on resource sourcing and availability. Generally, the stakeholders or team members with the most relevant experience regarding certain activities also perform the duration estimations for those activities. The estimations derive the amount of work necessary to complete activities, all while factoring in constraints and external requirements to the usage of time. Many factors contribute to the estimations of each activity, including resource availability and effectiveness. Duration estimates exclude lead and lag times; these are added when mapping network diagrams.

Factors to Consider When Estimating Durations

Diminishing returns occur in duration estimation when resources are increasingly added towards the effort of producing work output for an activity and the additional effort does not yield any improvement in obtaining the outputs sooner or in better quality. Technology serves as an estimation factor because of the gains in speed, efficiency, and accuracy with advances in technology. For example, automated sorting operations may complete an activity at a fraction of the estimated duration when hand-sorting methods are used. Resource quantity refers to the caveat that a linear increase in resources applied to an activity does not necessarily result in a corresponding decrease in duration. Resources at some point become a burden upon the duration as more support and work must go into each activity. Lastly, organizational motivation serves estimation work by preventing procrastination as well as expansion of work performed to fit the pre-existing duration.

INPUTS

FUNCTION OF KEY INPUTS

Input	Description
Activity attributes and list	The activities list is a compendium of all activities to be sequenced and executed. Attributes are attached as supplementary cut sheets that provide added detail, such as logical relationships and lead/lag durations.
Assumption log	Useful assumptions and constraints known to the project team and valuable to factor into duration estimates.
Milestone list	Ordered listing of key milestones marking progress through the project schedule.
Lessons learned register	Past knowledge gained from experience in the organization and compiled for repeating successes and avoiding mistakes in the future.
Schedule management plan	Provides guidance on accuracy and other requirements for duration assessments.
Scope baseline	Project scope information as well as work breakdown structure dictionary.
Resource breakdown and calendars	A detailed account and breakdown of the resources needed for each activity and their temporal availability to work at each activity. For example, human resources and equipment resources must be adequately scheduled to maximize schedule attainment.
Resource requirements	Requirements linked to the resources needed for each activity. These requirements serve as specifications needed to be met by resources in order to meet duration and quality expectations.
Risk register	A compendium of identified risks that may impact the project.

TOOLS AND TECHNIQUES

ANALOGOUS ESTIMATING

Analogous estimating is a version of benchmarking whereby past objective duration and cost data is used to estimate similar parameters in a present or future project. Parameters such as budget size, project scope, and schedule duration of the project, when comparable to the present project undergoing activity duration estimations, can be used to support these estimates, especially when reliable present information is not available. The technique is a relatively modest investment of time and cost, but it can be riddled with inaccuracies.

PARAMETRIC ESTIMATING

Parametric estimating uses computer software calculations and past project cost and temporal data to derive duration estimates based on statistical models. Other variables are factored into the calculations based on the past project parameters. The process can also provide statistical estimates of cost. The assumptions included in the calculations become increasingly accurate as the historical data is more reliable. Though the underlying assumptions of total necessary hours for an activity need calculating, the durations for each activity can be easily derived by the multiple of the work quantity and the labor capability. These calculations support resource allocation, costing, scheduling dependencies, and relationship determination.

Example duration calculation:

$$\frac{\text{Total activity work}}{\text{Labor capability}} = \text{Duration (hours)}$$

$$\frac{\text{200 pallets}}{\text{5 pallets per hour}} = \text{40 hours}$$

Three-Point Estimating and Bottom-up Estimating

Three-point estimating of durations is an average calculation of the most likely, best case (optimistic), and worst case (pessimistic) activity durations calculated. This average provides a useful duration value when indicators and uncertainties provide differing estimates with similar probabilities; it is especially useful when historical precedent for duration is lacking. This resulting average is based on the (non-statistical) range of possibilities. The most likely duration (tM) has the highest probability given the resource productivity, availability, and dependencies. The optimistic duration (tO) is the analyzed best outcome given the inputs and assumptions. The pessimistic duration represents the worst-case outcome (tP). By calculating the mean of these three durations, the triangular distribution (tE) is calculated.

$$\text{Triangular distribution (tE)} = \frac{\text{tM} + \text{tO} + \text{tP}}{3}$$

Bottom-up estimating is similarly useful when the project duration is difficult to estimate. The most elemental branches of the WBS are decomposed into work; the work is estimated individually to the farthest extent possible; and the aggregated durations (including dependencies) are summed to represent the activities, packages, and project itself.

Reserve Analysis

Reserve analysis is useful in deriving the level of contingency or management capacity needed for a project. When uncertainty exceeds an acceptable threshold, the project management allocates reserves to the schedule, generally in the form of additional percentage of the estimated duration or in the form of additional work hours. Given the uncertainty, as the project work is performed and actual durations and resource requirements are experienced, the reserve quantities may be reduced or eliminated. The project schedule often denotes core durations from reserve proportions and distinguishes both in performance reporting. Furthermore, management reserves are built-in contingency resources that are available to project management in the event that unforeseen variation in project risks, assumptions, and external factors diverge the project from its scope or schedule unexpectedly. These management reserve resources allow the project manager and stakeholders to make on-the-fly resource allocations to get the project back on track. These reserves are outside of the schedule baseline but may require a baseline change process if determined that the management reserves need to be used.

Outputs

Features of Duration Estimates as Outputs of the Activity Duration Process

Duration estimates that result from the estimate activity duration process are characterized as a duration of time estimated to complete the activity, phase, or project. The estimates may also have calculated range of variation that the team may experience when executing the activity or larger portion of the project. Such indicated variation can be displayed as additional work periods (e.g., days or hours) or as probabilities of exceeding or meeting the expected duration. The basis of the duration estimates includes several factors that were used to create the estimated durations. Such supporting data can be in the form of project risks, assumptions made, constraints known to the project team, the approach used to develop or calculate the estimates, how much statistical confidence exists for each estimate, descriptions of variance around the estimate, and the calculations of three-point or bottom-up calculations. The basis information can be highly valuable as historical information when planning future projects or iterations within a project life cycle.

Develop Schedule

OVERVIEW

The develop schedule element reflects precisely what its name describes. The collective analysis of activity sequencing outputs, duration outputs, resource requirements, assumptions, and constraints yield a schedule of the activities and work to be executed by the project team and stakeholders. The schedule includes start dates, divergent and convergent work streams, and milestones in a format that is easy to understand. Such an important element to the schedule management phase requires careful and often repeated analysis to reach optimization. Key inputs include the project management plan, several project document sources, agreements, and organizational factors. Key steps include schedule compilation (often by software), schedule review by the project staff to identify conflicts or resource constraints, review of dependencies for correctness, and approval/baselining of the schedule itself.

INPUTS

ESSENTIAL PROJECT DOCUMENTS

Essential project documents needed to effectively develop the project schedule:

Document	Explanation
Duration estimate	Details the specific quantity of work periods the estimation work has determined for completing activities.
Basis of estimates	The supporting details used to derive the duration estimates.
Resource calendars	Calendars that show the ebb and flow of resource availability during the project.
Activity list	The ordered list of all activities to be included in the schedule.
Activity attributes	Specific details that supplement each activity and support determining the schedule.
Milestone list	Markers within the schedule on specific dates that represent required achievements and demonstrating performance.
Project schedule network designs	A visual representation of the predecessor and successor dependencies between activities.
Resource requirements	Specific data on what resources are needed for each activity and in what quantity.
Project team assignments	Defines the human or personnel resources required for each activity; in other words, who is performing each activity.
Project management plan	An essential reference source that includes the schedule management plan, scope baseline, lessons learned, risk register, assumption log, and risk register.

Tools and Techniques

Schedule Network Analysis

Schedule network analysis is a broad term that represents the process of using schedule development input materials to create the schedule model. The process is rarely straightforward and often requires review and reanalysis throughout the project in order to reach an ideal network relationship between activities and phases. Furthermore, the network analysis includes supplementary practices of slip prevention and risk attack as iterations and reviews are performed. Part of scheduling is baking in management reserve resources in the event the project goes off track for unplanned reasons. Reserve execution can correct slip, especially at activity convergence or divergence points in the schedule. Such activation of reserve resources is also positive where critical path methodology indicates the potential for slip and delay. The critical path method is one of several commonly used network analysis tools.

Critical Path Method

The critical path is the primary constraint throughout the project and is also the length of the longest single chain of activities linked together, showing the shortest collective duration of start to finish. The critical path generally has no available slack time. Within this path, all other non-critical path activities can be scheduled with varying degrees of slack time. Slack time refers to the flexibility of delaying one or more project activities without causing delay to the overall project. The method uses relationships, sequence, duration, early start, late start, early finish, and late finish estimations to visually depict the critical path. Late and early finish and start dates provide the model with estimations of timeframes where activities could be completed.

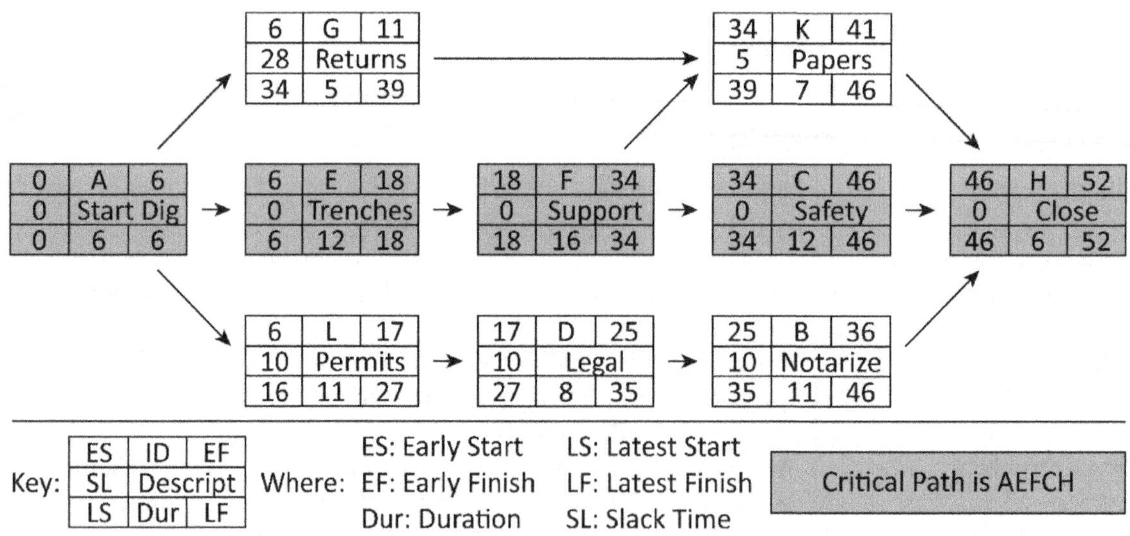

Resource Optimization and Leveling and Smoothing

Resource optimization refers to the modulation of activity start and finish dates to better align with the supply availability of resources such as labor, equipment, and funding. The optimization ensures that resource constraints due to overloaded demand are avoided where possible. Optimization can vary based on which variable is modified: the activity durations or the schedule sequence. Resource leveling is a type of optimization where start and finish dates are aligned to the availability of resources. Resource constraints that may prompt leveling include multiple activities requiring the same resources or severe time or quantitative limitations on the availability of those resources. Resource smoothing is the second alternative in optimization options and has the added benefit of not impacting the critical path. Smoothing changes the sequence variable; the activities are adjusted in the schedule so that resource constraints do not exceed a predetermined threshold.

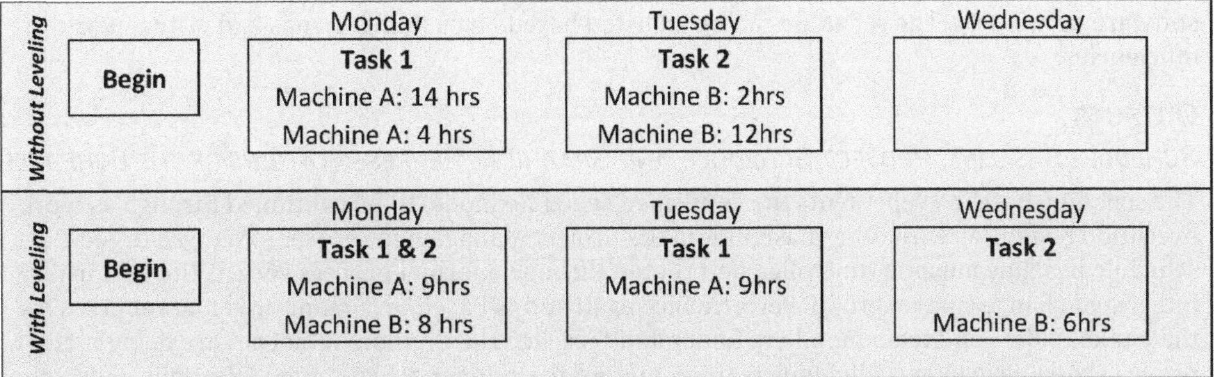

Benefits of Simulations, Probability Distributions, and What-if Analysis

The use of simulations in schedule development is based on *in silico* experimentation of scenarios where risk and error can be evaluated safely without wasting valuable project resources. Simulations can help explain the effects of changes and alternatives when uncertainty is abundant during schedule development. For example, Monte Carlo analysis analyzes risk and uncertainty to provide different schedule outcomes and probabilities that each model will meet timeframe expectations. Probability distributions that arise from such simulations allow project teams to reduce the uncertainty in their model schedule as they are able to optimize the activity sequencing and durations. As adjustments are made, probability distributions reach higher certainty that models will meet the schedule and end date expectations. What-if scenarios are evaluations where different combinations of factors are created to predict the effect upon objectives. What-if analysis provides tested outcomes and quantitative project impact as different variables are adjusted for one or multiple activities within the project. This analysis also supports the project team's preparation for reserve resources and contingency planning.

Schedule Compression Techniques

Schedule compression is a technique where the project team can analyze the project activities and durations against objectives and contractual dates to squeeze the schedule duration to a shorter timeframe. Crashing is a form of schedule compression where resources are added while controlling cost increases so that the critical path activities are prioritized and given a greater chance to be performed faster. Some additional resource allocation to the critical path activities may be diminishing returns. Added labor or parts may not shorten completion; a threshold may also exist for resource allocation where more effort is needed to manage the additional resources. Fast tracking refers to the maximized use of parallel work execution where the baseline schedule may indicate sequential work. The parallel activity in fast tracking is only beneficial as a compression option if it can hasten the critical path. Cost overruns and risk introduction must also be managed in both compression techniques and have a net benefit if able to hasten the project timeframe.

Agile Release Planning

Agile release planning is a deliverable schedule management process that works in reverse from a fixed deliverable date. Batches of completed work are planned sequentially prior to the expected deliverable (or release) date. Each batch, termed a sprint, is an iteration of customer-centered features that are developed by the project team to satisfy stakeholder and customer requirements. Generally, these requirements are gathered through quantitative and qualitative customer data collection methods. Work is broken down within each iteration among the team members. The team works with higher levels of flexibility and agility when given a fixed schedule and batch-separated sprints. The process is ideal for dispersed and non-co-located work teams, such as software developers. The schedule can be adjusted based on customer needs and virtual work efficiencies.

OUTPUTS

SCHEDULE BASELINE, PROJECT SCHEDULE, AND GRAPHICAL REPRESENTATIONS OF THE SCHEDULE

The schedule baseline represents the confirmed schedule model to be continued through as work execution begins. As with other baselines in the project management process, changes to the schedule baseline must be controlled and routed through a formal process such as the perform integrated change control group. Performance against this baseline is monitored and reported so that stakeholders and team members understand if schedule attainment metrics are being met. The project schedule itself visually depicts the activities, their dependencies, time durations, milestones, and supporting detail as needed to convey the sequential process to complete the project work. Schedules are commonly constructed with a combination of listed sequential activities and a visual guide to their durations, relationships, and sequence. Network diagrams may be used to show durations as well as interconnectivity between activities. More simple models such as bar charts and milestone markers explain durations and sequence sufficiently in low to moderately complex projects.

Bar Summary Schedule **Project Schedule**

Task #	Description	Units (days)	Phase 1	Phase 2	Phase 3	Phase 4	Phase 5
A.10	Permit Submission	45					
A.20	Procedure Draft	10					
A.30	Negotiate Agreement	13					
A.40	Interview and Hire	55					
B.10	Background Checks	6					
B.20	Train New Hires	11					
C.10	Remove Flood Debris	29					
C.20	Clean and Dry Factory	77					
C.30	Gap Review	14					
C.40	Return Facility to Owners	9					

Milestone Schedule **Project Schedule**

Task #	Milestone Description	Units (days)	Phase 1			Phase 2			Phase 3			Phase 4			Phase 5		
A.10	Permit Process Complete	0					X										
A.20	Final Procedures	0		X													
A.30	Signed Agreement	0			X												
A.40	Staff Hired	0								X							
B.10	Clean Backgrounds	0						X									
B.20	Training Complete	0							X								
C.10	Debris Removed	0										X					
C.20	Cleaned and Dry Factory	0															X
C.30	No Remaining Gaps	0														X	
C.40	Finalized Occupancy	0															X

SCHEDULE DATA, PROJECT CALENDARS, AND DOCUMENT UPDATES

Project calendars provide labor with more realistic timeframes within defined work days where scheduled activities and work are performed and distinguished from those times when work is not expected to be scheduled. For capturing faster schedule completion, work forces and their associated activities are likely to be scheduled in parallel, around the clock in shifts, and/or with added overtime or human capital. Project calendars provide a more focused and granular version of work to the persons performing the work. Schedule data is generated for the schedule model and should be able to capture all features and information in the schedule. The data can also be in the form of supporting material, such as reserve information; simulated alternative schedules as contingencies; and resources needed per timeframe of the schedule, financial reporting, and resource histograms. Document updates most significantly resulting from the schedule development include assumption logs, resource requirements, duration estimates (especially if crashing or fast tracking), and the cost baseline.

Control Schedule

Overview

Schedule control implies that the baseline schedule that was thoroughly created, validated, and optimized will be followed as work is executed. Tools must be implemented that can reasonably assure control to baseline is achieved. Where changes must occur to the baseline, a formalized schedule change process is employed. For example, the perform integrated change control (PICC) process serves to control proposed changes to the schedule, the reserves (if any), and the progress on the active schedule execution. Agile project life cycles are similarly concerned with maintaining control over the schedule and performance against its baseline. Agile—an iterative planning process—promotes mantra for controlling the schedule, including backward-looking reviews for future improvement, numerical estimations of project completeness, and managing any work backlogs.

Tools and Techniques

Common Data Analysis Techniques Used in Schedule Control

Iteration burndown is a technique for visual communication of work commitment and completion during iterative schedule planning. Displayed in a linear chart or bar chart, the visual shows the progress of smaller amounts of remaining work as the iteration days continue and work is completed. The burndown chart can also show differences between actual and predicted work remaining in the iteration. Earned value analysis (EVA) is a set of calculations to objectively show schedule performance variance compared to baseline. The analysis includes calculating schedule variance and a schedule performance index for the purposes of performance appraisal and reporting. Similarly, variance analysis can be performed on the actual and planned start and finish dates for all tasks to identify a quantitative variance compared to baseline. Weighted calculations may be imposed for variances within the critical path as opposed to variances outside the critical path having less impact on the project duration overall. Trend analysis provides a longer term visual on how performance changes over time.

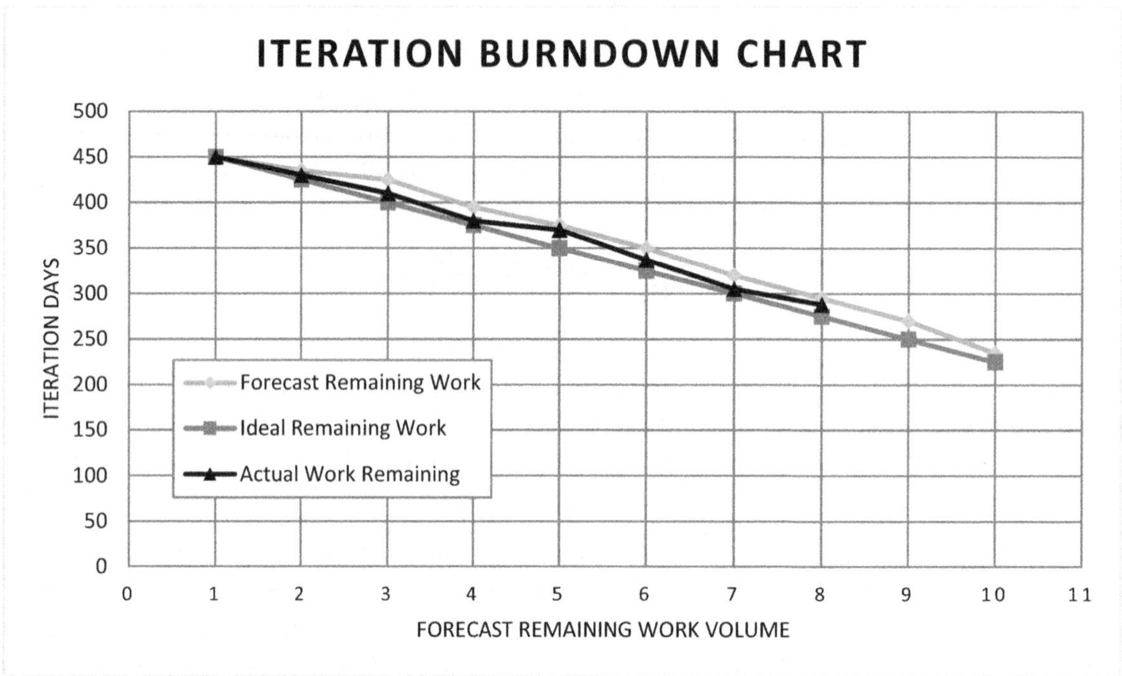

Project Cost Management

Plan Cost Management

Overview

Project cost management refers to the set of processes where project costs are estimated, the budget planned and implemented, and the costs controlled through formal procedures. The cost management is coordinated through a cost management plan. The plan details how costs must be estimated, monitored, and controlled. The plan also describes the budgeting process and cost management steps. The budget process results in an approved cost baseline against which the project leadership can perform variance analysis with actual expenses. Lastly, costs are expected to be well controlled compared to the cost baseline.

Financial analysis and modeling are likely different between projects based on the industry where the project is being executed. How costs are allocated may also be different based upon accounting standards within the organization. These accounting practices may be widely different between private and publicly traded companies. Independent financial performance prediction may occur by third party analysis or by analysts within the same organization. Project managers are expected to consider tailoring approaches regarding cost management so that the uniqueness of any given project would not be hindered.

Inputs

The plan cost management process involves the project team determining and documenting how project costs will be estimated, budgeted, distributed, monitored, and controlled. Several essential documents support this process, including the project charter, the schedule management plan, and the risk management plan. The resulting cost management plan guides the team through cost estimation, budgeting, and cost control. Other inputs to the cost management plan process include external environmental factors, like regional or global market conditions, productivity, monetary exchange, and overhead costs. Several organizational assets, such as financial skill, costing and estimating expertise and tools, and past project history provide a positive influence on the cost plan development.

Outputs

Cost Management Plan as an Output to the Plan Cost Management Process

The cost management plan guides the team in performing cost estimation, budgeting, cost management, cost monitoring, and cost control procedures. The plan resides within the overall project management plan and clearly describes all important financial factors to the project execution. The plan often conveys key details to stakeholders.

Type of Feature	Description
Additional cost details	Further footnote-type financial information may be included for reference, such as exchange rates.
Control thresholds	Cost control weakening to where variance would exceed a tailed threshold provides a warning to key stakeholders and the project manager.
Accuracy	Cost estimate level of accuracy acceptable to the organization. Expressed as a percentage about a mean.
Organizational procedures	Reflected in the work breakdown structure; costs are represented as a control account.
Precision	Rounding by the accounting practices of the organization is defined.
Reporting	The financial reporting requirements and frequency are defined for the project.
Rules of performance monitoring	Describes how performance measurements (such as earned value management) will be calculated.
Unit of measure	Defining the unit of measure for time, weight, distance, and currency for consistency across all stakeholders.

Estimate Costs

Overview

Cost estimation is the series of work performed by the project team to assess the expected costs associated with the activities to be performed in the project schedule. The estimation derives quantitative figures of the predicted expenses for labor, resources, and services to complete the project. Assumptions and constraints are factored into the estimations. Alternative cost models are also generated with differing scenario options for buying, leasing, or making parts and services needed in the activities. The cost estimation process is iterative during the life of the project. More information is gained as the project work is completed and as purchasing decisions become due during that project progress. Several rounds of review of the cost estimation are expected. It is also helpful to stakeholders to understand the degree of confidence around each cost estimate.

Input

As the preliminary task performed prior to using inputs to create the project cost estimates, the cost management plan outlines the procedures and specifications to be used for performing the estimations. Similarly, the quality management plan is incorporated as an input into the cost estimation process. The quality plan includes customer and stakeholder requirements and measures of project success. The scope is also highly important to the cost estimation. Thus, the scope baseline serves as another key input to the cost estimation process. Within the scope baseline, key elements such as the WBS, the WBS dictionary, and the scope statement itself give more specific reference information for cost estimation. Other inputs include common project documents such as the project schedule, resources requirements, and the risk register. External factors such as market conditions, exchange rates, and trade fluctuation are inputs that may vary in usefulness project to project.

TOOLS AND TECHNIQUES

USE OF COMMON ESTIMATING TOOLS

Analogous estimation is defined as the use of past project cost estimation data to derive similar (or analogous) estimates for the current project under the assumption that similar expenses, project execution, and constraints exist in the present project. Scope, cost, schedule, and resources may all be derived from analogous projects. Parametric estimation uses more statistical analysis with past data and parameters when analyzed against similar parameters in the current project. The uncertainty of the estimation may be reduced if the analytical model is validated and uses sound technique. Bottom-up estimations focus the estimation analysis on the most granular work in each activity within the project. This uses the line of thought that estimations of the lowest elements of the work will aggregate into a highly accurate estimation of total project costs. The roll-up of costs may however overlook macro-level risks, cost assumptions, and market forces. Three-point estimations use a range of probable cost analyses to derive a triangular distribution representing a pseudo-confidence interval of the likely costs. Three-point estimations can also employ a beta distribution calculation that adds weight to the most likely activity cost scenario. In both calculation approaches, confidence in the optimal estimation is gained.

COST OF QUALITY

The cost of quality is the expense incurred by an organization to meet customer and stakeholder quality expectations or to rectify product or service quality and customer satisfaction when quality has deviated from the acceptable limits. Quality costs can come in four different types based upon their degree of failure: conformance costs such as preventive and appraisal, or non-conformance costs such as internal failure and external failure. Preventive costs have little failure evident and are designed to use resources to avoid the multiples of quality costs in failure when preventive controls are not in place. Appraisal costs are those that perform quality evaluations and control upon processes, products, or services in order to ensure that customers are going to receive expected satisfaction and that the process worked as designed. Shifting appraisal costs towards preventive costs is an ideal to quality professionals. Internal and external failure costs occur when finished products or services do not meet specifications and must be reworked, scrapped, or recalled from the client. External failures incur the most significant expenses in retrieval of non-conforming output and in legal fees and remuneration. Cost estimates balanced heavily on prevention likely require little expense on failure.

OUTPUTS

FORMAT AND FEATURES OF RESULTING COST ESTIMATES

Cost estimates that result from the process are quantitative in nature and show a monetary value after historical, risk, external, and customer analysis of what the cost should be. This is expressed for the project as a whole and for each activity or phase within the project schedule. Contingencies are also tallied within the cost estimate given risk and constraint input. Specific direct cost details summarized within the cost estimate can include equipment, supplies, labor, materials, facilities, and financing interest. Furthermore, the cost estimate output includes a basis of estimates summary that describes the decision-making baked into each estimation. This basis also summarizes constraints, assumptions, risks, and ranges considered in the analysis. Once the cost estimation is complete, there may be more document revision in the project plan, including to the lessons learned log, risk register, and assumptions log.

Determine Budget

Overview

After the activity costs have been estimated using one or a combination of estimation approaches, the project team (or the organization's financial experts) compile the estimated costs into an approved baseline budget. Setting the baseline gives the project team and stakeholders a benchmark against which performance can be measured. Because the charter formally authorizes the use of resources towards the project, the budget creates the boundaries of authorized funding. The budget often includes contingency reserve funding in the event of unplanned issues or threats to the project schedule. The budget determination process is the aggregation of the cost estimation work. Several inputs are required for the budget process. Foremost, the cost estimations are needed. Additionally, the cost management, resource management plans, project schedule, and scope baseline are pulled from the project management plan.

Tools and Techniques

Historical Information Review, Data Analysis, and Funding Limit Reconciliation

When analyzing the cost estimates and supporting input documents, the project team must use history and data analysis as primary means for arriving at a budget. A straightforward approach is the aggregation activity costs following the pattern of the work breakdown structure. Phases and levels of the project have their aggregated costs tallied, as well as for the project as a whole. Historical information is reviewed to ensure analytical estimates, such as parametric or analogous methods, are as consistent with past patterns as possible. Accuracy of historical data, validity of the mathematical models, and scalability of the analysis are features that support effective historical review. Funding limit reconciliation is a budgeting element that monitors and identifies funding variances between budgeted limits and planned commitments of expenditure. Figurative red flags indicate expenses are exceeding planned costs, which would prompt adjustments in the scheduled allocation of funds as well as date constraints for future project work.

Outputs

Cost Baseline

The cost baseline is a detailed budget that includes cost allocations approved at various intervals throughout the schedule. The cost baseline, as observed with other project baselines, serves as the comparison point for actual performance when monitoring adherence to budget. The cost baseline covers all budget elements for the project, including contingency reserves but excluding management reserves. The baseline is commonly portrayed as a time-based graphic of the cost estimates incurred as the scheduled activities occur over time. When the project team factors in the management reserve funds, the complete project budget takes shape. The baseline is also used as a planning model for financial resource allocation as the project work progresses in time. This projection ability allows for smoothing or planning of expenditures by the organization. The baseline, when presented as a graph, would show step-wise increments of funding allocations as the cost curve increases over time. For comparison, actual expenditures are plotted with the cost baseline and funding outlays to provide a performance visual.

Control Costs

Overview

The control costs element involves ensuring that budgeted costs planned in the project schedule are monitored against the known cost baseline for performance assurance and expected use of resources. The control costs phase relies heavily on tracking value added per project expenditure (earned value analysis). Implying that the metric of expenditures compared to completed project work is important. Several important factors and deliverables are achieved through the cost control element. These factors can be grouped as monitoring, managing, and preventing activities. The perform integrated change control group must have oversight on cost baseline or budget change requests.

Deliverables Found in Effective Cost Control Outcomes

Control Costs Activity	Description
Monitoring	Cost variances as they occur, work performance based on actual funds expended, monitoring funding use by various segmentation of the project schedule (WBS, phases, activity, etc.).
Managing	Timely evaluation, execution, and communication of change request and approvals in real-time, regaining control of cost overruns.
Prevention	Leading baseline revisions through the change process, employing systems and controls to prevent unauthorized use of funds or change to baselines.

Tools and Techniques

Earned Value Analysis

Earned value analysis (EVA) is used in cost control to monitor actual expenditure and schedule progress compared to the budget and schedule. This metric provides an assessment of the value—in financial and schedule terms—of the investment spent to date in the project. EVA has three primary monitoring dimensions: planned value, earned value, and actual cost.

- Planned value (PV) is defined as a roadmap of the project work expected to be completed at any given point in the scheduled budget allocation point. The budget at completion (BAC) is a term used for the project's total planned value.
- Earned value (EV) is defined inversely from the planned value. EV is the proportion of work completed compared to the budget authorization distributed to date. EV is commonly used to express the percentage completion or work-in-progress in a project.
- Actual cost (AC) is the booked expenditures truly incurred and accounted for the work activity performed. AC can be monitored and reported at intervals in the schedule. AC is the true cost incurred given the budgeted funds.

Variance Analysis

Variance analysis is the process of mathematically expressing actual performance against an expected baseline performance. Variance analysis in the context of cost control and the earned value analysis can mathematically express variances in cost, schedule, and at completion. Variance analysis is a precursor to root cause, corrective, and preventive actions for resolving and preventing variances found.

- Schedule variance (SV) – The difference between earned value (EV) and the planned value (PV). The calculation factors in work performed against budget (EV) and negates the authorized budget for the planned work to derive a schedule metric.
- Cost variance (CV) – The difference between earned value (EV) and actual cost (AC) to express the degree of over/under budget with current performance.

- Schedule performance index (SPI) is the ratio of EV to PV. Cost performance index (CPI) is the ratio of EV to AC. SPI represents schedule efficiency while CPI, arguably a more important metric, represents cost efficiency for the work finished to date.

Schedule variance (SV)	Cost variance (CV)	Schedule performance index (SPI)	Cost performance index (CPI)
$SV = EV - PV$	$CV = EV - AC$	$SPI = \frac{EV}{PV}$	$CPI = \frac{EV}{AC}$

Forecasting

As the project team standardizes and effectively monitors project costs and value, the team may seek to predict an estimate at completion (EAC) that represents the expenditures estimated to be incurred at the time of schedule completion. Such forecasts are made using work performance information collected and analyzed from the project activity made prior to initiating the forecasting. Bottom-up summation where actual costs are summed with an estimate to complete (ETC) is an effective approach for estimate at completion forecasting. Risk is an important factor when developing forecast scenarios. Multiple options are available for deriving an EAC forecast for the estimate to complete metric.

Estimate at Completion Model	Description	EAC Calculation
For ETC work performed at budgeted rate	Uses actual cost data to represent work performed and forecast ETC at budgeted rates	EAC = AC + (BAC – EV)
For ETC work performed at present CPI	Bases forecast on present performance, assuming continuation of that performance and at same CPI. Expressed as a rate.	EAC = BAC / CPI
For ETC work using SPI and CPI	Expressed as a rate of efficiency by factoring in schedule and cost indices and allows for more management judgement in the calculation.	EAC = AC + [(BAC – EV) / (CPI x SPI)]

TCPI

A to-complete performance index (TCPI) metric provides cost control efforts with an endgame perspective on the cost control performance necessary to meet a defined management goal. TCPI is a ratio of the remaining cost to the remaining budget. Using the budget at completion (BAC) value, the earned value and the actual costs are factored to derive the ratio. Work remaining is the difference between budget at completion and earned value. Cost remaining is the difference between BAC and actual cost (AC). By setting control limits around the TCPI index, the team can assess the budgetary behavior needed to keep the expenses within range of the budget at completion. The TCPI can indicate performance above baseline (estimate at cost) or below baseline (budget at cost).

To-Complete Performance Index

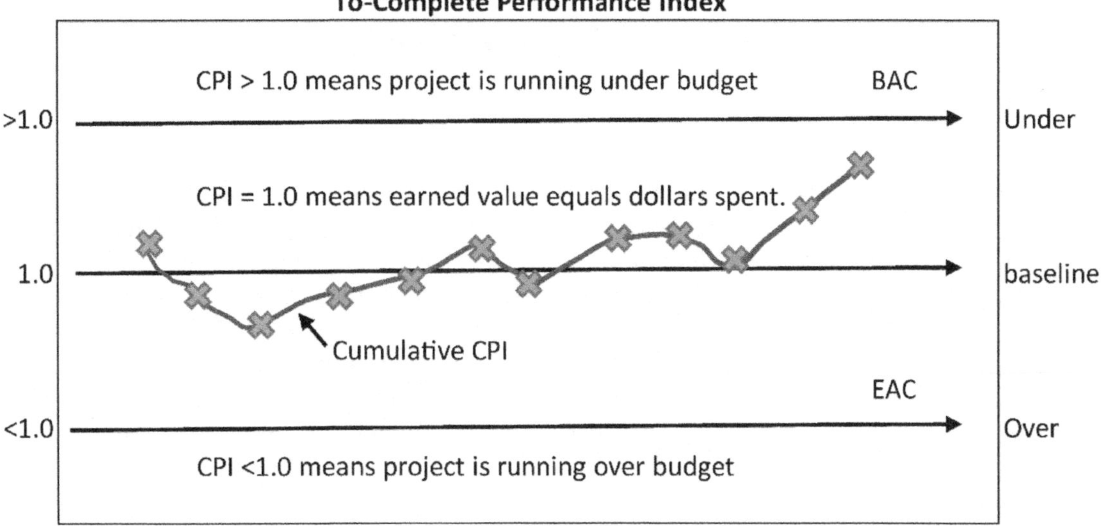

Project Quality Management

Plan Quality Management

Overview

Function

Project quality management serves the project management process by collecting and enforcing project and customer quality requirements upon the project work. The quality management system involves methods for monitoring, controlling, and managing quality requirements significant to stakeholders and customers. Related activities in the quality management system include continuous improvement programs. Similar to other project management plan elements, quality management begins with setting a quality management plan, followed by monitoring and controlling quality performance. Quality systems tend to have wide-reaching impact and influence on the organization or project processes. Interrelation between key quality processes—such as the quality management plan itself, scope validation, management activities, and quality assurance—are unavoidable. Behaviors such as product or service testing, quality reporting, auditing, and quality metric tracking are all supportive of effective oversight of project quality.

Quality

Quality is defined as the degree to which a product or service meets expected performance characteristics. Quality is primarily based on stakeholder and customer requirements or preferences. Quality can be expressed both qualitatively and quantitatively. The latter uses descriptive statistics, attribute measurement, and various graphical methods. Statistically, quality can be defined as the prevention of variation from the expected performance. Forward thinking quality assessments also must account for changing needs and desires of stakeholders and customers so that quality expectations are continuously being monitored and controlled for customer satisfaction. Quality is kept at high levels when balanced towards preventive activities. The costs and efforts associated with prevention are more effective and valuable than failure recovery and expenses. Preventive actions include auditing, design for experiments, and obtaining the critical-to-quality and voice of the customer for quality parameter development. Attribute sampling is an appraisal activity that performs in-process evaluations of quality performance as outputs and in-progress work is performed. Tolerances are the measurable boundaries that separate acceptable quality from unacceptable. Organizations often set internal tolerances tighter than customer-approved tolerances in order to deliver higher customer satisfaction over time.

Inputs

Plan quality management is the set of processes that result in having well defined customer-based quality parameters established for the project and its deliverables. The process is further defined as having documented procedures executed to monitor and control quality via assurance practices. These two elements ensure that customer requirements are captured and activities and outcomes of the project are verified to meet those expectations. The plan details how quality parameters are defined and controlled through the project. Common inputs are required for plan development, including the project charter, the requirements management plan, risk management plan, and a stakeholder engagement plan. Furthermore, inputs such as requirements documentation, customer specifications, regulatory references, and the requirements traceability matrix serve as essential data sources to setting quality standards.

Tools and Techniques

Baseline Data Collection Techniques

Interviews serve as qualitative data collection, primarily to gather quality specification, customer preferences, and stakeholder concerns. These interviews capture and aggregate such data to be translated into critical to quality specifications, ideally to the point where they can be monitored and controlled quantitatively through statistical and mathematical means. Various formats of interview data can be collected, including formal and informal feedback, as well as implicit and explicit details. Relevant stakeholders are subjected to the interviews in unbiased and positive settings so that the most high-quality information can be collected.

Benchmarking refers to the practice of evaluating other projects, organizations, or industries for best practices or optimal approaches to managing output quality and performance. The organization performing the benchmarking studies seeks to obtain and emulate such best practices in their own project operations.

Brainstorming involves the collective participation of stakeholders, project staff, and leadership in ideating and compiling ideas and approaches for the quality plan development. The unbiased collection of innovation serves to build incremental creativity to prevent and solve problems.

Similarities and Differences Between Cost of Quality Accounting Models and Cost-Benefit Analysis

Cost of quality is a management and accounting tool that tracks organizational or project costs based on impact to the quality of the product or service being created. The logic behind cost of quality is that of a dichotomy between costs of conformance and costs of non-conformance. The objective is to balance more costs onto the conformance activities to prevent costs in the non-conformance bucket. Often, the more resources spent on conformance activities, the less overall total quality costs are incurred, at least up to a point of diminishing returns. Conformance costs include preventive expenses, such as audits. Conformance costs also include appraisal expenses, such as product testing, raw material analysis, and record reviews. Non-conformance costs include internal and external failures. Internal failures are costs related to waste, defects, and inefficiency. External failure costs are those related to recalls, market withdrawals, insurance claims, and reputational damage. Cost-benefit analysis refers to the analytical comparison and decision-making between two or more alternatives. The cost or resources to be used must not outweigh the benefits likely to be obtained if the decision is accepted. Cost effectiveness is the objective when using the cost-benefit tool. It is important that project managers be wary of focusing solely on cost for decision-making. Such shortsightedness can miss the opportunity to strengthen preventive quality costs.

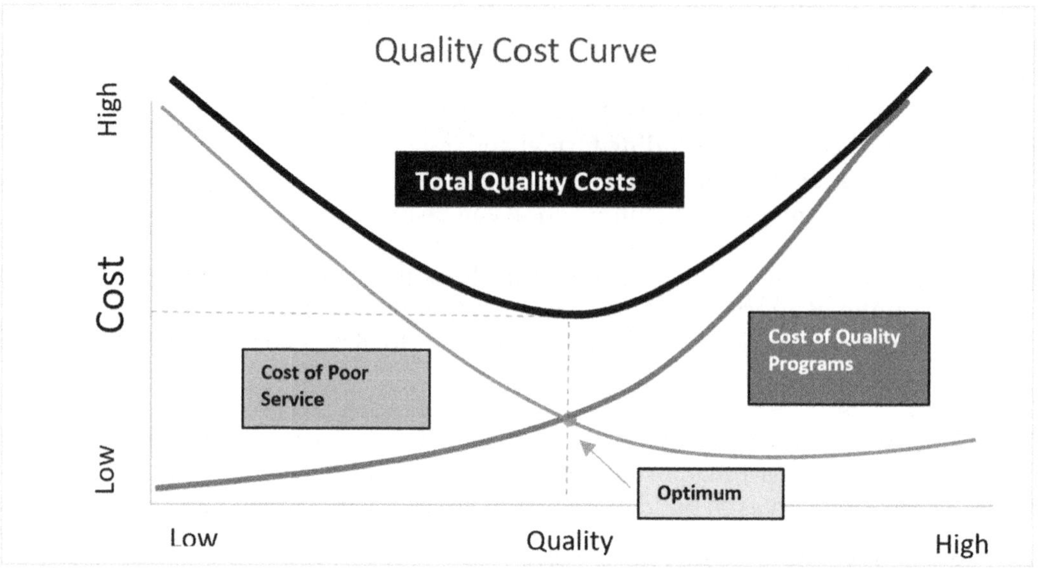

QUALITY DATA REPRESENTATION APPROACHES

Mind-mapping is defined as an information organization tool to group thoughts, ideas, and topics into groups based on shared characteristics. The technique can help capture all relevant details related to product or process quality so that key controls may be developed.

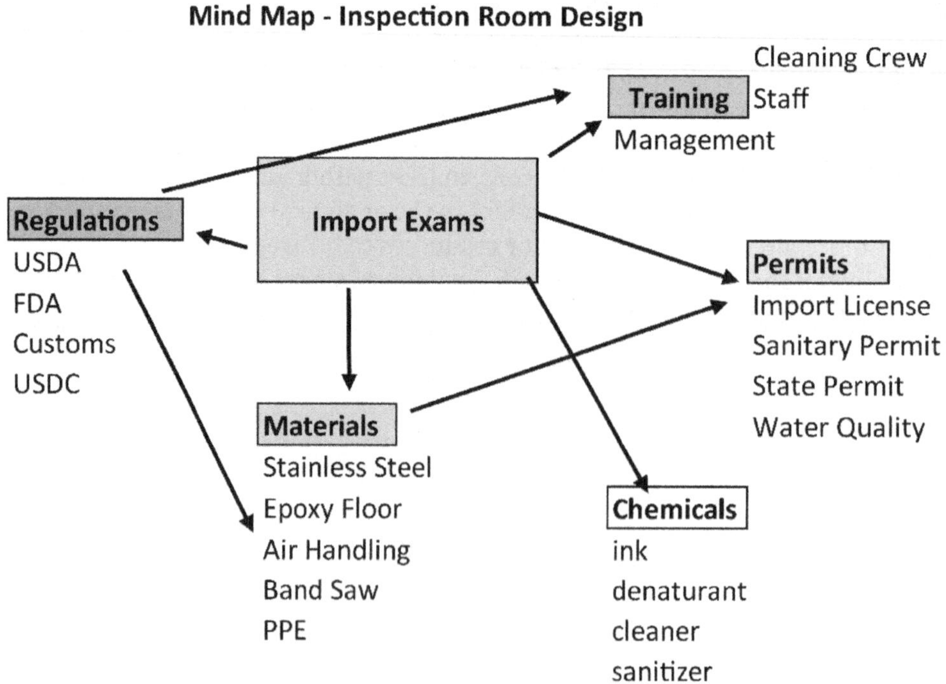

Matrix diagrams serve to give insight into the relationships between different datasets facing an improvement project or quality initiative. It is an essential management tool that comes in many forms based on how many types of sources are to be analyzed. By comparing relevant datasets amongst each other using any of the several diagram methods, a team can gain useful information and knowledge for improvement or strategic planning. The six common types of matrix diagrams used in quality and continuous improvement systems include X, Y, C, L, T, and roof-shaped diagrams.

Stakeholder	Unaware	Resistant	Neutral	Supportive	Leading
USDA		C			D
FDA			C	D	
USDC	C		D		
US Customs			C D		
Customer				D	C
City Health Dept		C		D	

Flow charts are visual diagrams that map a process and show the interrelations or sequential workflow of a process. Flow charts are useful when a quality or improvement team needs to fully understand all aspects of complex processes to control all steps and ensure the overall process functions appropriately to deliver compliant output. Examples of flow charts include failure mode mapping, SIPOC diagrams, and swim lane diagrams.

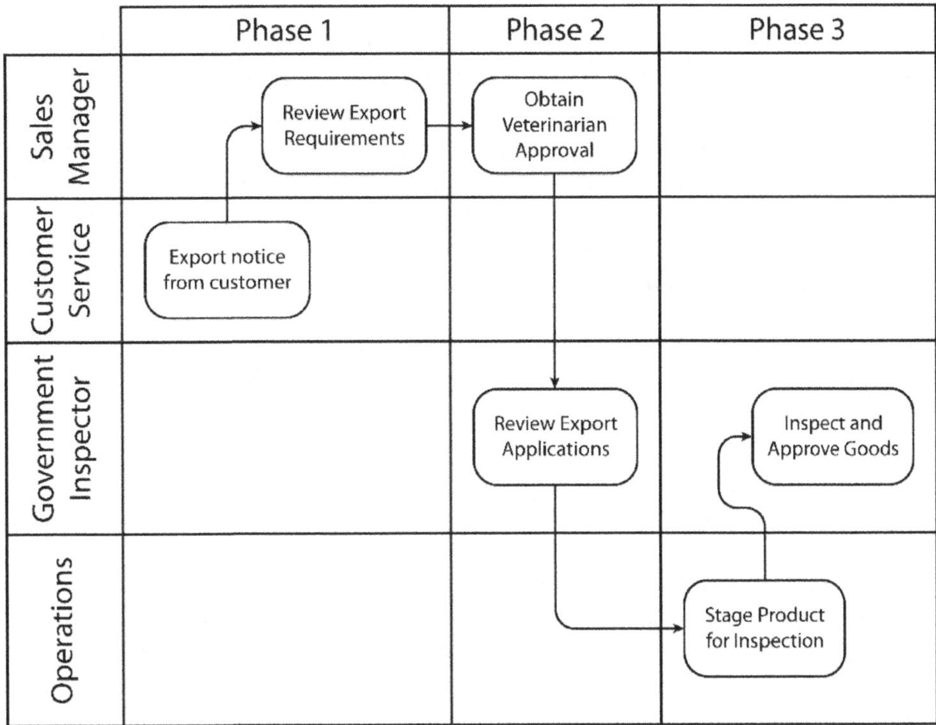

OUTPUTS

QUALITY MANAGEMENT PLAN AND QUALITY PARAMETERS AND METRICS

Once complete, the quality management plan must outline how the project team and stakeholders will manage, monitor, and control project quality requirements and ensure deliverables meet customer quality expectations. The quality plan also outlines how policies, procedures, and performance measurement systems for project quality will be implemented for the project. Stakeholders and the project team members must be clearly familiar with the quality plan and how it will be executed. The plan also includes quality standards or specifications, quality objectives and measurement approaches, roles and responsibilities, planned quality control and assurance activities, the frequencies of quality activities, and relevant standard operating procedures regarding quality impacts to the project.

Common quality parameters and metrics:

- First pass quality percent
- Defects per million opportunities (DPMO)
- Six Sigma
- Audit scores
- Defects per million units
- Net weight control
- Statistical process control conformance
- Cost of quality performance

Manage Quality

Overview

Quality Assurance

Quality assurance is the practice of ensuring that quality systems are being performed as designed and are operating at a high probability to produce outputs that meet or exceed customer expectations. The manage quality element of the project management process involves performing quality assurance activities in the project execution process so that customer and stakeholder expectations are verified as met. Data collected from the quality management element is communicated to stakeholders of the project. Manage quality also includes product or service design elements of the project and process improvements. Four essential facets to the manage quality process within projects include:

- Verification that quality standards are being performed and meet project quality objectives.
- Performing product or service design processes to ensure deliverables meet customer expectations.
- Perform preventive and process control functions to ensure outputs are highly reliable with little unwanted variation.
- Use quality tools to drive improvement in efficiency and customer satisfaction.

Although larger organizations are likely to have dedicated quality assurance personnel working as key stakeholders or project team contributors, the responsibility for quality performance lies with all employees in the organization, especially those with direct impact on project results. Quality assurance leaders may also be project managers, which is common with lean Six Sigma project initiatives.

Tools and Techniques

Data Analysis Techniques and the Procurement of Strong Data to Be Monitored

The old saying of "garbage in, garbage out" applies when considering the analysis of quality assurance data. First, data collection must be reliable, accurate, and representative of the systems being monitored for conformance. Traditional approaches such as checklists, run charts, and inspections are good examples. Second, the analysis methods must be appropriate in order to obtain relevant and useful information that helps the project team and stakeholders understand quality performance against requirements and objectives. Though there are many quality assurance tools useful for data analysis, four common tools for project quality management include root cause analysis, document analysis, alternatives analysis, and process analysis.

- **Root cause analysis** – The deliberate and structured analysis of the underlying reasons that led to a result or non-conformance. Finding the true root cause allows quality teams to deliver the most effective solution to the problem. Common tools include 5 Why analyses and fishbone diagrams.
- **Document analysis** – A form or record review that finds quality issues and feeds into corrective action processes.
- **Alternatives analysis** – The analysis of different options based on criteria, weights, or customer requirements.
- **Process analysis** – The assessment of processes and any opportunities to implement improvements for increased efficiency, customer satisfaction, and lower waste.

Data Presentation Tools

Scatter diagrams plot coordinate datasets where observations have two related parameters. For example, a plot of output defectives over time has a quantity value and a time value associated with each measurement. Scatter plotting shows the relationship between two variables, and best fit or trend lines can be added to further define those relationships and create predictive models.

Matrix diagrams translate variable and factor relationships between multiple criteria to derive meaningful information that is otherwise hidden.

Histograms are bar-chart plots of data by frequency in order to show a distribution pattern across a range of likely output values. Visualization gives insight into process behaviors and cause/effect.

Flow charts are mapped steps that show direction of a process to help others better understand the flow of materials and information.

Affinity diagrams can be used in project management to group common types of non-conformance causes, allowing greater focus on the most important causes.

Cause-and-effect diagrams visualize the relationship between an effect and the underlying cause or causes. This allows quality teams to attack multiple contributing causes and change outcomes in the future.

Auditing

Auditing is the planned review of an organization's performance compared to a set of agreed criteria or parameters. The audit is performed by one or more auditors and looks to gain objective and first-hand evidence to assess how strongly a process, organization, product, or service meet expectations. The expectations or standards used as the criteria for the audit are typically compiled or enforced by stakeholders, leadership, customers, or regulatory agencies with a vested interest and ensuring conformance. Auditing benefits the quality assurance process as a preventive cost of conformance. Proactively seeking out performance weaknesses or conformance risks reinforces the project team and organization to adopt and enforce the behaviors that ensure quality standards are met or exceeded.

Outputs

Outputs unique to the quality management process include quality reporting and quality testing documentation. Quality reporting includes aggregated performance measurements against customer quality requirements and quality objectives for the project. The reporting that is derived from the quality assurance and quality management procedures provides key status information to the project leadership and stakeholders. Reporting also includes current quality risks, probabilities of non-conformance, defect rates, waste and rework, and any open corrective actions or continuous improvement opportunities. The reports themselves can contain a variety of data and information formats, including observed quantitative and qualitative graphs and summarized statistics. Quality testing and evaluation documentation includes performance and durability testing on finished outputs of the project to confirm consistency with specifications. Stakeholders to the project may request certificates of analysis or other verifications that outputs of the project were tested and proven to conform to requirements.

Project Resource Management

Plan Resource Management

Overview

Project managers and project teams must have resources available in the necessary quantities and at the right points in the project schedule. Project resource management ensures that resource needs are determined, procured, and made available to the project team when and where needed. Resource management involves creating a resource management plan, estimating activity resources, acquiring the right resources, and controlling the resources. This management process must also develop strong team performance to strengthen project performance. After all, personnel and employees that support the project are resources too. Risks are mitigated when project managers can effectively manage and control both physical and human resources. Emerging trends in resource management include constraint management, the development of emotional intelligence in personnel, and non-classically distributed (or virtual) teamwork.

Inputs

Self-Organizing Teams, Tailoring Considerations, and Inputs

Self-organizing teams (SOT) are used in agile iterations of projects in decentralized organizational structures. No single person serves as the sole project manager. A person may be loosely designated to give support and guidance to the other team members. Decentralized SOTs share common characteristics among members: strong commitment to the vision, trustworthiness, self-reliance, and high levels of team performance. These people must be able to adapt well to changes.

Tailoring the resource management process must consider human resource acquisition, specific industry requirements, organizational management and design approaches, and the range of the project team skill and expertise.

Key inputs to the development of a resource management plan include the quality management plan, the scope baseline, the project schedule, requirements register, and the risk catalogue. Human resources are a critical element to the resource management plan. Thus, organizational process assets, including expertise in organizational design and leadership, are important inputs.

Tools and Techniques

Importance of Subject Matter Expert Support and Organizational Theory

Subject matter experts (SME) skilled in project resource management give a project manager important guidance. Expert consultants or organizations can provide guidance in three main areas: resource selection, procurement, and performance. SMEs can have specialized training or skills in determining the resources needed for activities and the levels of support needed. Furthermore, SMEs improve procurement practices by having skill in negotiating buying terms, managing supply chain details, navigating resource risks, and coordinating resource lead times with the project schedule. Lastly, SMEs can drive project performance by developing talent, resource management performance metrics, and communications.

Organizational theory collects data regarding how human capital interacts and behaves in groups, teams, and the organization as a whole. Organizational development uses this people data to design better work structures, operating policies, and leadership approaches to get the highest performance possible from personnel.

Data Representation Tools for Resource Management

The RACI matrix is a communication chart used by the project manager so team members, stakeholders, and other personnel resources understand responsibilities, accountabilities, consulted experts, and information flow.

The chart lists several tasks relevant to the project or may list all activities in the project schedule. On an opposing axis, the chart then lists relevant names—either team members or stakeholders or experts supporting the team. For each combination of name and task, the letters R, A, C and I are documented to indicate who is responsible for completing tasks, who is accountable to ensure tasks get done, and how communication and information is to flow among the team and stakeholders.

The resource assignment matrix (RAM) shows the resources assigned to each activity or work package in the project. This allows the project team to clearly visualize resource requirements, team member responsibilities, and resource usage over the life cycle of the project.

Hierarchical charts express how physical and/or personnel resources are divided among all activities of a project. The work breakdown structure, organizational breakdown structure, and resource breakdown structure illustrate how deliverables, the organization's personnel resources, and the physical and team resources are all broken down through a hierarchy into elemental packages or groupings for the project.

Outputs

Output Features

The finalized resource management plan describes to the project leadership how resources are organized, decided, allocated, managed, and issued to each activity or work package within the schedule. The two pieces to the plan include instructions for people management and for materials management. Each piece requires different management approaches and different procedures. Resource management plans generally include details on roles and responsibilities, how the resources will be obtained and managed, and how resources will be inventoried and verified for performance capabilities. Also, the plan typically includes personnel organizational charts, corrective action procedures, training requirements, team development guidance, and approved methods for rewarding or recognizing successful team members. Other documents and plans can be updated as a result of the resource management plan creation. These updates can occur to the charter, risk register, and assumption log.

Estimate Activity Resources

Overview

After the resource management plan is completed, the project team must estimate the resources needed for each activity within the project schedule. The team makes estimates for human and material resources. The estimations focus on several key dimensions: quantities, duration of time, cost, type of equipment, and any service provider support. Inputs for the activity resource estimation process include the resource management plan, the activity list and attributes, cost estimates, project schedule, and resource calendars. Procurement of resources requires financial investment. The methods and tools used in estimating activity resources are similar to the methods for estimating costs. Subject matter experts are also selected to support the estimation process.

Outputs

Activity Resource Estimation Process

The resource estimation is a documentation package that explains the resource requirements of the project activities. Details in the package include quantities, types, and sources. The resource requirements are aggregated and tallied in a similar way as the costs in the cost estimate output. To ensure clear communication of decision-making, the package also includes a summary basis of estimates. The basis outlines several factors, including risk and confidence level information, estimate ranges, detailed methods used to create the resource estimates, assumptions and constraints considered, and the references or resources used to create the estimation itself. The estimation provides a road map for the project team regarding procurement and inventory for project activities. Project document updates, updated from the resource estimation process, include the lessons learned register, the assumption log, and (most significantly) the activity attributes.

Resource Breakdown Structure

The resource breakdown structure (RBS) is a tool like the work breakdown structure. The RBS outlines the resources as categories—materials, equipment, services, and labor—needed for the project and separated by category and type. Each breakdown level may also include quality or grade information to identify the quality level of each resource needed. The breakdown makes the resource procurement quantities clear. The breakdown also makes the labor qualifications and material quality clear so that procurement and work assignments can begin.

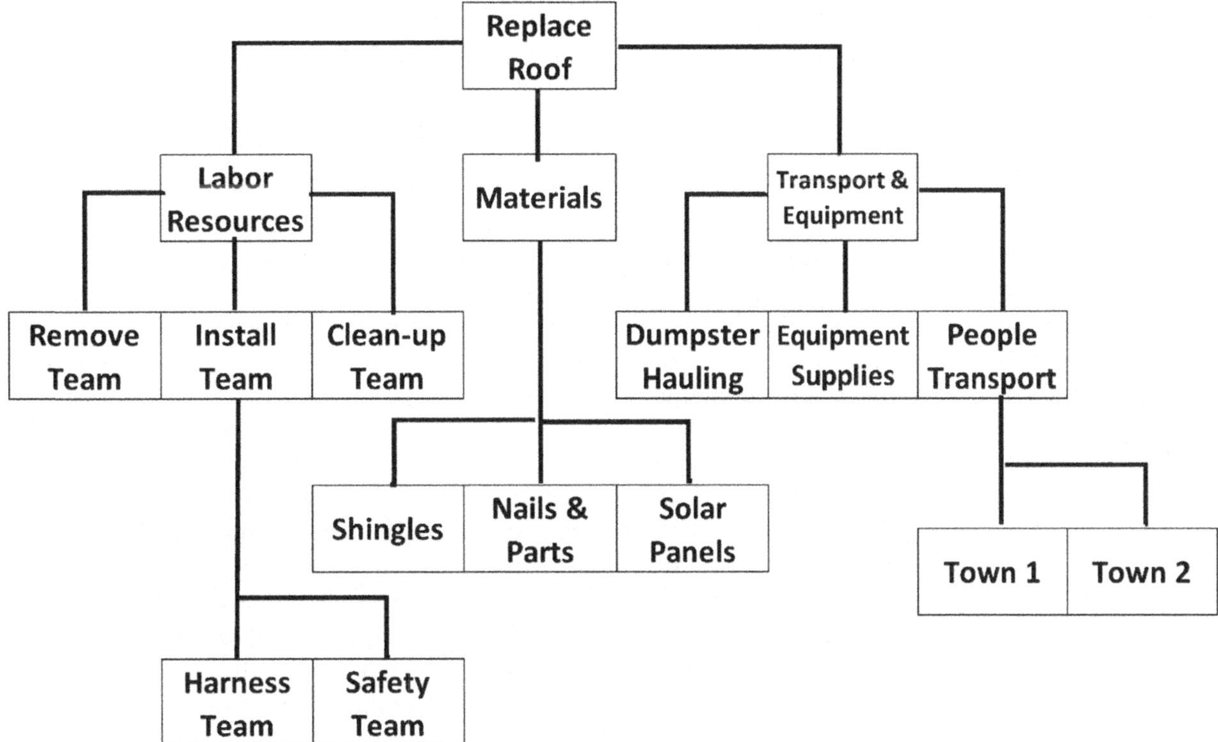

Acquire Resources

Overview

The acquire resources process involves hiring or assigning labor and procuring materials and services needed to complete project activities. Project teams and stakeholders must have clear descriptions of the acquisition requirements and the needs for each activity over the course of the project schedule. Inventory, labor, and expertise within an organization may be sufficient to keep procurement internal. Most organizations working in complex projects must make external resource acquisitions. The process of acquisition must be well managed to ensure project success. The project leadership must have several key skills, including negotiation, substitution, and alternatives planning.

- Specialists assigned to purchase materials for the project must be skilled in negotiation. This enables the project team to be more likely to out-compete other sources requesting the same resources.
- The limitation of resources, especially resources critical to the project, leads to the project team to have alternative resources options available so that delays or project failures are not likely.
- The failure of the project team to acquire materials, labor, services, or equipment for completing the project tasks may lead to scope changes, major delays, or project cancelation. Project leadership must be aware of procurement risks and ways to mitigate the impact to customers.

Tools and Techniques

Decision-Making and Negotiating

Resource acquisition for project management often has many factors and risks to consider before selecting a material source or making a personnel hire. Instinct and expertise are positive examples of decision-making ability. Analytical approaches to decision-making can benefit project resource acquisition decision-making through rational calculations. Multicriteria decision analysis is a tool that combines several important factors and scores several resource options against one another to derive the best sourcing to pursue. The criteria are weighted based on internal stakeholder criteria and project team assessment of importance. Commonly cited criteria for materials or services include capability to meet performance expectations, cost, and availability. Commonly cited criteria for labor include emotional intelligence, knowledge, expertise, attitude, and skill set. Negotiations are an important element to acquiring resources. The ability of a project manager to cut through the various acceptance criteria should be documented and communicated or enforced in a distinct way. Negotiating is a beneficial skill when scarce resources are required by the operation and limitations are abundant (or at least negatively impacting the operation).

Virtual Teams

Virtual teams consist of team members operating from a variety of physical locations, time zones, and work schedules within the same project. The virtual nature of the team means that its members are led and evaluated remotely across discontinuous communication methods such as internet, email, conference call, video conferencing, and shared computer-based work platforms. Several other staff resources may be included in a virtual nature, including home-based employees, remote consultants, off-shift activity execution, and follow-the-sun project teams in multiple continents. The coordination and monitoring of project performance are increasingly important when the team shifts towards virtual. Deliverables, milestones, progress reporting, and verification gain importance to ensure commitment is high with the remote staff. Resource needs may also be lower because some virtual contributors do not need infrastructure such as offices; other virtual or freelance contributors may be contracted as well.

Outputs

Resources Assignments, Calendars, and Project Management Plan Changes

Resource assignments are categorized as physical or team assignments. The physical assignment of tangible procured materials, parts, and equipment are assigned as detailed in the activity resource estimation process. These resources are acquired in the indicated quantities, locations, and timing per the previous estimates. Team assignments include the personnel who will be completing the work. Personnel are hired or assigned to the team with roles and responsibilities defined. The assignments are documented accordingly in project plans. Resource calendars are a compilation of team member work shift details. The resource calendar indicates all open and available work time for each resource: personnel, equipment, or facilities. Utilization can be monitored and reported as a metric when collecting calendar data. Geographic location, skill level, and resource cross-utilization are also factored into the resource calendar data. Lastly, and in a similar way to previous project phase outputs, the project management plan elements are subjected to updates throughout the resource acquisition process. Updates may be needed in the resource management plan, the cost baseline, the project schedule, the resource breakdown structure, and the resource requirements.

Develop Team

Overview

Team Development Process and Characteristic Behaviors of High-Performing Teams

Once acquired, the team members performing project work must be assimilated into the system and culture of the project team. Development must involve expansion of abilities, team building, training to work standards, and leadership support of a positive work culture. Project leadership must also be aware of methods to sustain high morale, develop interpersonal skills, and utilize team members by maximizing their strengths. Project and organizational leadership should develop several key behaviors in team members to make high performance more likely:

- Boost and champion collaboration in problem-solving and decision-making.
- Provide team-building opportunities.
- Promote honest and open communication lines to make conflicts less likely.
- Resolve conflicts quickly and effectively.
- Focus on crafting high levels of trust between team members.

Objectives and Stages of Team Development

Foremost, the first objective of the development of a well-functioning project team is to effectively complete project work within plan parameters. Team development should also enhance trust, skills, productivity (both individual and team), cross-training, and decision-making skills among team members. Teams hasten the development process when beginning with a prepared set of team norms or organizational cultural standards. Although these norms may adjust or change as the team develops, the baseline of cultural behaviors sets a strong foundation.

The common path for team development includes five characteristic steps. Team dynamics shift as the project team interacts with each other and faces challenges together. The development phases may not all occur, and some may not be in the same order as the model process describes.

- Forming – As the team begins working together, each person learns of their roles, responsibilities, and basic processes.
- Storming – As the team begins evaluating and working through activities, collaboration is minimal and team functioning is minimal. Conflict is highly likely.
- Norming – As more work is performed, behaviors that work well for the team are taking shape. Collaborative work strengthens.
- Performing – The team functions smoothly together and demonstrates interdependence when problem-solving.
- Adjourning – When the project work is completed, the team most often disbands without any further deliverables.

Tools and Techniques

Utility of Communication Tools, Colocation, and Virtual Work

Communication between team members and with project management helps hasten the time to high performance. Various situations of team work locations require multiple communication options. Collocated project teams, virtual teams, and blended styles will require savvy use of tools available. Common tools include email, conferencing, video/audio, shared scheduling, and information-sharing tools within localized intranet or cloud-based services. Virtual teams require distributed online platforms to share information and communicate. Virtual teamwork may enhance development if outside experts participate from a distance when physical presence may not be feasible. Colocation is an effective approach where all team members work from the same location and can strengthen team bonding and performance quickly.

Interpersonal Skills

Negotiation is a skill used to derive compromise outcomes on decisions within the project team. Conflict management is very important to maintaining a high-performing team without strife that may reduce performance and engagement. Conflict is inevitable, but unhealthy conflicts are detrimental to performance. Influence is a skill that builds trust and aligns team members and stakeholders with reliable evidence, persuasion, and relationships. Motivation is enabled in team members through healthy empowerment of team members to contribute to the mission of the project. Motivation is also enabled through respect, fair treatment, accountability, and a clear and positive mission for the project team. Rewards, such as financial, can also be motivators of performance. Lastly, skilled team building, where the right people are given the skills to perform the right jobs optimally, will lead to higher performance. Common themes in effective team building include fostering a collaborative environment, effective communications, and interpersonal skill development.

Outputs

Team Performance Assessments

The project team development phase produces team performance assessments as evidence of monitoring and opportunities for improvement. Team performance data collected periodically will help both project and organizational leadership to assess where efforts at team facilitation and development are working effectively and where such efforts need change or support. This evaluation of performance often includes assignment performance data, turnover rate, net competencies held by the cumulative project team, and strengthened team solidarity. By collecting team development and performance data, project leadership can analyze strengths and weaknesses in skills, training, coaching, and realignment necessary to improve project performance and team development.

Manage Team

Overview

The project team management process involves monitoring, evaluating, adjusting, and coaching team members and defusing conflicts to collectively ensure the team executes project work at high performance levels. The team management process focuses on optimization of human resources, behaviors, and skills for project success. Project leadership must have key project plans, information logs, and performance data. These sources are analyzed with various tools or techniques to achieve team optimization. Ongoing or periodic team member assessments are also used as means to ensure the team is functionally ideal.

Tools and Techniques

Conflict Resolution

Low to moderate levels of conflict among a project team is common and supports a healthy level of team performance and decision-making. When conflicts become detrimental to performance, it is important for project leadership to defuse conflicts quickly. Disruptive conflicts occur due to variation in resource expectations, schedule fluctuation, cost constrictions, and insufficient team development. The project manager or organizational leadership can help prevent disruptive conflicts by creating a culture of collaboration, trust, and communication. The project manager must assess the most effective approach to conflict resolution on a case-by-case basis while considering conflict intensity, team relationships, and impact to team motivation. Five key techniques—differentiated by degrees of active or passive engagement as well as win/lose combination—are commonly used in management to resolve conflicts.

Approach	Active/Passive	Description
Collaborative	Highly active (win-win)	Assessing the conflict from multiple viewpoints in a shared approach to solve the root cause problem(s).
Forced resolution	Active (win-lose)	The authoritative party (the project manager) forces the decision upon the team or individuals without feedback.
Compromise	Neutral (neutral)	Both sites of the conflict make concessions to a satisfactory outcome. The root cause of the conflict may not get resolved and the situation may be win-win or lose-lose.
Accommodation	Passive (lose-win)	By accommodating one party's desires to avoid conflict, the underlying root causes remain for a future day.
Avoid	Very passive (lose-lose)	The conflict resolution is avoided and may increase in severity if ignored further.

Leadership, Influencing, and Emotional Intelligence

Leadership, emotional intelligence, and influential abilities are traits that can be developed in project managers. Leadership is defined as the ability to motivate and inspire other people towards a common mission. Strong leaders are passionate about the project and driving their team towards success. Emotional intelligence is defined as a leader's ability to gauge and respond effectively to their own emotions and the emotions of those in their sphere of influence. Emotional intelligence also includes the ability to be empathetic, acknowledging of others' concerns, and the ability to reduce team tensions. Influence is developed skillfully over time by project leaders. Their influence can have three dimensions: role-based, relationship-based, or expertise-based. Influence based on role-power or one's authority over others is effective only in the short term. Relationship and expertise influence are more sustainable options for influence.

Control Resources

Overview

Resource control is focused on resource utilization against the project schedule and resource management plan. The expected timing and usage of physical resources are monitored and controlled. Corrective actions are implemented where deviations from the baseline plan create a negative performance impact. This level of control helps ensure that the necessary resources are made available, costs incurred, and schedules maintained in the sequence expected. Key parameters monitored in the resource control phase include resource costs, quantity variances, accuracy in release and timing, navigating resource availability constraints, and change management.

Tools and Techniques

Problem-Solving

Problem-solving is a technique used by project managers to face challenges with a defined process so that the obstacle is overcome or eliminated and the project work can continue within the expectations established. Project managers and teams are faced with internal or external problems, each presenting different methods to approach solutions. Many problem-solving techniques are available. Generally, problem-solving techniques follow a similar set of steps. Identifying and defining the problem begets the ability to collect the right types of data before beginning analysis. Analysis searches for possible solutions to the problem's root causes. Implementing solutions resolves the immediate issue, but resolution is not sustained without methods to verify and control the improvement in the future.

Project Communications Management

Plan Communications Management

Overview

Project communications management involves the implementation and support of project communication systems used to share project information to stakeholders within and outside the organization. The management system components include strategic communications planning and the execution of that plan. Essential communication approaches in effective project management include written, verbal, body language, choice of media, and level of formality. These approaches may differ in effectiveness when considering multiple potential dimensions to communication. In addition to internal, external, formal, and informal dimensions, communication activities may be along organizational design paths. For example, up or down the chain of command or lateral among colleagues. Communication dimensions can also be publicly formal, such as securities filings or press releases. Communications could also be unofficial, such as stakeholder meetings and working groups.

Trends

Social computing is best defined as the beneficial use of public communication networks, such as public internet, social media, and mobile systems, to challenge or improve project collaboration and performance. Stakeholder engagement can diverge into two sub-categories: stakeholder participation in project meetings and stakeholder participation in project reviews. The former sub-category gives a greater voice to stakeholders that will be impacted by the project work or its outcomes. Participation in periodic project meetings opens an opportunity for the project team to receive feedback, ideas, or low- to mid-level conflict for better decision-making and focus on stakeholder needs. The latter category ensures stakeholders are informed of project work, status, and performance through reviews. Stakeholders that are considered essential to project success are primary recipients of review communications. Multifaceted communication strategies exist where project management delivers project communications in a variety of forms, platforms, and styles to ensure all participants and stakeholders receive information and messages in the model they prefer.

5 C's of Written Communications

The 5 C's of Written Communications are as follows:

- Control idea-flow - Using mixed approaches (written, verbal, charts, graphs) to convey ideas and information smoothly.
- Clear purpose - The content and purpose of the information must be relevant to the audience.
- Concise - Communications delivered without unnecessary wording will keep audience misunderstandings minimized.
- Coherent flow - The art of denoting sections, topics, and a logical flow of information to the audience. Also, providing summary and introductory elements.
- Correct grammar - Accuracy of language and grammar used will prevent misunderstandings.

Supplementary Ways to Enhance the 5 C's of Written Communications are as follows:

- Active listening - Capturing and summarizing the speaker's words to ensure understanding.
- Skill enhancement - Using several concepts to enhance team performance: coaching, persuasion, motivation, negotiating, and conflict resolution.
- Stakeholder expectation management - Ensure stakeholders are satisfied that the project will meet their expectations.
- Cultural intelligence - Developing empathy and cultural understanding among team members.

INPUTS

PLAN COMMUNICATIONS MANAGEMENT AND KEY INPUTS TO THE PRELIMINARY PROCESS

The communication management plan is a set of standards and policies set by the project management team to ensure that the communication needs of stakeholders are met. The approach to meeting these expectations involves balancing the available communication assets within the organization as well as the project needs. The project team collects the communication preferences and needs from stakeholders early in the project life cycle and implements communication systems to ensure those preferences are met in a timely manner. Information management is an important element to the plan.

Key inputs to the development of a communication management plan include the resource management plan and the stakeholder engagement plan. These inputs are part of the overall project management plan and detail communication needs for personnel resources and project stakeholders. Related documents to these plans, including the stakeholder register and the requirements documentation, are also used.

TOOLS AND TECHNIQUES

TECHNOLOGIES AND ANALYSIS

Important technologies used for developing the project communication plan are implemented based on underlying characteristics of the project. The project manager must adapt the communications technologies to the project using several potential approaches. Foremost, security of the communication is considered based on the sensitivity of the project objectives. Confidentiality may be increased if the project is within a military or highly-competitive environment. The physical environment where the project will take place—virtual, blended, or collocated—and the geographic distribution of the project team will require consideration of cultural, time zone, and technology considerations. The methods of communication must also be easy to use for the project team and stakeholders.

Many sources are investigated to obtain input for development of the plan. These inputs can include:

- Stakeholder requirements
- Regulatory requirements
- Communication path network diagrams
- Organizational charts
- RACI matrix and related responsibility documents
- Internal and external information requirements
- Project staffing levels to gauge level of involvement with communications

Baseline Interactive and Cross-Cultural Communication Model for Project Management

The interactive communication model presents the standard flow of effective communication within a project between a sender and receiver. The baseline process involves the recipient acknowledging the information, reviewing it, and issuing their feedback to the sender. The sender must take responsibility to ensure the communication is clear and delivered correctly to the recipient. The recipient must take responsibility for receiving the complete communication, interpreting the material, and providing an acknowledgement or response to the sender. As layers of complexity are added to this model, communication effectiveness can decline if care is not taken. Cultural differences in language, ethnicity, socially acceptable behaviors, work methods, and social roles will impact how well senders encode their message and how recipients interpret and affirm their feedback. Furthermore, each individual within the communication will have personal influential factors impacting encoding and decoding the communication. The project manager must be aware of these factors and adjust communications accordingly.

Communication Methods for Sharing Project Information with Stakeholders

The three main types of communication methods for project stakeholder communication are push, pull, and interactive. Push communications involve the project manager and/or team distributing communication materials downwards to the stakeholders on a schedule and format that is dictated by the project leadership. These results are discontinuous and are only provided periodically by select persons. Information asymmetry may exist between sender and recipient. Push techniques include reports, emails, newsletters, blogs, and meetings. Pull communications result when recipients can access and retrieve relevant project communications and reporting when they so desire. Real-time information is obtained by the recipient as desired. Pull systems are better suited for larger stakeholder groups. Pull technologies include intranets, training portals online, and knowledge databases. Interactive methods involve multiple persons or parties sending and receiving information among each other simultaneously. This common approach is found in meetings, conference calls, and seminars.

Outputs

Project Communications Plan

The project communication plan is the result of the analysis of stakeholder communication requirements, cultural and organizational communications characteristics, organizational technology dedicated to communications, and project standards for communications. The plan describes to internal and external stakeholders how project communications will be designed, executed, and controlled. Plan elements can be grouped into several categories: linguistics, stakeholder, resource/responsibilities, and methods. The plan may also include controlled documents and templates for effective communications during the project and likely developed from previous work in the lessons learned register.

Plan Element Category	Description
Linguistics	Glossary of familiar terms used
	Information in the appropriate language, content, and format
Stakeholder	Stakeholder communication rules and preferences
	Regulatory constraints
Resources/responsibilities	Designated responsible person for communicating
	Defined distribution frequencies of communications
	Authorization controls for confidential information
	Defined resource allocation for communications
	Information flow charts and control requirements
Methods	Information flow charts that map out the distribution
	Procedures on how to escalate communications issues for more senior support
	Receipt acknowledgement process
	Approved technologies and media for communications

Manage Communications

Overview

Communication Management Process and Concepts for Effective Project Communication

The process of managing the project communications will follow the project's communication management plan. Managing communications involves the effective and accurate oversight of project information among the project team and with relevant stakeholders. Communications management addresses all steps in project information flow, including information creation, storage, distribution, control, monitoring, and review. The management process also addresses the functionality of communication methods, systems adjustments, and change requests. The communication management process also explains how the project team will address seven key communication techniques.

Technique	Description
Active listening	Strengthens comprehension by sending clear communications, actively acknowledging receipt, and achieving understanding between both parties.
Choice of media	Selection of the right communication medium (one or more) to deliver with effectiveness to all stakeholders.
Facilitation	Management of decision impasse and conflict to keep team member engagement strong.
Meetings	Performing effective meeting behaviors such as agendas, timeliness, minutes, action lists, and participation.
Presentations	Conveying information through effective visuals, concise content, and clear delivery.
Sender/receiver models	Lowering barriers to effective feedback and interactive communications to strengthen understanding.
Writing style	Maintaining active voice and effective writing skills.

Tools and Techniques

Communications Skills for Effectively Managing Project Communications

Competence is a communication skill characterized by strong leadership qualities, delivery with clear purpose, and effective information sharing. Experience in managing project communications develops project manager communication competence.

Feedback is a communication tool commonly used in the speaker/listener model. Interaction by the recipient when digesting the sender's information results in providing a feedback loop to clarify and verify understanding between the two parties. Furthermore, leadership behaviors such as coaching and performance evaluation are considered effective project communication behaviors related to feedback.

Nonverbal communication skills can supplement the written and spoken delivery of information. Body language, preparation, facial expression, and tone of voice serve to enhance communication delivery.

Presentations are most effective when delivered with relevant information of importance to the concerns and schedules of the audience. Effective presentations in the project process are often focused on performance reports, key challenges, and creating project scope and deliverable understanding.

PMIS

The project management information system (PMIS) is a component of the project work phase that is often overseen by the organization's information technology (IT) division. PMIS is commonly computer software that collects, analyzes, and communicates project data into useful information for the management of project work. PMIS systems can often be integrated with enterprise resource planning software tools for procurement, costing, and human resource planning. PMIS provides a reliable and easy information retrieval source for communicating project status and information to stakeholders. Assuming the data in PMIS is accurate, several PMIS tools are available to support these communications:

- **Electronic communications** – Tools and integrations are common so that information can be pushed or pulled with stakeholders through email, web portals, and conferencing.
- **Social media platforms** – Information and feedback systems may integrate with social media and mobile platforms for ease of stakeholder interaction.
- ***In silico* management tools** – Computer-based technologies that support project communications, including collaboration software, project management software, and office platforms.

Monitor Communications

Overview

Project leadership performs monitoring activities upon the communications systems and processes to ensure effective, timely, and accurate delivery of project information to stakeholders and team members. Project leadership is responsible to ensure the information and communication expectations are met or exceeded for all stakeholders. The monitoring process for communications uses pre-defined information flow diagrams, stakeholder information requirements, and relevant subplans in the project to ensure the expectations and plan requirements are met. Activities including the collection and analysis of customer data, satisfaction surveys, complaint summaries, and collected corrective actions ensures that communications monitoring remains valid. As communications are issued or received, monitoring practices may need to be changed through formal project change systems.

Project Risk Management

Plan Risk Management

Overview

Key Elements and Non-Event Risks to Consider

Project risk management is an element of the project management plan that focuses on identifying, analyzing, and subverting project risks. The element also includes risk monitoring and response planning. By identifying, addressing, and monitoring project risks, the project manager is better able to prevent risks from negatively impacting project performance. The risk management plan includes components such as risk identification, quantitative and qualitative analysis, responses, and risk monitoring. The two types of project risks of concern include individual risk and overall project risk. Individual risks may impact certain objectives in the project while the overall risks are those, from multiple potential sources, identified to impact the project as a whole. Non-event risks are defined as those in a project that are not tied directly to future uncertain events. Rather, the non-event risks, including variability and ambiguity, being quantitative, statistical, or probability-based variations that add risk to the achievement of the objectives. Ambiguity risk arises where assumptions and available knowledge are weak and may impose a positive or negative risk.

Project Resilience and Integrated Risk Management

Resilience is defined in project management as the preparation in project planning to absorb and overcome unknown project risks as they impact the work. Resilience is created when project managers perform several strategic approaches. The three key resources must have allocated flexibility for unknown risk management, including schedule time, material and man resources, and budget. Continuing the flexibility theme, the project processes and personnel must remain flexible to unknown risks and be confident in using procedures to overcome the risks when faced. Clear project objectives, mission, and scope allow the team to get back on track when they face unknown risks. Preventive assessment of risks before they require resources and action is a way the project manager can avoid unknowns becoming detrimental to the project. Lastly, high levels of communication between project leadership and key stakeholders is essential, especially if these unknown risks require adjustments to the project scope, deliverables, or plan. Integrated risk management is defined as the process of organizational risk management when the organization has many subdivisions or teams working on separate and possibly related projects, programs, or portfolios. Some risks are best managed at the lowest level, while collective or higher scale risks can be managed using broader resources.

Inputs

Risk Management Plan and Inputs

The risk management plan is developed as the first step in the plan risk management element. The plan describes how the project team will perform risk analysis and management processes for the project. The plan and its execution highlight risks and make known the strategies necessary to minimize their impact to achieving project objectives and deliverables. The risk management plan is developed early in the project life cycle and is often revised or reviewed during various project phases. Inputs to the risk management plan development include essential material like the charter, project management plan, scope, and stakeholder requirements. Other key inputs from the parent organization overseeing the project can include a broader risk management policy, organizational risk management tools such as a risk breakdown structure, and the use of contracted experts skilled in risk analysis.

OUTPUTS

FEATURES AND IMPACT OF THE RISK MANAGEMENT PLAN

The risk management plan itself is a document that outlines the risk strategy, risk management methodology, and team roles and responsibilities regarding risk management. Furthermore, the plan describes how risk management will be financed, scheduled, and the levels of severity for certain risk classifications. The risk strategy gives stakeholders a thorough understanding of how the project team and the organization will assess and manage through risks. The methodology section details the specific tools the team will use to identify and manage the risks. Roles and responsibilities provide stakeholders confidence that tasks in the management plan are assigned to specific functions or team members. Resource allocation is described in the financing and timing sections. Both describe how money is allocated and human resources are scheduled for risk management functions. Project budgets are expected to include risk management funds based on the analysis. Finally, risk categories are detailed in the plan; the categories are organized in a risk breakdown structure that groups like risks or bases the dichotomy on organizational knowledge.

IMPACT MATRIX AND SCORING SCHEME

The impact matrix is a prioritization tool that gives project managers a quantitative method for ranking risks relative to each other. The matrix is precluded by a set of definitions for known risk probabilities and impact. This set defines risk severity based on several factors, such as time, cost, quality impact, and probability of occurrence. The impact matrix plots probability of occurrence against degree of impact on either a positive or negative scale. Positive impacts are considered opportunities, while negative impacts are considered threats to project performance. The matrix is filled in with unitless scores in which higher values represent high impact/high probability risks, while lower scores represent lower impact/lower probability combinations. The rankings give management a tool to visualize the likelihood of positive or negative risk impacts to the project.

Threats

Probability \ Negative Impact	Very Low 0.05	Low 0.25	Moderate 0.50	High 0.75	Very High 0.95
Very High 0.95	0.05	0.24	0.48	0.71	0.90
High 0.75	0.04	0.19	0.38	0.56	0.71
Moderate 0.50	0.03	0.13	0.25	0.38	0.48
Low 0.25	0.01	0.06	0.13	0.19	0.24
Very Low 0.05	0.00	0.01	0.03	0.04	0.05

Opportunities

Probability \ Positive Impact	Very Low 0.05	Low 0.25	Moderate 0.50	High 0.75	Very High 0.95
Very High 0.95	0.05	0.24	0.48	0.71	0.90
High 0.75	0.04	0.19	0.38	0.56	0.71
Moderate 0.50	0.03	0.13	0.25	0.38	0.48
Low 0.25	0.01	0.06	0.13	0.19	0.24
Very Low 0.05	0.00	0.01	0.03	0.04	0.05

Identify Risks

Overview

The risk identification process includes detection of likely risks, including their sources and features. The collection of profile information on the known risks supports project decision-making and risk mitigation strategies as the risk plan is further executed. Knowing the risk enemy well can allow a project team to attack it correctly. It is wise for the risk profiles to have similar formats and information captured. Stakeholders and team members reviewing these risks benefit when viewing familiar information and categories. Identification may also lead to assigned risk observers and document initial responses the team will take if the risks occur. The risk identification process occurs throughout the project life cycle. As the project progresses, new risks may be identified, especially when deviations occur from the project plan.

Inputs

Inputs to the Risk Identification Process

Input	Description
Baselines	Documents including schedule, cost, and scope baselines. Each document is assessed for uncertainty in estimates or assumptions made. External factors may also impact the risk profile of each baseline.
Cost management plan	Uncertainty elements are included within the cost management plan.
Logs and registers	Commonly used documents include the assumption log, issue log, lessons learned register, and the stakeholder register.
Quality management plan	The quality plan often lists areas of uncertainty regarding quality performance and stakeholder perceptions. Risks to shifts in quality perceptions are also commonly addressed.
Requirements management plan	Describes the project objectives highly subjected to risk impact.
Resource management plan	Details the risks associated with material and personnel resources.
Risk management plan	Provides the framework for analyzing and managing the known and unknown risks.
Schedule management plan	Details the risks associated with the project schedule and its assumptions.
Estimates	Documented quantitative estimates for cost and duration contain underlying variance. Risk occurs if estimates lose accuracy over time.
Requirements documentation	Stakeholder and resource requirements documentation used as a frame of reference for which requirements are exposed to varying degrees of risk.

Tools and Techniques

Brainstorming, Checklists, and Interviewing

Brainstorming is a tool used for collecting all comprehensible risks to individual project elements and collectively to the project overall. The team assembled includes project team members, stakeholders, and often subject matter experts; an unbiased flow of ideas culminates in a comprehensive list of risks to be analyzed. Checklists are a basic quality tool that is used to remind a person or group of important points to be inspected or assessed routinely. The items within the checklist have been added with insight and justification based on lessons learned, regulations, or project policies. The checklist can gather objective data on risk exposure in project operations. Lastly, interviewing is a project risk data gathering technique when the interviewees have experience in risk management scenarios like what is found in the project. In all data gathering, the project team must prevent bias, untruthfulness, and inaccuracy in the results collected.

Document Analysis, SWOT Analysis, Constraint Analysis, and Root Cause

Document analysis is a simple review of the relevant project documents for signs of project risks. These documents can include plans, schematics, policies, schedules, budgets, contracts, and stakeholder reports. **SWOT analysis** is the assessment of strengths, weaknesses, opportunities and threats from collective sources internal and external to the project or organization. These compilations can be further analyzed in permutations to develop approaches to prevent the identified risks. **Constraint analysis** involves validation of the assumptions and constraints that were baked into the project. Validation can expose the true likelihood of impact for each of the assumptions and constraints. Validation is best performed early in the project, soon after the constraints and assumptions are identified. **Root cause analysis** is a technique used to derive the right corrective and preventive action for project issues or non-conformances requiring resolution. When a project is a continuous improvement initiative, the root cause analysis follows the crafting of the problem statement.

Prompt Lists

Prompt lists are a compilation of known risk categories that serve as a useful reference and reminder to the project team. When the team encounters risk or must use risk identification, the prompt list will provide supportive ideas for assessing the type of risks observed. Risk prompt lists can be generated in multiple ways. The most common approaches include the risk breakdown structure (RBS) and broader mnemonic acronym devices. The lowest identified risks on the RBS can be tallied into a prompt list. These are especially useful for identifying individual risks in a project. More strategic prompt lists may focus more on overall sources of risk. Examples of strategic project management prompt lists include VUCA (volatility, uncertainty, complexity, and ambiguity) and PESTLE (political, economic, social, technological, legal, and environmental).

Outputs

Risk Register and Risk Reports

The risk register is a central file where known individual risks are documented. The risk register is the primary output of the identify risks subprocess of project risk management. The results of other subprocesses such as qualitative risk analysis, planning risk responses, implementing risk responses, and risk monitoring are also documented in the risk register. The risk register lists out all identified risks categorized with a unique identification number. It is essential that the identified risks are described as completely as possible. The register also may include contributor names designated as the responsible owner for each risk. Additionally, the register may offer response concepts for each risk so that action can be performed when risks are monitored in the project execution. Risk registers may also vary between different projects or organizations; relevant information is included based on organizational needs. Sufficient information to tie the risk to WBS activities, timing, and severity are common considerations.

The identified risks are compiled into a risk report that summarizes overall project risk as well as individual risks that may occur. The report eventually includes risk-related information and performance from several points in the project. The report typically lists sources of overall project risk, summarization of individual risks, and relevant analysis of risk across the project life cycle.

Perform Qualitative Risk Analysis

Overview

After the risks have been identified, the qualitative risk analysis process serves to analyze each known risk in terms of severity and likelihood of occurrence. The analysis results in a risk profile ranking where the project team or organization can prioritize certain risks over others. While the severity and likelihood rankings can generally be subjective, internal or external studies may be available that can provide a more objective assessment of the risk profile. Some risks may be regulatory or customer-driven in nature, and these risks are more easily defined for priority. The internal team that performs the qualitative risk assessment must be calibrated so that bias and variation in risk perception is absent or minimized from the analysis work. Once all risks are provided a prioritization score, each is assigned an owner and efforts may be made to eliminate or reduce the risk severity to a more acceptable score. The risk quantitative analysis and response is continuous throughout the project, especially as new risks are encountered.

TOOLS AND TECHNIQUES

RISK DATA QUALITY ASSESSMENT AND RISK PROBABILITY AND IMPACT ASSESSMENT

Risk data quality assessments examine the accuracy and precision of data generated for the individual quantitative assessments. This check of risk data reliability ensures that decision-making is not weak. The quality assessment is performed by surveying stakeholders regarding several risk data perspectives, including data relevance and objectivity. The project team takes the weighted average of the returned rankings and derives quality scores for each measured perspective. The risk probability and impact assessment are related tools used to gauge the likelihood and effect severity of the identified risks. These concepts are very similar to failure modes and effect analysis (FMEA) in lean Six Sigma projects. The effect focuses on how the risk would impact cost, schedule, resource, quality and performance objectives. The impact analysis is gauged on a scale where negative impact represents threats while positive impact represents opportunities. By plotting the impact against likelihood, a graphical impact matrix of the risks improves interpretation. The project team must gather meaningful and well supported probability and impact data using qualitative techniques.

ASSESSING ADDITIONAL RISKS TO THE PROJECT

Additional risks that must be assessed by the project team beyond likelihood and impact are categorized into those affecting time, control, and social interconnectivity.

Category	Risk parameter	Description
Control	Controllability	High controllability occurs when the project team (or owner of the risk itself) is best able to govern the outcome of a given risk.
	Detectability	Highly detectable risks are those that the project team can most easily identify as they are occurring or are forthcoming.
	Manageability	Highly manageable risks are those that the project team or risk owners are best able to manage the effects of.
Social interconnectivity	Connectivity	Connectivity refers to how extensively the risk is related and connected to other individual risks. High connectivity implies many other risks are connected.
	Perception	Termed propinquity, the level is high when multiple stakeholders perceive the risk to be very significant.
	Strategic impact	High strategic impact refers to those risks that will have a very significant effect, either positive or negative.
Time	Dormancy	High dormancy risks are those where there is a long period of time between the occurrence of the risk and the point when the risk was detected.
	Proximity	High proximity occurs when a risk's occurrence is a short duration of time prior to impacting a project objective.
	Urgency	High urgency is reflected in a short period of time between when the risk occurs and an effective resolution is implemented.

Hierarchical Bubble Chart for Visualizing Project Risks

Bubble charts are used to visually express more than two risk parameters within the same chart. A traditional x and y axis plots two of the three variables, while the size of the bubbles represents the third risk parameter to be visualized. Any applicable combination of three risk parameters relevant to the project can be plotted and visualized using a bubble chart. Further expansion on the chart model, each quadrant can be qualitatively categorized to communicate a label or grouping of certain risk combinations. The added information to the chart provides improved decision-making when assessing multi-risk impact to the project. Large bubbles in the high proximity/high detectability fields are unacceptable. Small bubbles in the low/low area are ideal. The bubble size reflects intensity of the third parameter, such as impact to the project.

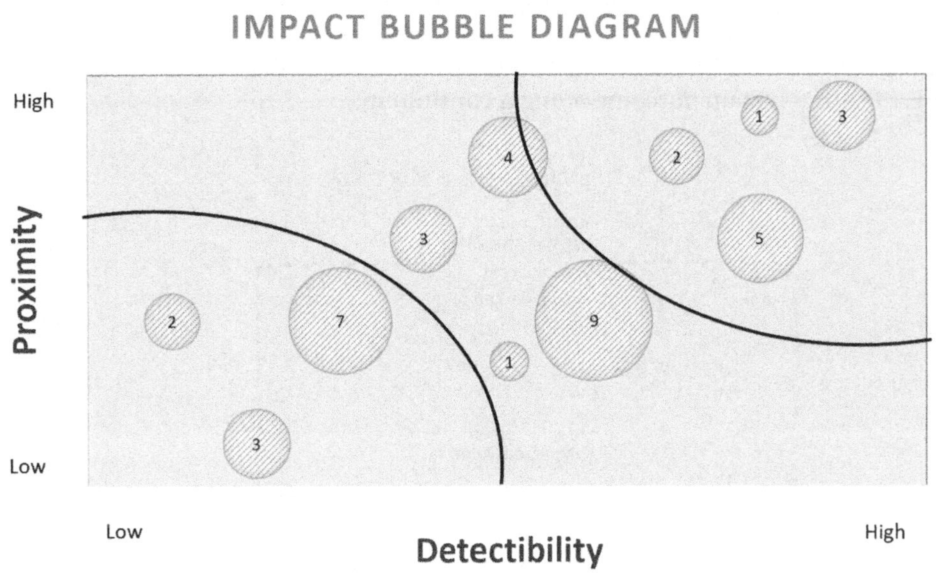

Perform Quantitative Risk Analysis

Overview

Quantitative Risk Analysis and Inputs

The quantitative risk analysis takes mathematical approaches to analyze the effects of all identified individual project risks as well as their impact upon the project objectives. Numerically quantifying the risk levels benefits data-driven organizations and stakeholders. The project team performing the risk analysis must rely on strong data collection techniques; thorough data analysis for the risk quantification; and the support of well-crafted assumption and baseline documentation, including that of the scope, schedule plan, and cost plan. Quantitative risk assessment is highly reliable and must have necessary costs allocated within the project for its execution. Larger or complex projects often require this form of analysis, especially where the project is of high strategic importance to the organization. The qualitative risk analysis phase outputs of high significance are used as inputs into the quantitative analysis phase. Thereafter, the mathematical analysis results in planning risk responses. Inputs to the quantitative risk analysis include the project management plan and its sub-elements, baselines such as cost and schedule, and nearly the full gambit of project documents.

Tools and Techniques

Expression of Uncertainty and S-Curve of Quantitative Cost Analysis

Uncertainty can be expressed in the quantitative risk analysis by transforming data for schedule, cost, or resource uncertainty into one of several probability distributions. This transformation communicates the likelihood of different outcomes across a distribution of all potential outcomes. Common distributions used in this phase include uniform, beta, normal, and lognormal. Individual project risks are either directly covered with an assessed probability distribution or with a probability branch model to visualize likely impacts that would occur as potential risks happen. The S-curve is an output of a Monte Carlo simulation of risk. The simulation factors in the effects of multiple individual risks in the project and provides greater certainty on the effects those risks may have upon the project achievement of objectives. The S-curve is a cumulative probability distribution of the simulated outcome for a given project objective, such as schedule adherence, cost, or other performance metric. Further up the S-curve indicates a higher probability—approaching 1.0—of a certain outcome along a continuum.

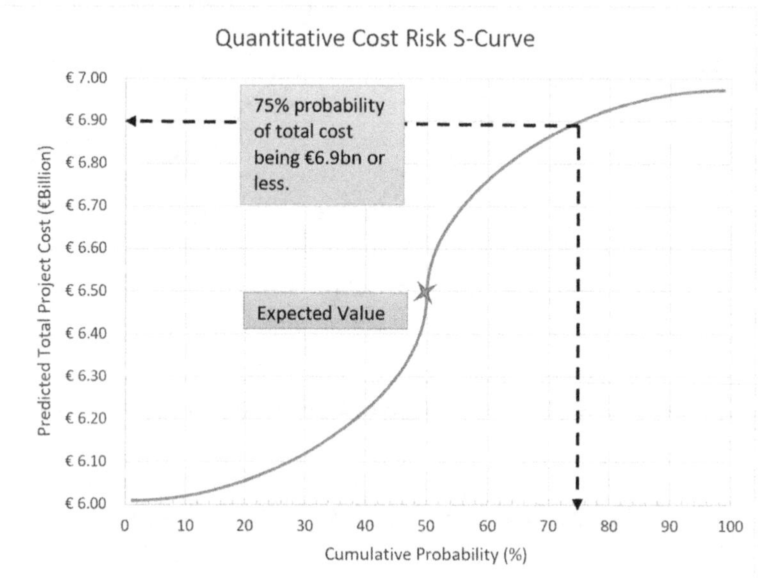

Tornado Diagram and Decision Tree Analysis

The tornado diagram is a visual output of a sensitivity analysis used in the quantitative risk analysis phase. Sensitivity analyses take the risk analysis of individual risks one step further than simply defining them. It is positive to analyze how much impact individual risks may have upon the project outcomes. The tornado diagram plots the relative correlation coefficient for each analyzed element in the quantitative model. Correlation is between each risk or uncertainty and the outcome of concern. Stronger correlated risks are plotted on top and descending downward to lesser correlated risks. Correlation can be either a positive or negative direction on the plot. The resulting graph resembles a tornado and expresses risk correlation intensity and direction for each outcome.

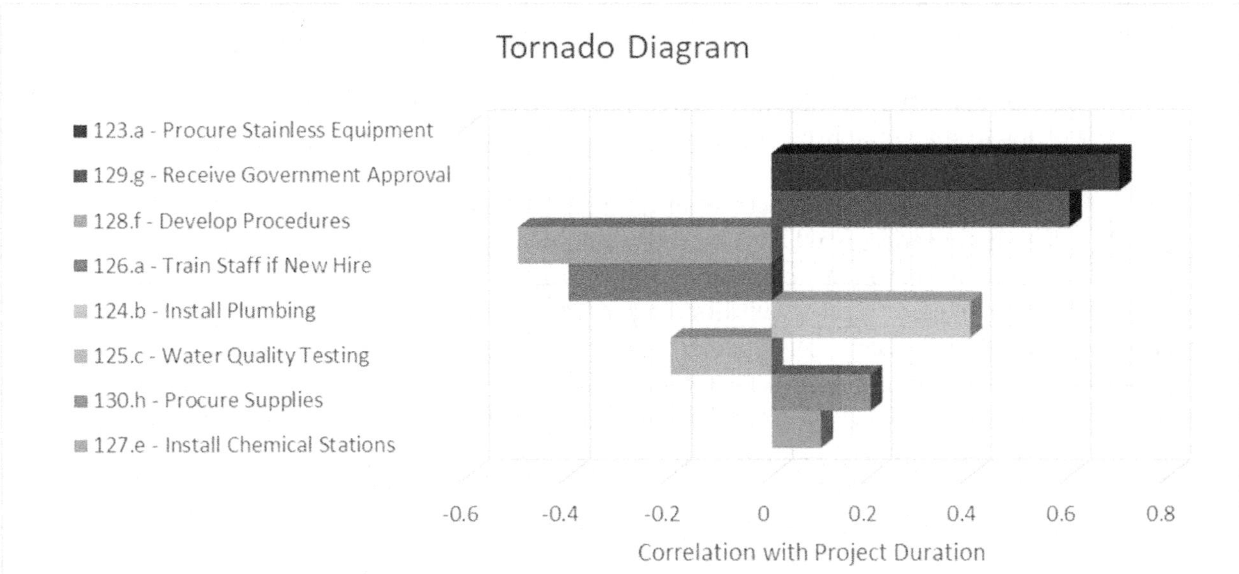

OUTPUTS

PROJECT DOCUMENT UPDATES

The primary document updated because the quantitative risk analysis is the risk report. The report is updated with an assessment of the overall project risks and validated likelihood for those identified project risks. The assessment of overall risks contains two key measures: success probabilities and inherent remaining variation among potential risks still pending in the project at the time of the assessment. The probabilistic success information is based on the individual project risks and compiled sources of uncertainty. The second most common element updated in the risk report is the detailed likelihood analysis for the project. This update contains the analysis information, including S-curves, tornado diagrams, and criticality for the project risks. Additional updates include individual project risks listed and described by priority, identified trends captured from the quantitative analysis, and the risk analysis team's recommended responses to each risk.

Plan Risk Responses

OVERVIEW

The risk response planning phase involves the project team defining specific actions that will be taken, presently or in the future, to diminish the impacts of the proposed risks. The subjugation of the risks through action generally begins with tasks that carry the highest risk probability. Prioritization can be done through a combination of quantitative likelihood and severity and detectability measurements. The process also must have allocated budget resources to execute these potential response plans as needed. Responses must be valid for the risk presented. Constraints may still force the organization to have several contingency strategies for each response, should full planned resource allocation be a challenge. Multiple strategies, including back-up procedures, are important. Key inputs include the resource, risk, and cost management plans; the resource calendar; the risk register; and the risk report.

Tools and Techniques

Strategies for Neutralizing Project Risk Threats

Strategy	Description
Accept	Acceptance strategies allow the risk to occur with full understanding that there may be positive or negative impact to the objectives. This strategy is generally used for low-priority risks and the related resource constraints that occur can be easily absorbed by the project plans. Active acceptance includes budgeting a reserve of resources in time, money, or resources. Passive acceptance keeps an ongoing view of the risk level and impact rather than setting aside reserves.
Avoid	Avoidance occurs when the project team works to neutralize the risk threat. Elimination can be achieved by significant adjustment to the schedule, scope, objectives, or strategy within the project.
Escalate	Escalation occurs when project experts assess that the project manager is not suited to manage the risk and the resolution must be performed at the organizational level. Program and portfolio level leadership may also take on the responsibility of risk neutralization.
Mitigate	Actions are performed to lessen the impact and/or likelihood of risks. The mitigation strategy is preventive when started as early as possible when valid risks are identified. Mitigation may also require organizational investment to add redundancies or scale-up simulations.
Transfer	The transfer of risk responsibilities and mitigation can occur towards competent providers so that the project leadership can focus on the project work. Insurance and warranties are examples of risk transfer.

Strategies for Capitalizing on Project Risk Opportunities

Strategy	Description
Accept	Acceptance is a passive activity regarding the acknowledgement of an opportunity without acting. Considerations such as low-impact, cost-benefit, and resource constraints may prevent these opportunities from being pursued.
Enhance	Known opportunities are deliberately strengthened early after they are recognized. Enhancement increases the benefit that is derived from the opportunity towards the project. The causes of the opportunity create the effect of the probability that the opportunity will occur. Enhancing the causes will increase the benefit derived.
Escalate	Escalation refers to the hand-off of the opportunity to another leader of the organization, program management, or portfolio levels. This is generally due to the opportunity being outside the scope of the project or outside the capabilities of the project manager and team.
Exploit	A beneficial strategy for high-benefit opportunities where the project team or organization act to manipulate the opportunity to increase the likelihood of stronger positive outcomes. For example, exploiting process bottlenecks by adding more processing capacity.
Share	Opportunities may be transferred to another team or to a third party for further pursuit, especially if the opportunities are out of the project scope. Companies may also form spin-off organizations or new corporations built around the shared opportunity. Negative risk sharing may also involve paying risk premiums to the firm overtaking responsibility.

Outputs

Project Document Updates and Revision of the Risk Register Based on Outcomes

Updated project documents contain several project management plan sub-plans, including those for quality, cost, schedule, resources, and procurement. Key baseline documents such as the cost, schedule, and scope baselines are updated as a result of the risk response determination. Project document updates outside of the project management plan itself are highlighted by changes made to the risk register. The risk responses must be captured in the risk register, and the process includes many informational elements. Foremost, the agreed response and specific related actions are detailed for each relevant risk. To support decision-making, the conditions or causes that would lead the team to activate each risk response is detailed for clarity. Also included are relevant budget or schedule actions that must be added when the responses are activated. Contingency and back-up plans are also described where necessary, should the planned risk response not work as expected. Lastly, the responses each detail secondary risks that may remain after the initial response is performed.

Implement Risk Responses

Overview

The implement risk responses element serves as a process to establish the agreed risk responses and the underlying support systems needed for effective execution. Detailed plans laid out in the risk response planning process support effective execution in the implementation phase. Implementation serves to minimize known risk impacts to the project and minimize individual known threats. Key inputs to the process include the project management plan, the risk register, and risk reports. Techniques for implementation include effective interpersonal skills and sound judgement. For more complex projects or organizations, a project management information system (PMIS) would also drive implementation. The output of the process, other than implemented responses, includes project document updates, notably to the risk register and the risk report.

Monitor Risks

Overview

Monitor Risks Element and Inputs

The monitor risks process includes oversight by the project manager and team on the progress of risk response implementation. The process also evaluates conditions for adding new risks to the project and to monitor the effectiveness of the risk process. Monitoring also serves to ensure project team members and key stakeholders are kept updated on the status of risk exposure as the project continues. The objective information gathered regarding project performance aids the risk monitoring function to ensure response effectiveness, adequacy of the risk responses, that assumptions remain valid, and that contingencies are available. Key inputs include the project management plan, the risk register, the risk report, and work performance data.

Tools and Techniques

Reserve Analysis and Technical Performance Analysis

Reserve analysis provides information to stakeholders on the relative ratio of resource reserves allocated for risk mitigation compared to the amount of remaining risk at any given point within the project execution process. The resulting figures provide stakeholders and project members with an assessment of the capability of the reserves to meet the ideally expected demand. Technical performance analysis benchmarks the expected technical performance progress with the actual technical performance achievement. This ratio of planned versus actual performance must ensure that data collected is reliable without bias. The measurements and actionable limits for each performance parameter commonly include defects, transfer times, and capacity.

AUDITS

Auditing is the planned review of an organization's performance compared to a set of agreed criteria or parameters. The audit is performed by one or more auditors and looks to gain objective and first-hand evidence to assess how strongly a process, organization, product, or service meet expectations. The expectations or standards used as the criteria for the audit are typically compiled or enforced by stakeholders, leadership, customers, or regulatory agencies with a vested interest and ensuring conformance. Risk-focused audits serve to ensure the risk management processes are effective. The organization creates detailed risk audit criteria and execute the audit (or have a third party perform the audits) on a defined frequency. The project manager bears responsibility for scheduling and preparing for risk audits during the project.

Project Procurement Management

Plan Procurement Management

Overview

Project Procurement Management Process

Procurement management focuses on obtaining resources, services, or results effectively and within constraints from outside of the project team. These assurances are obtained using formal contracts, purchase agreements, and service agreements with clearly defined criteria and terms. Procurement stakeholders and responsible persons are part of either the project team or the organization at large. The process includes having a defined procurement plan, executing that plan, and performing control methods to ensure providers meet their responsibilities. The contractual process and language influences much of the outcomes in the procurement process. Various parameters are commonly included in procurement contracts, such as cost, timing, quality, and customer service metrics. There are also many laws that impact the contractual deliverables for procurement. The financial, legal, and executive level of the project's parent organization may have full responsibility for entering into procurement agreements; such situations may require careful planning and influence by the project manager. Alternatively, smaller organizations without dedicated procurement teams likely have the project manager lead procurement efforts for projects. Risk mitigation is critical when contracting services or supply, and contracts and service agreement language, audits, and performance evaluations can help mitigate likely risks. Procurement strategies may also require supply chain systems working concurrently to ensure cost and schedule parameters are met.

Features of Purchasing Contracts and Relationships Between Buyers and Sellers

Purchasing contracts describe the transactional, legal, and deliverable requirements that the buyer will impose on the seller should the two parties enter into the agreement mutually. Purchasing contracts within the context of the project management responsibility include ensuring the contracts include all relevant terms, conditions, specifications, and requirements necessary to receive goods or services that help achieve the requirements of the project itself. The project manager may also need to adhere to organizational procurement requirements or defer procurement responsibilities to the organization's support colleagues. The agreement can take one of many forms, including service-level agreements, purchase orders, contracts, or memorandum of agreement. Buyers seek to include all necessary details, requirements, and restrictions so that the seller output will meet their expectations else the imposition of claims and penalties. The seller seeks to obtain the business to service the buyer in favorable terms within their known capabilities and for an equitable fee.

Procurement Management Plan

The procurement management plan ensures that the project team has a formal procedure for selecting suppliers, defining how procurement decisions are made, and outlining the procurement requirements and process. The plan also describes the project resources to be obtained from within the organization or obtained externally. Lastly, the plan outlines the roles and responsibilities within the project team and organization for procurement related to the project. When preparing the project procurement plan, key steps are grouped into preparation, evaluation, and selection:

- **Preparation** – The project team, with or without support from the parent organization, documents the specifications in the form of a statement of work (SOW) or a terms of reference (TOR) file. The team prepares a cost estimate and budget for the total project procurement using supporting project documentation.
- **Evaluation** – After advertising the opportunity, the team narrows down a short list of qualified suppliers and opens the bidding process. Suppliers submit bids. The project team analyzes the bids compared to criteria and project expectations.
- **Selection** – The final analysis of cost and quality among the narrowed bids identifies the winning provider or supplier. The procurement negotiations and contract signing finishes the process.

Tools and Techniques

Cost-Reimbursable Contracts, Fixed-Price Contracts, and Time and Material Contracts

Cost-reimbursable contracts are defined as terms where the buyer makes payments to the seller for approved incurred costs as they occur. The model benefits buyers when project work variation is relatively high. No up-front payments are made prior to the phased completion of work elements. Three self-evident variants of the cost-reimbursable model include cost-plus award, cost-plus incentive, and cost-plus fixed fee.

Fixed-price contracts define the overall total price to be paid for the procurement agreement without embedded payments or incentives based on variation or flux in work. The fixed price contract is useful when the deliverable purchased is highly familiar and procurement variation is limited.

Time and material contracts are a blend of both fixed cost and cost-reimbursable versions. Time and material contracts are common when there is no clear statement of work available from prospective sellers.

Source Selection Analysis

All projects and organizations have competing spheres of influence that impact which criteria are prioritized when making procurement decisions. It is advantageous for buyers and sellers to ensure that all parties are aware of the buyer's selection method and criteria. Sellers must prepare proposals and may invest significant resources to submit a strong bid, especially if the contract is very large or the proposal is very complex. Several common selection methods are used and differ on project elements as highest priority parameter.

Selection Method	Description
Quality-based	A technically superior product or service with high quality may cost more but will inherently be more reliable and meet expectations better. Financial perspectives are considered after firms exceed technical baselines.
Low cost	When supplies or services are of minimal variation among providers, cost is often the key differentiator.
Qualifications	A streamlined approach where the cost-benefit ratio of the project team performing a formal procurement analysis is weak. The team selects based on commonly known reputational factors.
Sole source	The buyer does not seek out bids among providers, rather the buyer negotiates with one provider only.
Combo (quality and cost)	The two criteria are blended; quality becomes more important when the seller's performance is not well known.
Fixed budget	The sellers are made aware of a fixed value of the procurement offer and a top bid is chosen from several choices that have adjusted cost and quality parameters to fit the budget.

OUTPUT

PROCUREMENT MANAGEMENT PLAN AND GUIDANCE FEATURES

The completed procurement management plan outlines the procurement processes that the project team will perform. The plan describes the bidding procedures and controls to be used and describes the resource allocations available for each procurement need. The plan also describes how the procurement process ties into the overall project management plan elements. For example, linkage is described to the schedule plan, cost plan, and the stakeholder requirements information. The degree of formality of the procurement plan is determined by the scope and complexity of the project itself.

Guidance Detail	Description
Coordination	Advising the project team how procurement requirements link to other elements of the project management plan (e.g., schedule, cost management, quality, and performance management).
Timetable	Temporal map of when procurement activities must occur relative to the project plans.
Metrics	Procurement metrics for assuring performance is achieved.
Stakeholder involvement	Defining the roles and responsibilities needed from key stakeholders in the procurement process.
Assumptions	Constraints and assumptions that drive procurement decisions.
Legal awareness	Details of any legal boundaries impacting the procurement.
Independent estimates	Advice on when external independent guidance is needed.
Risk mitigation	Details on insurance and risk mitigation options to prevent major negative impact to the project.
Prequalification	Pre-approval of trusted suppliers and providers.

Procurement Strategy

The procurement strategy is outlined within the procurement management plan, specifically when the team decides to purchase from sources external to their organization. The procurement strategy provides functional instructions for the logistics, legality, contract development, and flow of obtaining the goods or services contracted. The logistics and delivery of the good or service is chosen based on whether the team is procuring professional or commercial construction services. Professional services include options such as direct purchase, sub-contracting, joint ventures, and buyer-directed. Each option carries a different level of control and risk-taking. Commercial construction service options typically include design-build, design-bid-build, design-build-operate, and turnkey delivery methods.

Contract payment approaches are typically managed by the project team's financial colleagues, not by the project team itself. Verification may be requested by the financial team to ensure expenses are accurate. Several variations of procurement payment methods are used in projects, including cost plus incentive fees, labor/time and materials, and fixed-price. Different methods may be desired depending on the familiar or variable nature of the project work.

Procurement flow is monitored by the project manager through phased implementation, key performance indicators for sellers, stage-gate progress criteria, and phase knowledge transfer. Describe primary types of business bid documents, including RFI, RFQ, RFP, and SOW.

Bid Document Type	Description
Request for proposal (RFP)	The project team is seeking proposed solutions to a problem needing external expertise. The formal request seeks specific content and parameter responses from prospective sellers before a decision is made.
Request for information (RFI)	A preliminary step in procurement. Requesting further information on goods or services helps the project team request a quotation or proposal.
Request for quotation (RFQ)	A quotation is a commonly used document where the seller outlines how they intend to meet the buyer's expectations and at what costs. Buyers should be expected to communicate their needs and constraints prior to receiving a quotation. Accuracy in the quotation communication prevents project errors.
Statement of work (SOW)	A compilation of relevant parts of the project scope that a prospective seller would have to achieve to successfully meet expectations. Sellers use the statement of work to determine if they can meet those requirements. Clarity is important when the project team creates the SOW. SOW information can also include quality parameters, cost requirements, specifications, work location, and supply levels.

Conduct Procurements

Overview

Conduct Procurements Process

The conduct procurements process is the activity of comparing formal agreements from sellers, making a choice, and completing a legal contract with the chosen seller(s). Prerequisites to the decision-making process include the compiled RFQ, RFP, and/or RFI documents that the project team may have requested from each potential vendor. The decision itself can reference much of the project management plan, including sub-plans for risk, resources, requirements, communications, procurement, configuration, and cost. The combination of these references used in the conducting of procurement can vary between projects. When making yes or no decisions regarding conducting procurement with each potential vendor, teams are wise to keep good documented evidence of the decisions made. Supporting documentation for the conduct procurement element includes the independent cost estimates, statements of work from the potential vendors, bid documents (RFI, RFQ, RFP), and the source selection criteria. Furthermore, there are enterprise environmental factors and organizational process assets that are factored into the decisions, such as prior contractual agreements still ongoing, regulatory restrictions, internal policies that influence procurement choice, and internal accounting practices.

Tools and Techniques

Data Analysis, Advertising, Bidding Conferences, and Team Skills

Data analysis techniques used in procurement execution mainly focus on ensuring the proposal details match the bid expectations, the statement of work, and related criteria incumbent upon the chosen vendor. Advertising of procurement searches may be a prerequisite for certain projects, such as government contracts. Advertisement is also likely to expand the pool of interested or available sellers of a resource or service. Bidding conferences may involve large gatherings of vendors or contractors to collectively and competitively show and discuss their capabilities to prospective buyers or project organizations with relevant needs. More commonly, one buyer may arrange a bidder conference where all potential sellers present their proposals on a level playing field and benefit the single buyer with fair decision-making. Team skills such as negotiation tactics are important for both the buyer and seller in the conduct procurement process. Reaching an equitable decision where both the buyer and seller feel successful is the ideal outcome. Fine details often must be negotiated, such as payment terms, legal wording, corrective action obligations, performance capabilities, and service schedule. Ideally, the project organization should have a financial authority perform the negotiations with clearance to sign the contract when finalized and consult the project manager as necessary.

Output

Completed Procurement Agreements

Completed procurement agreements share common features. Foremost is the approved statement of work that both parties agree will be provided contractually. Related details regarding schedule, cost, and milestones are included to support the achievement of the statement of work. Accounting details regarding payments and terms are included. Any relevant performance reporting requirements placed upon the seller are detailed in the agreement. Key quality and performance requirements are also detailed in the agreement as needed. The agreements are also likely to include common legal clauses, warranties, hold-harmless details, and termination language. Lastly, the agreements may include incentive details or penalties, should either party exceed or not meet expectations.

Document Updates and Project Management Plan Updates Resulting from Procurement Decisions

Procurement agreements with sellers can disrupt previously planned elements of the project management plan based on the seller's capabilities or the available options buyers have in a marketplace for procured supply. The project manager may need to adjust quality and requirements plans based on seller capabilities. The project manager may also need to revise the risk management plan if the procurement agreement introduces new uncertainty. Changes are likely to the cost, schedule, and scope baseline (including the WBS) when initiating a procurement agreement. When outsourcing the supply or service, sellers introduce variation to the schedule and cost expectations because of the uncertainty that can impact their own ability to meet demands of buyers, often multiple buyers simultaneously. As the project becomes more dependent upon outside work and factors, the inherent supply chain risks become more likely. Documents that are often updated after procurement decisions include the requirements documentation and traceability matrix. Both documents expand to include supplier technical requirements, multiple levels of compliance standards that the suppliers are expected to meet, and the seller's capabilities that impact the requirements traceability. Any added risks from contracting a supplier would be added to the risk register, while any stipulations that must be met with the seller (performed by the project team) must be updated in the stakeholder register.

Control Procurements

Overview

Control Procurements Process and Administrative Control Tasks

Procurement control involves seller-buyer relationship management by the project team, contract performance monitoring, and related corrective actions when performance is not meeting expectations. Monitoring is performed by the project team continuously during the project while the seller or provider is expected to perform work. It is wise for the project manager to monitor the project team and organization's performance to the expectations listed in procurement agreements. These control processes must be replicated across multiple suppliers and vendors. Administrative tasks that must be performed in the control procurements process include data collection from procurement activities (including financial), schedule adjustments for procurement activities, procurement-related reporting to the project team and any impact procurement has upon the project objectives, payment of procured vendors by the organization, and quality assurance analysis upon project elements that are impacted by procurement behaviors and performance.

Input

Agreements, Procurement Documentation, Change Requests, and Work Performance Data

Agreements are contractual documents that place legally binding conditions upon the seller and buyer regarding the goods and/or services to be procured. Specific conditions within the agreements must be reviewed and implemented by both parties. The project manager and team must monitor procurement performance as part of the project management plan. Procurement documentation includes all contracts and supporting information related to their evaluation, execution, and performance monitoring. Key procurement documents include the performance evaluations, communications, contractual payment processes, and the statement of work. Change requests must be approved by the project manager and, in some cases, by the vendor. Subsequent revisions may be performed on related procurement documents, such as the vendor's statement of work, deliverable specifications, and payment terms. The project team must be cautious to avoid changes and disruption to a vendor's supply that may impact the supply of other procurement deals simultaneously. Lastly, work performance data is compiled for vendors with active procurement agreements. Relevant data includes work that is in progress or recently completed, financial transaction data, performance metrics, and schedule accuracy.

Tools and Techniques

Claims Administration, Earned Value Analysis, Performance Reviews, Trend Analysis, and Auditing

Claims administration is the technique used to resolve conflicts and poor performance issues between buyer and seller, though primarily directed towards the seller-side of the relationship. A claim indicates that either party has evidence or subjective opinion that argues that the other party has not maintained the expected level of quality, performance, or service necessary. The claimant seeks remuneration and/or corrective action from the other party. Claims may also include contested changes or disagreement regarding whether a change occurred. Both the buyer and seller have a desire to effectively negotiate an equitable resolution to any claim situation; the procurement agreement should indicate claims procedures and recourse.

Earned value analysis is used in procurement performance monitoring to track expected schedule and cost performance against actual performance, with the variances being the key performance indicator.

Performance reviews are documented and shared evaluations of a vendor or contractor's performance against the pre-defined measures from the agreement. Periodic performance communication to vendors supports continuous improvement and collaborative dialog to prevent future major problems with deliverables.

Trend analysis may be included in performance reviews as a proactive tool. Lastly, auditing serves as an independent assessment of vendor performance and can be the basis for continued procurement agreements.

Output

Closed Procurements, Work Performance Information, and Organizational Process Asset Updates

Closed procurement agreements are a key outcome of the procurement control process; the closed agreements indicate that both parties met their overall responsibilities and that the deliverables were achieved. Formal written notice from the buyer to the seller serves as confirmation of the closure of the agreement after fulfillment. The closure implies no outstanding and unfulfilled deliverables or payments remain. The project team has also approved all deliverables and performance.

Work performance information is collected following the procurement control process. Such data can be used to gauge future procurement searches among the same or similar vendors and benchmark procurement in future projects. The statement of work is used to compare actual vendor technical performance, budget adherence, and deliverable performance.

Furthermore, organizational processes may be improved or revised to account for experiences and information gained after contracts are closed. Payment processes, performance evaluations, seller pre-qualification records, lessons learned, and procurement history databases are all valuable information sources benefiting from contract closure.

Project Stakeholder Management

Identify Stakeholders

Overview

Project Stakeholder Management Process

Stakeholder management begins with identifying and compiling all relevant stakeholders that have an impact on or could be impacted by the project in positive or negative ways. From there, the expectations of each stakeholder are defined and prioritized based on their impact to the project. The project team then creates targeted stakeholder management plans so that such persons, groups, or organizations are engaged, well-communicated, and supportive of the project's objectives. The process begins with creating a stakeholder management plan and continues with monitoring and managing the engagement of each stakeholder. Stakeholder management is a primary objective of the project manager, and the effective management of expectations and requirements can drive success of the project. Periodic reviews of identification, prioritization, engagement, and satisfaction of stakeholders is the responsibility of the project manager, at least during project phase transitions, the influx or release of stakeholders, and during any significant changes to the project objectives or plans. Project team members have an important supportive role in stakeholder management; consultation with key stakeholders for their feedback and critique of project performance gives the manager room for improvement.

Tools and Techniques

Inputs and Analysis of Inputs to Create the Stakeholder Register

Input	Description	Analysis
Business case	The business case is an early project document that outlines the organizational and stakeholder benefits to doing the project.	The business case includes information regarding how initially identified stakeholders will be impacted by the project.
Benefits management plan	The plan that is derived after the business case and explains how the benefits to the organization and stakeholders will be achieved.	Select groups of stakeholders or individuals are described regarding the benefits they will see from the project.
Communications management plan	The project subplan that describes how the project team will execute communications with stakeholders and the organization.	Information and reporting needs in the form of communication are listed in this plan. Responsibilities to communicate with stakeholders are vital to stakeholder management.
Stakeholder engagement plan	The output of the first iteration of the stakeholder identification process. This document can be a reference for ongoing reviews of the stakeholder register and engagement.	Stakeholder engagement details are compiled in this plan and should correlate with the stakeholder register.

Input	Description	Analysis
Change and issues logs	Documented sources for project changes and issues that arise during planning and execution.	Changes and issues that have an impact on all or select stakeholders. Change and issues may also identify new stakeholders to the project.
Requirements documentation	Summary of the key requirements expected of the project and its deliverables.	Requirements may directly or indirectly identify stakeholders to the project.

Stakeholder Analysis and Stakeholder Mapping and Representation

Stakeholder analysis is the process of compiling several key details about each stakeholder to the project and each individual's stake in the project. The compilation allows the project team to prioritize and strategize stakeholder management practices. The analysis begins with certain vital information, including relative attitudes and expectations of the project, their role as a stakeholder to the project, and how much each is concerned with project communications. The stake component of the analysis includes several sub-parts:

1. Contribution – The individual may have provided resources, such as finances, labor, materials, or advice towards the project and expect some form of share of the project's benefits in return.
2. Interest – Decisions made by the project team will have an impact on some stakeholders more than others.
3. Knowledge – Knowledge can be powerful when a project team must navigate the workings of an organization and the nuances of human behaviors.
4. Ownership – The stake may be a legal title or ownership of some part or asset to the project.
5. Rights – Certain stakeholders have either moral or legal rights to common or competing interests to the project.

Stakeholder mapping involves creating characterization analyses of the stakeholders to find and strategize around stakeholder relationships and connections. Common versions include the power/interest grid, stakeholder cube, the salience model, and directions of influence model.

Outputs

Stakeholder Register and Updates to Project Documents and Plans

The stakeholder register lists all key details and requirements from each project stakeholder. The register begins with vital information for each individual or organization, including names, organization name, roles, and contact information. The stakeholders are classified by several binary terms that provide simple categorization to the stakeholders. These categories may include levels of power, influence, and impact; interest, whether internal or external; and direction of influence classifications. Assessment information is the third and most significant set of classification data in the register. Assessment information includes project life cycle relevance, stakeholder expectations, and key requirements held by each identified stakeholder. As the register is created and stakeholder requirements become well understood, changes may be necessary to project documents and plans. For example, the requirements plan, communications management, risk management, and stakeholder engagement plans may need to be revised to align with stakeholder data. Along those lines, other related documents such as the issues log and risk register may need to be revised given stakeholder data realization.

Plan Stakeholder Engagement

Overview

Stakeholder Engagement Planning Process and Inputs

Stakeholder engagement planning is the activity of the project team and/or organization to draw stakeholders into the project, increasing their involvement, and being attentive to their expectations and impact to the project. The stakeholder identification is performed early in the project life cycle, while the engagement plan is reassessed routinely throughout the project as new information is gained from stakeholder interactions. Events or milestones in the project should prompt the project manager to reassess the engagement process. Situations including the addition of new stakeholders to the register, parent organizational structure change, project phase transitions, and changes in project deliverables or objectives would all prompt a reassessment of the register. Key inputs to the engagement plan development include the resource, risk, and communication management plans; the assumption and issues logs; the risk register; and the stakeholder register. Related agreements for procurement or with stakeholders would also be factored into the plan development.

Tools and Techniques

Mind Mapping and Assessment Matrices

Mind mapping is defined as the organization of ideas and information according to their relationships with other thoughts, information, and ideas. The organization leads to greater understanding of the information and obtaining of key relationships and innovations from studying the connections made. Mind mapping stakeholder engagement information and register details stimulates creativity on how the team can effectively engage and manage stakeholders. Assessment matrices plot the current engagement conditions for each stakeholder against the desired state of engagement as defined by the project plan. The matrices include scales that define engagement levels in several buckets based on the degree of engagement observed. Buckets include unaware, resistant, neutral, supportive, and leading. Resistant stakeholders are aware of the benefits of the project but do not want to accept the outcomes as they may disrupt perceived aspects of their function. On the positive end of the spectrum, leading stakeholders are fully engaged and are helping to drive the outcomes of the project. The matrix plots "C" for the current state for each stakeholder and "D" for the desired state.

Stakeholder	Unaware	Resistant	Neutral	Supportive	Leading
USDA		C			D
FDA			C	D	
USDC	C		D		
US Customs			C D		
Customer				D	C
City Health Dept		C		D	

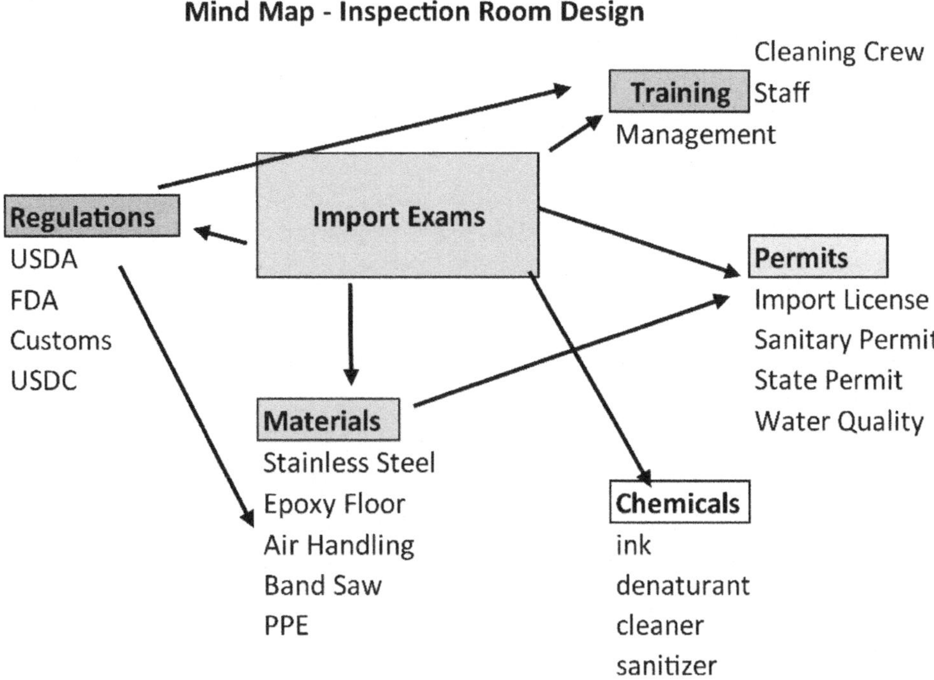

Manage Stakeholder Engagement

Overview

The engagement management process follows the development of the engagement plan. The physical work of meeting, communicating, and performing improvements related to engagement highlight this process. Furthermore, communications must meet stakeholder expectations and provide the information each individual or organizational stakeholder desires. Active engagement and management of stakeholders provides the project manager with leverage, flexibility, support, and power struggle related to impactful stakeholders. Key inputs include the project management plan and many of its sub-plans and project documents. These inputs are transformed into engagement activities with techniques such as communication skills development, internal or external expert judgement, and the development of interpersonal skills. Interpersonal skills such as active listening, conflict resolution, emotional intelligence, negotiation, and political awareness all serve to improve and maintain engagement. The primary output to the process includes measurably engaged stakeholders, verified by assessment matrices, and potential updates to the project plans or documents via change requests.

Stakeholder Engagement Monitoring Process

Monitoring stakeholder engagement follows the development of a stakeholder engagement management plan. Monitoring involves continuously assessing the stakeholder relationships, granular data regarding performance on factors most important to stakeholders, and revising engagement strategies based on performance results. Monitoring the relevant data and information allows the project team to be more effective at engaging the stakeholders, most notably those highly prioritized. Inputs include project management sub-plans such as the resource, communications, and stakeholder engagement plans. Also, the stakeholder register serves as a primary document input. Work performance data is included with these monitored materials. Analysis techniques such as alternatives, stakeholder, root cause, multicriteria decision-making, and data visualization all allow the project manager to derive effective monitoring and engagement strategies. Interpersonal skills such as active listening and networking also support effective monitoring. Work performance reporting and related updates to project plans and documents result from the monitoring process, all of which may be used as supporting information to reinforce customer satisfaction and involvement with the project.

PMP Practice Test

1. During resource control meetings, a project manager facilitates a discussion among team members regarding problem-solving. Specifically, the team discusses the most effective approaches to take when needing to solve resource control problems. What is NOT considered a step in the problem-solving process?

a. Define
b. Analysis
c. Eradicate
d. Control

2. What additional systems must be used in project management organizations looking to maximize gains from lessons learned registers?

a. Project management information systems
b. Coaching and communication among project managers of lessons learned
c. Project integrated change control
d. Agile development tools

3. During the charter and project management plan development processes, multiple stakeholders approach you with their concerns and uncertainties for the proposed national expansion project. You are the project manager leading the expansion; without the support of these key stakeholders, the project will not likely succeed. What types of resources BEST address the cost-benefit analysis needs of your stakeholders?

a. Time, temperature, and organizational pressure
b. Financial, labor, materials, and information
c. Human and natural resources
d. Financial, organizational design, and available consultant support

4. What is the purpose of the lessons learned register?

a. Serves as a transitioning tool to document valuable experiences such as issues, problems, risks, or opportunities for the benefit of future projects
b. To compile all completed training courses of each hired labor resource in the project to assure no safety risks exist
c. Serves as an accountability tool for stakeholders eager to know if the project manager is competent at his or her role
d. To advise organizational human resources departments on possible hiring and firing decisions

5. Which choice BEST describes the sequence used in the project schedule management process?

a. Define activities, sequence activities, estimate durations, develop schedule, control schedule
b. Estimate durations, define activities, develop schedule, create schedule management plan
c. Develop schedule, sequence activities, control schedule, create schedule management plan
d. Estimate durations, develop schedule, sequence activities, control schedule, create schedule management plan

6. An effective schedule management plan advises the project team and stakeholders of how the project schedule will be executed. Stakeholders to the project you are leading require reporting of variances to the schedule plan. What plan elements are MOST notable to achieve this stakeholder requirement?

a. Reporting formats and organizational procedure linkage
b. Level of accuracy and control thresholds
c. Project schedule model maintenance and iteration length
d. Units of measure and rules of performance measurement

7. During project activity execution work, a contracted seller of key components informs the project team that their supply capabilities declined as did their ability to meet quality specifications. All the following are beneficial actions for the project team EXCEPT

a. adjusting the schedule and quality baselines with stakeholder consent.
b. executing protective clauses in the procurement agreement while shifting orders to a backup vendor
c. developing an agile alternative supply from minor defective parts with relaxed critical-to-quality parameters
d. auditing the supplier and giving support by finding collaborative solutions to the failures.

8. Which information is NOT a reliable input source for creating the quality management plan?

a. Requirements traceability matrix
b. Voice of the customer analysis
c. Customer specifications
d. Financial break-even analysis

9. During the development of the schedule management plan, the level of accuracy calculations provides the team with which of the following?

a. Rules of performance measurement
b. Release and iteration length
c. Ranges acceptable in activity duration estimates
d. Schedule control thresholds

10. Which choice represents possible uses of subject matter experts during the phase or project closeout process?

a. Regulatory review by government
b. Legal fulfillment of contract details by the PICC team
c. Deliverable team review and approval
d. None of the above

11. As the portfolio manager for a series of complex building and logistics development projects, you are also acting as project manager for each individual project. The portfolio must be consistently monitored for alignment on cost, schedule, and scope attainment. Invariably, the portfolio will encounter variances and needs for adjustment. Which is the BEST approach for you to take?

a. Develop complex prediction models to gain insight into variance impacts.
b. Benchmark cost, time, and scope expectations with previous industry projects.
c. Establish baselines for projects and an integrated change process for adjustments.
d. Diverge the portfolio into separate projects solely led by project managers.

12. What is part of the five Cs of written communications for effective project management?

a. Content
b. Cross-referencing
c. Coherent flow
d. Cultural intelligence

13. The four parts of a RACI matrix include

a. reliability, authority, connection, and input.
b. resource, allocation, criticality, and importance.
c. responsibility, accountability, consultation, and inform.
d. required, assigned, considered, and important.

14. As issues are evaluated and resolved during the project, the project manager is responsible for translating such inefficiencies and solutions into which improvement program?

a. Baselines
b. Lean/six sigma
c. Lessons learned register
d. Root cause analysis tools

15. During the control project work phase, several types of project documents may be revised as the result of changes made by the change control board or through the perform integrated change control (PICC) process. What types of documents are MOST commonly revised?

a. Project management plan
b. Earned value analysis tools
c. Procurement contracts
d. Forecasts and registers

16. Which phrase BEST describes the key difference between the cost estimation plan and the budget determination process?

a. The use of net present value calculations supports planning for budget constraints.
b. Cost estimations aggregate into a larger budget process with added contingency resources.
c. Budget limits are flexible and can be exceeded; the cost plan must be strictly adhered to.
d. The baseline budget is less specific and is monitored less than the cost estimation plan.

17. In larger projects, development of the project management plan generally precedes which of the following?

a. Selection of the project manager
b. Review of lessons learned from a previous related project
c. The first full project team meeting
d. Crafting project objectives and sub-plans

18. Self-organizing teams are commonly found in agile projects or decentralized organizational structures. Which is NOT a common characteristic of self-organizing team members?

a. Trustworthiness and adaptability
b. High team-focused performance
c. Commitment to the team vision
d. Advanced engineering training

19. When faced with the decision to execute a risk response plan, project managers and the larger organization must be careful to execute which behaviors after deciding to respond?

a. Document key decisions, and adjust supporting budgets, action plans, schedules, and resources to maneuver the project with the risk response.
b. Input response plan into the project management information system, and await an analysis.
c. Consult with stakeholders regarding the necessary next steps.
d. Avoid creating contingency plans in case risk response fails.

20. A project team is co-located between Europe and the Middle East with engineering and scheduling teams divided among both geographies. Both co-locations are separated by time, responsibilities, and cultural norms. Your role as the new project manager includes communications management and ensuring alignment and understanding between both groups. The cross-communications have been historically poor. Neither geographic team understands or trusts the other group. What baseline behaviors should the collective team pursue to improve communications?

a. Pull technologies such as intranets and online training portals
b. Linguistics consultant support and translation mobile devices
c. Clear information from the sender with interpretation and acknowledgement from the recipient
d. Adhere to a RACI matrix detailing the communication responsibilities among all divisions

21. All of the following processes are necessary in the project scope management process EXCEPT

a. compiling evidence to support the sufficiency of the scope deliverables.
b. developing a work breakdown structure to achieve the deliverables.
c. auditing metric measurement methods and project organizational design.
d. capturing customer and stakeholder requirements to craft the scope language.

22. A cost control element of the cost management plan describes how expenses are managed to align with the expected use of resources. Which organizational group has oversight on the cost baseline and budget change requests?

a. Stakeholders and customer liaisons
b. Organization executives
c. Perform integrated change control group
d. The project team and manager

23. When faced with project quality improvement opportunities to efficiency, customer satisfaction, and waste reduction, what type of analysis is MOST commonly used?

a. Traditional root cause analysis
b. Alternatives analysis
c. Document analysis
d. Process analysis

24. For defects and waste generated in the project activity phases, what is the BEST choice regarding use of the project issues log?

a. Capture all defect quantities and waste values in the issues log for troubleshooting.
b. Only defects are routinely captured in the project issues log.
c. Only waste is routinely captured in the project issues log.
d. Capture defects or waste on the issues log that may affect ability to meet the deliverables.

25. What sub-plan within the overall project management plan will contain the criteria for acceptance of final deliverables?

a. Scope management plan
b. Deliverables management plan
c. Quality management plan
d. Requirements management plan

26. You are a project manager beginning a new product launch in a global manufacturing network. The organization has documented hundreds of lessons learned from past product research and development across 40 manufacturing sites, all making the same outputs. Lessons focus on several categories such as machinery, raw materials, and measurement methods. What is the ideal choice of tools to help you digest the volume of lessons presented to you?

a. Fishbone analysis
b. Cost of quality financial analysis
c. Multi-voting
d. Design of experiments

27. During the execution of early project phases, a project manager observes that certain communications tasks are not on schedule, interactivity between virtual and non-co-located teams is inefficient, and project data is not easily retrieved when needed. Which action can BEST solve these concerns?

a. Alignment of project objectives and organizational design
b. Project management information systems and related collaboration software
c. Team member survey and feedback collection tools
d. Training for team members on sender/receiver communication models

28. What are the general groups of documents requiring completion, sign-off, and archival during the project closeout activities?

a. Baselines, vendor contracts, and the project management plan
b. Logs, data servers, and budgets
c. Reports, standards, and registers
d. Communications, baselines, and marketing materials

29. When project managers approve change requests in a perform integrated change control process, they must

a. schedule the change's resources and implementation before integrating it into the ongoing project.
b. notify all stakeholders affected by the change through predefined communication modes.
c. perform ongoing assessments of impact as necessary given the scale and scope of the change.
d. do all of the above.

30. Which document bridges the project deliverable and performance requirements to the project milestones during work activity execution?

a. Milestone list
b. Work breakdown structure
c. Requirements traceability
d. Stakeholder register

31. The lessons learned register meets the following types of project tools EXCEPT

a. organizational process asset.
b. project documentation.
c. information management.
d. enterprise environmental factor.

32. When reassessing stakeholder engagement levels, which tool is BEST able to guide the project management team through a strategic improvement approach?

a. Stakeholder register
b. The advanced engagement "ring" approach
c. Stakeholder engagement assessment matrix
d. Direction of influence analysis

33. You are the project manager for a distributed, highly agile portfolio of projects. Your typical project has high variation and must adapt procurement strategies in iterations as each project progresses. What is the BEST contract strategy for your procurement management plan?

a. Fixed-price contracts
b. Time and material contracts
c. Bulk purchase contracts
d. Cost-reimbursable contracts

34. As the project manager you have compiled several feedback sources from a large pool of stakeholders. The results explain that stakeholders need to have key information at various times. Select high-impact stakeholders are expecting routine performance updates on key metrics. What is an ideal strategy regarding communication delivery?

a. Execute pull communications for high-impact stakeholders, and push communications for only the large pool.
b. Implement interactive seminar-style communications with all stakeholders equally for ease on your project team.
c. Consult the communications management plan from the previous project.
d. Perform pull communications for large pool; separate push communications for high-impact stakeholders.

35. During the early weeks of project activity, the project manager received multiple complaints from stakeholders regarding expected completion performance. His or her plans did not account for this analysis. The project manager realized that he or she needed the ability to forecast the project's completion based on schedule and budget baselines and data. Which data analysis technique is the BEST approach for this project manager?

a. Earned value
b. Variance
c. Cost benefit
d. Alternatives

36. Which choice BEST defines the purpose of the project or phase closeout process?

a. To complete remaining tasks, final reports, and provide final deliverable(s) to customers
b. To retroactively change project baselines to align with actual performance data
c. To demonstrate to the organizational leadership that your project team is highly capable
d. To disband the configuration control team

37. In early project phases, stakeholders provide the project leader or organization with key specifications for quality. These parameters reflect what will satisfy the stakeholder or customer once the deliverable(s) are complete. Which phrases best describe two stakeholder-focused quality tools used early in project planning?

a. Lean and six sigma
b. Voice of the customer, critical-to-quality planning
c. Balanced scorecards, Kaizen projects
d. Independent auditing, stakeholder engagement planning

38. As a project team member tasked with overseeing the utilization and availability of labor and physical resources, what is the key element you are responsible for?

a. Resource breakdown schedule
b. Procurement management plan
c. Resource contract negotiation
d. Resource calendars

39. During project performance meetings, the project team discovers that early winter weather patterns are creating unavoidable risks and disruption to activities in the coming weeks. The project management team decides to monitor the weather fluctuation and prepare activities and resources to complete tasks on call when conditions are suitable. Additional overtime work is planned before the weather risk hits its peak. Components of the project that can be made in safer climates will be an added redundancy to the project. What type of risk neutralization strategy is the team using?

a. Mitigation
b. Escalation
c. Avoid
d. Fluctuation

40. Following the weekly performance reporting of project progress, the project manager received complaints from multiple key stakeholders. The stakeholders complained that their concerns were not being met and that they do not feel integral to the progression of the project. What approach is the BEST action for the project manager to take to improve engagement?

a. Work harder at the project tasks to improve performance and speed.
b. Reassess the stakeholder engagement plan, and execute actions to improve attentiveness to expectations.
c. Contact the stakeholders, and review the report data with each.
d. Assign a team member to the stakeholders to prevent these stakeholders from disrupting project progress.

41. What is NOT an element of the PMI talent triangle?

a. Leadership
b. Strategic and business management
c. Advanced engineering degree
d. Technical project management

42. Which quality analysis tool provides a breakdown of the frequency of data to show a distribution pattern of a data set?

a. Histogram
b. Scatter diagram
c. Affinity diagram
d. Flow chart

43. Projects that differ in worker co-location, team disbursement, and "follow-the-sun" project coverage generally involves various degrees of virtual work. What must be considered in these project designs to ensure high levels of commitment?

a. Consultants are needed to build an effective organizational design that enforces commitment.
b. Subject matter experts must be seeded within virtual teams to ensure alignment.
c. Deliverables, milestones, and progress are clearly communicated among virtual teams.
d. Working hours are closely monitored for self-organizing teams.

44. When entering into a purchasing agreement, what are the primary goals of the buyer and seller?

a. Buyer seeks to receive all goods and services quickly; seller seeks to deliver all goods and services quickly.
b. Buyer seeks deliverables meeting all necessary criteria; seller seeks to service customers within capabilities and achieve profit margins.
c. Buyer seeks deliverables meeting cost requirements; seller seeks to receive payment prior to supplying goods and services.
d. Buyer seeks to obtain just compensation for any defects or mistakes; seller seeks to avoid strict requirements on quality.

45. During risk management planning, the project team considers several dozen risks to an international construction project on the Arctic Circle in Northern Canada. The risks vary in three key parameters including detrimental impact to deliverables, detectability, and time to recovery. Which tool is MOST appropriate for the project manager to analyze the relative nature of all the identified risks?

a. Impact bubble diagram
b. Risk probability analysis
c. Quantitative S-curve
d. Risk response plans

46. Which procurement bid approach serves as a request for competing vendors to offer details on how they can offer project solutions via their products or services?

a. Request for information (RFI)
b. Request for quotation (RFQ)
c. Statement of work (SOW)
d. Request for proposal (RFP)

47. During the project risk identification process, you as the project manager consult with your portfolio manager regarding how best to collect risk data from stakeholders, team members, and experts across multiple countries. Which of the following is NOT a commonly used technique to collect risk data from these groups?

a. Brainstorming
b. Life cycle assessment
c. Interviewing
d. None of the above

48. Which of the measurements is detailed in the project management plan and communicated regularly to key stakeholders as the project progresses into execution phases?

a. Creation of baselines
b. Scope development
c. Integration progress
d. Key performance indicators

49. During the execution of project activities, multiple nonconformances are documented on the project issues log awaiting corrective action. Many of these issues are related to poor performance against quality parameters in the hardware assembly process. What approach is BEST suited to resolve these quality issues?

a. Process and root cause analysis
b. Alternatives analysis by the project manager
c. Independent auditing of the assembly process
d. Reassessment of the quality performance baselines

50. Your project team resolved a quality plan development concern from a key stakeholder by collecting data within the project industry to develop critical-to-quality objectives, surveying stakeholders and industry experts, and ideating for the development of the plan. All of the following techniques were used EXCEPT

a. benchmarking.
b. brainstorming.
c. mind mapping.
d. interviews.

51. During project work activity, the project manager receives notice that performance data and vendor communications are presenting a schedule lapse risk that may severely delay the next milestone and ultimately the final deliverable schedule. The project manager recognizes the features of the pending risk; what resource aids in risk identification to the project management team?

a. Constraint analysis
b. SWOT analysis
c. Prompt lists
d. Detectability plans

52. Your project team is beginning to analyze stakeholders. Specifically, the team seeks to better understand how the stakeholders may be interrelated, if they have shared interests, and how to make common connections among persons or organizations. As the project manager, what tools are ideal for supporting the analysis?

a. Power/influence grid and mind mapping
b. Risk register and issues log
c. Stakeholder cube, salience models, and the directions of influence model
d. Power/influence grid, a salience model, and procurement contracts

53. Which sentence BEST describes the difference between configuration and change management?

a. Configuration focuses on organizing planned changes; change management executes the solutions.
b. Configuration deals only with choosing the few critical stakeholder issues to resolve; change management fixes project documents.
c. Configuration controls the project or deliverable features; change management deals with resolving issues in the execution tools.
d. Configuration avoids contacting stakeholders and customers; change management is primarily concerned with affecting deliverable criteria.

54. Which phrase BEST defines resource control?

a. The measurement of resource utilization against the schedule and resource management plan
b. Identifying key resource data prior to performing improvement analysis
c. The correction of deviations from the resource baseline, which creates a negative performance impact
d. Implementing sustainable controls to resource systems after completing post-failure corrective actions

55. You are the project manager working with a high-technology company to develop artificial intelligence hardware based on a body of preliminary research. The project scope is well-known, yet the feasibility must be validated before progression into later development activity. Which is the MOST appropriate process flow for meeting these objectives?

a. Phase-gate development
b. Agile development
c. Sustainability governance
d. Intelligence mapping

56. During the scope management plan development process, the acting project manager becomes aware that the project scope does not fit previous and familiar template project models used in the organization. Specifically, the client requesting project management services has not finalized deliverable requirements and may not do so until various stages in the project process. What tailoring consideration is the MOST important for the project manager to evaluate?

a. The use of agile or hybrid scope management approaches to lessen requirements backlogs
b. Analysis of how the organization uses stakeholder requirements in scope development
c. The assessment of internal validation and control tools for project scope management
d. Using the project governance and organizational design to affect scope development

57. You are a project manager leading the development and launch of a new consumer good on behalf of a major retailer for the winter season. Consumers of this product demand high quality. The stakeholders to the project provide you with a detailed set of specifications for the product and for the logistics to deliver inventory into the supply chain on time. Which choice BEST represents key success measures likely included in the project charter?

a. Project management plan finalization
b. Payback period and cost savings to the stakeholders
c. Schedule adherence, quality, and customer satisfaction
d. Key successes depending on inventory accuracy

58. During the latest perform integrated change control (PICC) meeting, several team members and organizational staff expressed concerns that members and stakeholders do not fully understand the processes used for controlling change. What approach can the project manager use to reduce this uncertainty?

a. Implement work instructions, error proofing, and standard documentation.
b. Replace the PICC team with prior trained individuals.
c. Disband the PICC team, and let the project manager perform all changes alone.
d. Implement changes to the change control processes by using the PICC.

59. In addition to the five Cs of effective written communications, which phrase BEST describes supplementary communications skills that enhance the effectiveness of project management?

a. Clear purpose, correct grammar, and control of the idea flow
b. Active listening, skill enhancement, and cultural intelligence
c. Stakeholder expectation management, coherent flow, and system redundancy
d. None of the above

60. Relevance of project deliverables is BEST achieved by project management in which way?

a. Requiring that the development of deliverables be performed by the project champion
b. SMART objectives without restrictive time and cost boundaries
c. Deliverables aligning within the project charter and project schedule
d. Verifiable linkage between customer requirements and resulting project goals

61. During the development of the stakeholder management plan, the expectations of stakeholders to the project are defined and prioritized based on which of the following?

a. Relative impact to the project
b. Reputation in their industry
c. Personal relationships with the project manager
d. Guidance from the RACI matrix

62. Which key document is a phase closure output used to drive future change in project management systems of an organization?

a. Lessons learned register
b. Change control board meeting minutes
c. Resource allocation timetables
d. Closed-out contractual agreements

63. What project process includes the steps used to implement the identified changes to the project management plan?

a. Direct and manage project work
b. Project closeout
c. Project scope management
d. Configuration management

64. In an existing manufacturing operation, a new product launch is subjected to internal project management processes and the project manager is seeking to better capture the voice of the customer in delivering the next product. The customer is general consumers of a retail product. The quality management planning phase of the project must define what the quality parameters for the deliverable. What quality tools best achieve this early element?

a. Critical-to-quality house diagram
b. Design of experiments
c. Lean and six sigma
d. Descriptive statistics

65. You are the project manager for an operation that works for a customer to redesign and relaunch a consumer product with lagging market share. Given the provided stakeholder engagement matrix, what strategy should the project manager adopt to relieve stakeholder pressure on the project?

Stakeholder	Unaware	Resistant	Neutral	Supportive	Leading
1. Raw Material Provider		C			D
2. Labor Force		C		D	
3. Maintenance Union			C	D	
4. Quality Assurance	C				D
5. Customer				C	D

a. Focus on neutralizing the customer and maintenance elements.
b. Raw material providers, QA, and the customer are in detrimental situations; address these first.
c. Align quality assurance with customer expectations, and develop stakeholder engagement plans for material vendors and labor teams.
d. The gap is greatest for quality assurance; the quality team is the only area of focus needed.

66. As the project manager, you have negotiated a final charter with key organizational leaders and stakeholders. Your top five stakeholders to the project each have three separate criteria that gauge acceptable performance. These criteria are specific to the interests they hold in the project. As the manager, you implement these stakeholder-focused objectives in the charter document. What additional performance measures are likely of high value to your organization and your stakeholders?

a. Negotiation effectiveness scores
b. Cost, schedule, quality, and scope
c. Risk mitigation number
d. Risk exposure, deliverable complexity, and charter delivery method

67. During the execution of project activity tasks per the schedule, the team encounters unforeseen risks to achieving the next deliverable. Along with several key stakeholders and subject matter experts, the project team begins to collaborate on how to adjust the activities, work, and resources to get the project back on track. What is the name for this project strategy?

a. Elementary
b. Trial and error
c. Agile
d. Embracive

68. What are the two primary inputs necessary to build an effective communications management plan?

a. A virtual and collaborative communication platform
b. A RACI matrix and related responsibility documents
c. A resource management plan and stakeholder engagement plan
d. A communication path network diagrams and regulatory requirements

69. Which project documents or elements are MOST likely to be updated at project or phase closeout?

a. Organizational process assets, functional deployment capabilities, and tornado diagram metrics
b. Lessons learned register, communications methods, and baselines for all future projects
c. Lessons learned register, organizational process assets, and project operational support documents
d. None of the above

70. Which of the following is NOT an essential facet of the manage quality process according to the Project Management Institute?

a. Use quality tools to drive improvement and customer satisfaction.
b. Design products and services so deliverables meet customer specifications.
c. Analyze cost of quality data for organizational financial reporting.
d. Perform preventive and control functions to ensure reliable outputs with low variation.

71. What are three primary responsibilities of the project manager during the project work phase?

a. Lead task completion, achieve deliverables, and analyze work performance data.
b. Change management, perform many activity tasks, and collect payments from vendors.
c. Compile performance reports, perform accounting functions, and coach team members.
d. Perform vendor audits, calibrate test equipment, and facilitate all change management meetings.

72. Prior to the evaluation and selection of procurement options for a project, what process must the project leaders perform?

a. Preselection analysis
b. Pre-procurement negotiation
c. Preparation of budgets
d. Approval for funding

73. To complete several activities in the project schedule, the project manager has outsourced the work to third-party labor services. To avoid lapses in project performance, how can the project manager ensure expectations are met?

a. Use predictive modeling to find the lowest cost provider for the least risky activities.
b. Retract the use of outsourced labor, and use project team members to get the work done internally.
c. Assign a team member to monitor the workmanship of the hired labor after activities have been completed.
d. Require formal performance agreements when procuring labor service providers.

74. Several milestones within your project describe deliverables that must be finalized before moving to subsequent phases of the scheduled work. As your project team nears completion of a deliverable, you decide to perform a preliminary review of the acceptance criteria necessary to close out the deliverable and move on to the next stage of the schedule. What key document will provide you and your team a reference to the acceptance criteria?

a. Work breakdown structure
b. Phase transition road map
c. Scope statement
d. Requirements traceability matrix

75. Projects often employ a variety of tools and techniques to satisfy stakeholder needs and requirements. During project planning phases, what process supports the employment of such variation?

a. Tailoring
b. Drum-buffer-rope
c. Business benefits management planning
d. External environmental factor assessment

76. How is the issues log beneficial to project managers, stakeholders, and the organizational executives overseeing the project team?

a. The issues log is the sole source of personal conflict issues in the project.
b. The issues log uses additional overhead expense and is an opportunity to save costs.
c. The issues log supports informing these persons of issues and what is being done to resolve such issues.
d. The project team members receive performance evaluations based on the issues in their functional areas.

77. Which procurement control tactics involve monitoring schedule and cost variances against contractual expectations?

a. Trend analysis
b. Claims administration
c. Earned value analysis
d. Auditing

78. Which of the following are approved and critical elements of the project management plan that support stakeholder understanding of project performance during execution phases?

a. Baselines including scope, schedule, and cost plans
b. Subsidiary plans
c. Analytical tools for continuous improvement
d. Project management information systems (PMIS) reports

79. Which list BEST describes supplemental techniques beneficial to project managers seeking to enhance communication practices in projects?

a. Active listening, skill enhancement, and cultural intelligence
b. Multifaceted communication strategies
c. Social computing, virtual teams, and press releases
d. Strategic communication planning and meeting management

80. Which project improvement processes are supported by an accurate issues log?

a. Current reporting on the project schedule, budget, and scope
b. Assumption log and basis of estimates reports
c. Stakeholder management plan and assumption log
d. Lessons learned register, risk register, and organizational process assets

81. When assessing two presented risks—first to the project schedule attainment and second to the cost management plan—the project manager identified the schedule risk as high negative impact and low probability. The cost plan risk was identified as moderate positive impact and high probability. How are these risks characterized if the project manager analyzes them using an impact matrix?

a. Schedule risk is a weak threat; cost risk is a moderate opportunity.
b. Schedule risk is a strong threat; cost risk is a weak opportunity.
c. Cost risk is a moderate threat; schedule risk is a strong opportunity.
d. Cost risk is a weak threat; schedule risk is a moderate opportunity.

82. A project management organization wins a contract to oversee the construction of a new office tower. The building is partially taxpayer funded with half of the office space being controlled by government agencies. The clients are adamant about completing the building within 2 years to avoid conflicts with other local construction for the next Olympic Games. Congressional representatives and senators are eager to ensure the project remains on budget because it is partially funded through Congressional appropriations. What are likely to be the MOST important deliverables facing the project management team?

a. Completed office building, meeting planned budget and achieving planned schedule
b. Congressional and stakeholder satisfaction indicators
c. Completed office building and government approval
d. Project plan, scope, charter, and the completed building

83. All of the following are inputs to the perform integrated change control (PICC) process EXCEPT

a. a formal written change management plan.
b. scope, cost and schedule baselines.
c. human resource management plan.
d. a requirements traceability matrix.

84. During project performance evaluation meetings for a new military vehicle, the project team reviews any outstanding nonconformances for opportunities for improvement. Functional team A within the project has encountered a need to improve the design of the vehicle's engine. Functional team B has encountered a weakness in the procedures used to verify quality parameters are met. How should the project team approach these opportunities for change?

a. Both team A and B use change management tools.
b. Both team A and B use configuration management tools.
c. Team A uses change management; team B uses configuration management.
d. Team A uses configuration management; team B uses change management

85. During the procurement selection process, the project leadership team determines that customer criteria dictate highly specialized components within the deliverables. Critical-to-quality analysis using customer specifications determines that high part reliability and infinitesimally low variation are the drivers of selection. What is the BEST source selection analysis method given these criteria?

a. Fixed budget
b. Low cost
c. Quality based
d. Reputation based

86. Which phrase BEST defines mind mapping tools used in planning stakeholder engagement activities?

a. Listing all engagement levels for stakeholders using a sliding scale to create a full matrix
b. Comparison charting of stakeholder engagement levels with desired levels of engagement
c. Plotting stakeholder information to create connections and insights that increase engagement
d. Revising the stakeholder register with physical location mapping for each person or firm on the register

87. What is the preparation done in project planning to absorb and overcome known risks before or as they affect project work known as?

a. Resilience
b. Risk identification
c. Qualitative risk analysis
d. Risk probability assessment

88. During a project you are leading, multiple divisions of the larger organization are involved to support planning and execution of the project and several other nonrelated projects. Projects may have unique risks or may share several common risks to meeting performance goals. What strategy BEST solves the problem of shared organizational risk?

a. Risk validation brainstorming
b. Cascaded risk management
c. Value-added risk management
d. Integrated risk management

89. Work execution data is the basis for performance metrics but must first be transformed into what intermediary?

a. Key performance indicators
b. Work breakdown structure
c. Stakeholder assessments
d. Work execution information

90. Which is a primary objective when using a cost of quality accounting model?

a. Reducing overhead expenses used by the quality management team
b. Tilting quality expenses away from failure costs toward prevention
c. Proving that the project cost accounting is meeting quality objectives
d. Modifying customer quality specifications and project plans to reduce costs.

91. Project management is best defined as achieving project objectives using a skillful combination of which of the following?

a. Subject matter experts, outsourced staff, and advanced software
b. The resources of other organizations
c. Communication, knowledge, tools, and resources
d. Deference, recycling, and matrix data sets

92. During critical path activity in your project, you receive threatening phone calls from major stakeholders seeking updates on deliverable status, key performance indicators, and any risk or changes observed to date. Upon close evaluation, you realize that no formal communication plans exist. How can this error be prevented?

a. Collect stakeholder communication preferences when they call with complaints.
b. Deny stakeholders access to such information due to confidentiality requirements.
c. Avoid agreeing to key performance indicators and reporting requests by stakeholders.
d. Collect stakeholder communication preferences early in the project life cycle.

93. During the development of the project scope and the scope management plan, what tool is BEST suited to enjoin the validated customer requirements to the determined project deliverables?

a. Work breakdown structure
b. Requirements traceability matrix
c. Quality management plan
d. Project constraint matrix

94. Project integration involves two key responsibilities for the project manager; often these responsibilities overlap as non-mutually exclusive events. Along with aligning project deliverables to the executive organizational strategy, what other responsibility is essential?

a. Coaching newly assembled team members in the early phases of team development
b. Filtering out distractions and clearing a path for the team to focus on deliverables, charter, and objectives
c. Developing the work breakdown structure and the resource breakdown structure in advance
d. Synchronizing the communication systems of the organization and relevant stakeholders

95. Which of the following are considered organizational process assets?

a. Internal culture
b. Reporting and information sharing
c. Organizational governance
d. Telecommunications infrastructure

96. What are key elements found in project charters?

a. Objectives, procurement requirements, occupational hazards, and resource allocation
b. Purpose statement, key stakeholders, project scope, and objectives
c. Team responsibilities, external environmental impacts, and corrective action procedures
d. Business case summary, brainstorming results, and a list of the organizational process assets used

97. During procurement management planning, the engineering-focused members of the project team conclude that supplier A should be selected due to their superior quality reputation. Conversely, the finance-focused team members argue that supplier B has better pricing terms than supplier A. No predefined selection method was established in the project, and several other suppliers are also being considered. Which of the following is the BEST method the project manager should use to resolve the conflict?

a. Allow the project champion to decide.
b. Allow the project manager to decide.
c. Employ multi-voting among all team members
d. The team member best able to influence the other members must choose the supplier.

98. When evaluating the relative detectability, proximity, and severity of risks that the project faces, which tool can BEST visually summarize these factors (or any combination of three factors) for the project team?

a. Impact bubble diagram
b. Tornado diagram
c. Quantitative S-curve
d. Vision statement

99. Which choice BEST explains why the process to change key project documents must be tightly controlled?

a. Regulatory agencies always require management of change record keeping.
b. Project management information systems are not reliable for document control.
c. Organizational leadership demands authority over all project documentation.
d. Changes to project documents can drive the decision-making of many stakeholders.

100. Your project enters the closeout phase where registers and reports are finalized and archived. Performance against stakeholder requirements was monitored throughout the project. What formal part of the project management plan details how the performance to stakeholder requirements is handled?

a. Risk register
b. Project management information system
c. Specification register
d. Communications management plan

101. Material and service vendors supporting a project should be expected to meet performance standards and quality expectations aligned to the project stakeholders and customers. When a vendor produces a product to be used as an input into the project activities, what is the BEST tool for the project manager to gain assurances that the goods meet quality expectations?

a. Destructive testing of all production lots for quality compliance
b. Independent lab testing of all output units for compliance
c. Statistical sampling and testing of material performance before use in the project
d. Evaluation of the project activity performance after using unverified vendor materials

102. During project work execution after baselines have been set, the management team is faced with a change proposal that would positively affect the project deliverables and schedule. The project manager and key stakeholder are not sure how the proposed change will affect other aspects of the project. The proposed change is presented to the perform integrated change control (PICC) group for evaluation. Which tool is MOST commonly used by the PICC group when evaluating a project change?

a. Risk register and stakeholder communication strategy
b. Alternatives and cost-benefit analysis
c. Multicriteria decision-making and work breakdown
d. Change control board record keeping and scope revalidation

103. Which of the following statements regarding project charters is NOT accurate?

a. The project is not authorized to begin without an approved charter.
b. The charter is an acknowledgement that the project aligns with the strategy and business case
c. The charter cannot be started without prior review of the completed project schedule.
d. The charter is one of the outcomes of successful integration performed by the project manager.

104. How does lessons learned register content connect former projects to future projects in an organization?

a. Lessons learned from each project are sent to a database and randomly applied to future projects.
b. Lessons learned analysis and problem solutions serve as outputs of a project or phase and can be used as inputs to subsequent projects or phases.
c. Organizational risk analysis teams and cost accountants must give approval to which lessons are worth learning.
d. Future projects must learn these lessons through trial and error, only reviewing the lessons learned register after experiencing a failure.

105. As a new member of an existing project, your task is to become familiar with the cost management plan and current variance performance. What element of the cost management plan would BEST describe current variance performance?

a. Performance monitoring rules
b. Control account procedures
c. Reporting requirements
d. Control threshold levels

106. Key stakeholders are listed within the finalized project charter. What benefit does the project charter provide to the key stakeholders?

a. A review of how the project management process works
b. Thorough summaries of the risks and resources planned in the project
c. A list of all other stakeholders that are affected by the project
d. Information regarding the project scope and execution

107. In which project phase is the work breakdown structure developed?

a. Project schedule management
b. Project scope management
c. Monitor and control project work
d. Project human resource planning

108. Which phrase best describes the ideal approach for planning project kick-off meetings based on project size?

a. Smaller projects kick off in planning phase; larger projects kick off in implementation phase
b. Smaller projects kick off in analysis phase; larger projects kick off at stakeholder discretion
c. Both sizes kick off when all personnel and labor resources have been hired or procured
d. Both sizes kick off when all financial resources have been secured

109. Rolling wave schedule planning for an agile project approach combines which two scheduling techniques?

a. Schedule validation and optimization
b. Critical path method and "wet" optimization
c. Stage-gate schedule review and reporting
d. Decomposition and long-term work packaging

110. A project specialist working with the project manager is responsible for executing the project communication plan with the manager and for developing any incomplete plan elements. The project communications process includes data compilation and report creation tools, a project management information system (PMIS), data and communication monitoring, and a formal process to review communication effectiveness. What communication plan elements remain undeveloped?

a. Active listening and facilitation
b. Communication distribution and control
c. Sender/receiver models
d. Nonverbal feedback loops

111. During monitoring and controlling project work, the project manager encounters performance reporting requirements as part of customer contracts. The manager has previously created template reports and has secured the data sources to be able to capture actual data. What other elements must the project manager obtain to create valuable reporting of performance?

a. Quality and risk reports
b. Lessons learned register
c. Project charter
d. Schedule and cost forecasts

112. Which description represents key benefits of compiling all agreement and procurement closeout documentation, such as performance evidence on cost, scope, schedule, and quality?

a. Allowing vendors to create future project procurement management plans
b. Giving additional work to fill downtime among project team members
c. Growing the lessons learned register and improving future procurement negotiations
d. Maximizing the business case, retroactively, to past completed projects

113. How are project procurement activities established by the project manager and/or the parent organization?

a. Through formal contracts, purchase agreements, and service agreements with clear terms and criteria
b. Through lessons learned registers from past projects
c. Using the low-cost vendor in the local market only
d. Using random selection methods to prevent conflicts and biases among project team members

114. Which choice is an example of a configuration management tool?

a. Change request form
b. Change control board
c. Verification audit
d. Issues log

115. When monitoring procurement performance, what guidance is generally included in the procurement management plan?

a. Coordination advice on how procurement requirements will alter the project management plan elements
b. Procurement timetables relative to project plans and schedule
c. Key metrics used to assure performance achieved by stakeholders
d. All of the above

116. Which of the following is NOT a project management knowledge area (PMKA)?

a. Integration management
b. Closeout management
c. Quality management
d. Stakeholder management

117. Which description best represents behavior to develop or expect from newly hired labor into a high-functioning team build?

a. Expressing high levels of collaboration and trust
b. Making early decisions quickly regardless of project plans or risks
c. Assimilating into the moderate habits and systems
d. Seeking conflicts so that ineffective members can be weeded out

118. What is the process of allocating protective levels of scheduled time, material, and labor resources to mitigate risk impact to a project called?

a. Resilience
b. Risk-breakdown structure
c. Impact matrix and scoring scheme
d. SWOT analysis

119. As the project manager, you are evaluating multiple vendors of key parts used for building advanced military equipment. The equipment requires high levels of reliability (infinitesimal defect levels); each part contributes a cumulative impact to the overall reliability performance of the final deliverable. What type of procurement contract is the BEST option for your project?

a. Sole source contract
b. Low-cost contract
c. Fixed budget contract
d. Quality-based contract

120. During the project management plan development, the quality and manufacturing representatives working with the project manager argued that the description of the deliverable manufacturing process was weak and did not clearly define the activity likely at each step of the process. The representatives stated that they will not be able to support the project without a better understanding of the process. What is the BEEST tool to use to improve their understanding?

a. Matrix diagrams of output data
b. Risk register
c. Process flow diagram
d. Stakeholder engagement matrix

121. Which is NOT a common feature of the risk management plan?

a. Impact matrix and scoring scheme
b. Work breakdown structure
c. Resource allocation
d. Functional responsibilities

122. During a post-employment exit interview, a project manager described some of the weaknesses she experienced during a recent internal improvement project when developing the charter. The former project manager described difficulty in boosting stakeholder participation, delivering clear communication, and gaining buy-in from all participants in meetings. What skill set would overcome these challenges?

a. Conflict management
b. External stakeholder involvement
c. Facilitation
d. Use of meeting task lists

123. As your project team identifies risks within the execution phases, what is the BEST approach to use when analyzing each risk relative to the collection found in the risk register?

a. Consultation support for risk organization
b. Survey of all critical stakeholders aware of these risks
c. Deep-dive analysis of cost accounting methods
d. Quantitative assessment of severity and likelihood

124. Which tools are MOST appropriate for supporting the stakeholder benefit analysis?

a. Benefits management plan, pro forma statements, and business cases
b. Stakeholder management plan and quality program cost-benefit calculations
c. Market research, customer testimonials, and interviews
d. Agreements made between stakeholders and the project team or project management organization

125. Which list BEST describe the process of monitoring stakeholder engagement?

a. Auditing of the stakeholder register, adding capital investment to communications tools, and calibrating messaging
b. Standardizing data measurement systems, analyzing stakeholder data, and implementing cost-savings tools
c. Conducting customer surveys, developing critical to quality plans, and developing internal auditing programs
d. Assessing relationships, tracking performance aligned to expectations, and revising engagement strategies as needed

126. Which choice is NOT a widely useful quality tool for identifying root causes when evaluating an issue on the issues log?

a. Ishikawa—fishbone diagram
b. Tornado diagram
c. 5-Why analysis
d. Plan-do-check-act cycle

127. At what stage of the project does risk identification occur?

a. At project closeout
b. During risk management plan development
c. Throughout the project life cycle
d. Only during the preliminary planning stage

128. During project closeout activities, the portfolio manager directing your project begins to transition into communicating overall project performance and evaluation. Following the communications management plan, the portfolio manager must deliver convincing summary results to all key stakeholders face-to-face. Which BEST reflects the communications skills needed to complete this task?

a. Feedback and nonverbal communication
b. Competence and feedback
c. Nonverbal communication and presentations
d. Presentations and feedback

129. As the project manager you are working with the human resources leadership within your organization to ensure that the organizational structure of the complex agile project aligns with your needs. Which is the BEST choice as a focal point with the human resources team?

a. Adaptability and simplicity of design
b. Structuring alignment to objectives
c. Performance efficiency
d. Delegation authority

130. Which quality plan element provides stakeholders with unbiased assurance that quality expectations and processes are being met by the project team, vendors, and those persons executing tasks?

a. Data monitoring
b. Defect evaluation
c. Benchmarking
d. Auditing

131. Completed lessons learned information from a finished project is documented and stored in the lessons learned repository of the organization. How is the information thus classified?

a. Continuous improvement project
b. Business case document
c. Organizational process asset
d. Administrative norm

132. Which series BEST describes data analysis techniques used for risk identification in project management?

a. TOWS analysis, failure modes analysis, and cost of capital analysis
b. SWOT analysis, constraint analysis, and root cause analysis
c. Document analysis, alternatives analysis, and voice of the customer
d. Root cause analysis, process hazard analysis, and stakeholder benefit analysis

133. Which choice BEST describes the process of managing stakeholder engagement during the execution of project activities?

a. Monitor work performance data and key performance indicators of concern for each stakeholder prior to reporting.
b. Engagement inputs are transformed into engagement activities using communication skills development only.
c. Voice-of-the-customer immersion sessions are planned to receive verbal updates from customers and stakeholders.
d. Create a current state assessment matrix that does not change throughout the project life cycle.

134. Key elements to the communications monitoring process include

a. audio-visual equipment to support high-performing virtual teams.
b. interview and survey teams communicating to stakeholders regarding performance.
c. telecommunications surveillance equipment.
d. information flow diagrams and stakeholder communication requirements.

135. Which phrase BEST describes the steps needed for scope decomposition when developing a work breakdown structure?

a. Verification, tagging, organization, deliverables analysis, and division to subsidiaries
b. Analysis, division, control, deliverables review, and audit
c. Validation, measurement systems analysis, organization, buildup into subsidiaries, and evaluation
d. Organizational assignment, delegation, brainstorming, and scheduling

136. You are the project manager of a complex project and are currently developing the cost management plan. Which of the following are optimal inputs sought by you and your stakeholders for developing an effective cost plan?

a. Charter, risk management plan, and schedule management plan
b. Budgeting strategy, cost control strategy, and cost estimations
c. Performance monitoring rules and past project history
d. Exchange rates, stakeholder contact information, and work-breakdown structure

137. After brainstorming sessions for project scope development, the project team members and several stakeholders ranked several dozen choices into a manageable list of preferences based on expertise and opinion. What method is being used by the project manager to narrow the scope?

a. Affinity diagraming
b. Brainstorming
c. Facilitation
d. Nominal group technique

138. During the closeout of a project, when lessons learned are institutionalized into the organization's project management knowledge base, which approach BEST describes how to conduct a comprehensive project review for such lessons learned?

a. Evaluate each potential lesson learned against gauges of business case accuracy and how risk and issues were handled.
b. Extract key points from the final project report to give brief highlights into the lessons learned review.
c. Only adjust external environmental factors based on the lessons learned; external factors negatively affect projects the most.
d. Hand off the project review to an independent third party based on project performance data.

139. Which is NOT a key component of the scope baseline?

a. Work breakdown structure
b. Work breakdown structure dictionary
c. Project scope breakdown
d. None of the above

140. A long-time vendor supplying routine engineering services to your project has lapsed in several key contractual metrics without showing improvement. You are seeking a new vendor to supplement or replace this underperforming service provider. What type of business bid document can you MOST likely expect to receive first from prospective vendors?

a. Request for proposal
b. Request for information
c. Request for quotation
d. Statement of work

141. As the project manager, you are evaluating the documented lessons learned from five past completed projects. With the help of the continuous improvement manager within your organization, you have selected several lessons where evidence-based improvement can be achieved. What is the MOST effective tool for executing improvements based on the lessons learned?

a. Agile development
b. Plan-do-check-act cycles
c. Phase-gate development
d. 5 Why root cause analysis

142. Which phrase BEST defines the concept of a context diagram?

a. Performance validation models
b. A visual model of deliverable use and the business systems that create the deliverable
c. Simulations of iterative scope adjustments
d. A complex version of the quality function deployment tool

143. Which source BEST reflects the key success measures used by project managers and stakeholders in early project phases?

a. Customer satisfaction, return on investment, and achieving business case objectives
b. Payback period, vendor qualifications, and lessons learned evaluation metrics
c. Operating expense versus budget, schedule attainment, and project employee headcount
d. Quality performance, cost control, and lessons learned evaluation metrics

144. Part of your aerospace-focused project activity includes the commissioning of production equipment to create output that meets tight quality specifications. Variation beyond the allowed tolerances will lead to failure of the deliverable to achieve their mission. Which tool must be used in your quality management plan to ensure variation is minimized?

a. Quality function deployment matrix
b. RACI matrix
c. Lessons learned register
d. Statistical process control

145. During project execution, the project manager and key stakeholders analyze performance data and realize that he or she has an opportunity to neutralize risk with high benefit. Specifically, the engineering team of the primary vendor organization has the capability to neutralize a throughput bottleneck and increase production output by 500% to supply the project with materials essential to the critical path. What type of strategy is being employed?

a. Escalation
b. Share
c. Accept
d. Exploit

146. Which phrase BEST defines systems thinking?

a. The ability to analyze the interaction of organizational components and how each can affect shared goals
b. The ability to think about a single division within an organization
c. How a project manager focuses on multiple risks at the same time
d. The longest duration of advanced focus recommended for future project activities

147. During procurement contract review, you are faced with the challenge of developing a contract with vendors supplying raw materials and labor to construct an Artic energy generation factory. The project schedule is expected to have high variation based on weather and labor supply fluctuation. During stable periods of time, your lessons learned register suggests that your vendors must be incentivized to maximize productivity. The costing details within your procurement contracts must be designed with these factors in mind. What is the BEST cost approach to these contracts?

a. Fixed price
b. Cost reimbursable
c. Weather based
d. Low cost

148. What is the ability to absorb and overcome unknown project risks due to preparation and planning in the risk management phase known as?

a. Responsiveness
b. Strategic planning
c. Impact matrix
d. Resilience

149. As a project manager, you are faced with two demanding issues that are threatening to derail your deliverable schedule. First, an early completed step in the critical path was completed with significant quality errors. Second, the procured resources for the final activities on the critical path are delayed and threatening to cause the project to miss the customer's deadline. After some negotiations, the lead agents of all procured vendors indicate that resources will be delayed at least 14 days. What change management approach best resolves these issues?

a. Cancel the critical path, and employ an agile management approach.
b. Implement a rework or correction to the quality errors, and adjust the schedule baseline by 14 days through perform integrated change control (PICC).
c. Defer. the quality errors to after the project is closed out, and adjust the schedule baseline by 14 days through PICC.
d. Consult organizational leaders on how to end the project with no further losses.

150. Which threat neutralization strategy is BEST suited when a project manager becomes highly overwhelmed with the burdens of compounded risk impacts to a project?

a. Mitigate
b. Avoid
c. Escalate
d. Transfer

151. What does the appropriate use of a business benefits management plan involve?

a. Transforming business case files into a road map to how the organization realizes the benefits of the project
b. Explaining how the project will block value and market share from competitors
c. Describing and analyzing the project employee benefits within the human resources management plan
d. Developing external and internal organizational designs so the project can best achieve business objectives

152. A project manager, nearing the completion of the deliverables, received notice that the primary customer found critical defects in the sample test batch despite the customer having approved the test batch for further production. The critical defects will make the deliverables unsellable according to the customer. Which choice is the BEST tool for the project team to implement next?

a. Process analysis
b. Alternatives analysis
c. Root cause analysis
d. Document analysis

153. As a project team member supporting the project manager, you have been assigned to draft the final report when the final deliverable has been accepted and transferred. Which choice BEST summarizes the key elements of your report?

a. Performance against quality, cost, schedule and resource metrics; confirmation that scope was met; how risks were managed
b. Executive summary, risk summary, and final unpaid invoices
c. Explanation of how project and deliverable met business needs; list of employees fired during the project.
d. Cost, schedule, and quality variance summary; summary of the change log and open change requests

154. Which process grouping involves activities that create the project scope, objectives, and work breakdown structure?

a. Monitoring
b. Executing
c. Initiating
d. Planning

155. When using the precedence diagraming method, what relationship type is employed when an overlapping relationship is used and the successor activity does not begin until the predecessor activity finishes?

a. Finish to finish (FF)
b. Finish to start (FS)
c. Start to finish (SF)
d. Start to start (SS)

156. What features are commonly found when program managers assess interdependencies among several projects or programs?

a. Change requests and budget overlaps
b. Components, subprojects, and benefits realization
c. Scope alignment, risks, and resource conflicts
d. All of the above

157. Which of the following represents the forum used to review and decide upon proposed changes to elements such as baselines, schedules, scope, and management plan details?

a. Contract review alliance meeting
b. Technical committee
c. Start-up meetings
d. Perform integrated change control

158. Which BEST represents a clear charter problem statement?

a. "Customer satisfaction to schedule completion is 7% below the goal of 90% in the recent 2 months due to an average procurement delay of 12.5 days."
b. "Most of the project's customers are unhappy, and supplies are always delayed."
c. "Project stakeholders report high measures of dissatisfaction with the performance of the project team."
d. "Project deliverables have a defect rate 20% higher than the competitor's deliverables."

159. Which tools achieve scope deconstruction?

a. Project closeout
b. Project charter development
c. SWOT analysis
d. Work breakdown structure

160. As the project manager, when your team is faced with the need to perform corrective and preventive actions to resolve nonconformances or errors, what is NOT a suitable approach?

a. Continuous improvement tools such as lean and six sigma
b. Brainstorming possible solutions with stakeholder input
c. Employing subject matter experts to advise solution strategies
d. Deference of corrective action work to the project closeout phase

161. As the project manager, you are leading the perform integrated change control process for the organization. What three types of outputs are derived from this control process?

a. Work breakdown structure, risk matrix, and calibration forms
b. Project schedule, scope, and baselines
c. Plan updates, approved change requests, and document updates
d. Terminated contracts, final reporting, and project closeout

162. As the project manager, what is your MOST effective means to gain authority and commitment from stakeholders and support staff toward an approved project?

a. Establishing baselines for key measurements and performance standards
b. Communication from the project champion about work instructions to each stakeholder and team member
c. A finalized charter between stakeholders and the project team committing all to a common set of deliverables
d. Excess financial resources allocated by the parent organization so the project is not constrained

163. Which approach BEST achieves stakeholder needs during the development of the communication management plan?

a. Implement a one-way email system to push communications to stakeholders.
b. Compile stakeholder communication preferences, and establish capable communication delivery.
c. Update the stakeholder register for the project.
d. Evaluate stakeholder communication skills using coaching and conflict resolution.

164. Which choice represents time-based additional risks to be considered by the project team beyond likelihood and impact?

a. Controllability, detectability, manageability
b. Dormancy, urgency, proximity
c. Connectivity, perception, strategic affect
d. Proximity, detectability, duration

165. Which tool serves as the place to document threats and opportunities observed throughout the project life cycle?

a. Lessons learned register
b. Assumption log
c. Issue log
d. Risk register

166. The risk breakdown structure and a PESTLE analysis are examples of what type of risk tool?

a. Prompt lists
b. Scheduling resources
c. Root cause analyses
d. Validation studies

167. Project stakeholder agreement and alignment with the details of the charter are important. Disagreement among organizations and stakeholders is common. How BEST does the project manager obtain this alignment during charter development?

a. With pressure from the project champion upon resistant stakeholders
b. With leadership techniques including conflict management, facilitation, and meeting management
c. With randomized selection of elements important to each stakeholder
d. With execution of the stakeholder management plan and measuring key performance indicators

168. As the project manager, you are facing influence in the completion of downstream activities based on the pull within the marketplace for further progression. You must collaborate with your counterparts in the operations division of your organization to ensure throughput is sufficient when activities increase. What type of schedule management strategy should you be aware of in this situation?

a. Alternative scheduling
b. Rolling wave planning
c. On-demand scheduling
d. Activity sequencing

169. What are the three hierarchical charts used to express resource division among project activities?

a. Organizational, work, and resource breakdown structures
b. Work breakdown structure, RACI matrix, and mind maps
c. Budget, project schedule, and the quality management plan
d. Organizational design chart, risk matrix, and supplier bill of materials

170. Stakeholder classification in the stakeholder register is MOST commonly based on which data sets?

a. Vitals, measurements of power and influence, and assessment information
b. Quality specifications, market capitalization, and return on investment
c. Alphabetical, cost to the project, and geographic location
d. Size of operating firm, experience with project management, and number of deliverables

171. Projects benefit from leaders with strong emotional intelligence. Which features BEST describe features of emotional intelligence behaviors?

a. Vision, integrity, and respect
b. Focus, business acumen, and financial skills
c. Formal project management training
d. Systems thinking and a formal title in the organization

172. During project schedule planning, several stakeholders with extensive history performing similar projects report that the resource allocation is cost prohibitive in the current scheduling—so prohibitive that the current activity durations would not be achieved using the currently assigned resources—nor would such activities be achieved with any additional resource allocation. What element of schedule design must be revisited by the project manager to address these stakeholder concerns?

a. Diminishing returns
b. Organizational motivation
c. Material resource quantity
d. Technology use

173. During the development of the project charter, the project manager must compile valid sources of input including which of the following?

a. External environmental factors and internal organizational process assets
b. Business case files and shareholder interviews
c. Cost-benefit analysis and the stakeholder management plan
d. Lessons learned register and the project task schedule

174. During project performance meetings, the project manager begins discussing the required elements to monitoring for effective team management. What performance components should he or she be considering?

a. The resource management plan
b. Forming, storming, norming, performing, adjourning
c. Hiring supervisors, third-party training courses, and meeting schedules
d. Assignment performance data, competencies, and turnover rate

175. When faced with schedule variances, how can the project team discern between acceptable and unacceptable levels of flexibility for sequential work activities?

a. Calculating the variance between lead time and lag time for an activity
b. Referencing the dependency determinations of scheduled activities
c. Referencing the milestone list
d. Adopting a rolling wave planning process

176. During the development of the project resource needs, a resource management output is created that includes the quantities, types, and sources of labor resources likely needed for each activity. What is the name of this output?

a. Resource estimation package
b. Resource breakdown structure
c. Basis for estimates analysis
d. Resource assignment matrix

177. What formal process within the change management plan defines how to execute the approved changes?

a. Direct and manage project work process
b. The stakeholder's attestation process
c. Accountability matrix process
d. Closeout phase work instructions

178. Why are business case studies used early in a project life cycle?

a. To demonstrate validity of the project manager's business acumen
b. To compare vendor proposals for procurement contracts
c. To influence the overall strategic planning of key stakeholders
d. To align the project manager, team, and stakeholders through project execution

179. According to project management professional criteria, which statement is true regarding charter approval?

a. Final approval occurs before initiating process group work.
b. Project work may not begin until charter approval is finalized.
c. The project management plan is finalized before the charter is created.
d. A finalized charter legally binds project stakeholders to the objectives.

180. As the project manager, you are aware that tailoring will be necessary for an upcoming new project under early planning phases. Based on your early knowledge and expertise, you know that there is likely to be alterations to the project scope later in the execution of the project. What type of tailoring approach is BEST suited to overcome this challenge?

a. Development approaches
b. Governance
c. Stability requirements
d. Sustainability

181. During schedule planning, a key project task is determined to have a most likely duration of 10 days. During further analysis the project team considers an optimistic duration of 7 days and a pessimistic duration of 16 days. What is the triangular distribution of these duration estimates?

a. 33 days
b. 9 days
c. 11 days
d. 10 days

182. Integration complexity is caused by the interaction of key factors: uncertainty, human behavior, and organizational systems behavior. What two complementary behaviors can a project manager use to overcome integration complexity?

a. Balanced contextual and cognitive approaches
b. Dedicated use of power and contracts to force behavioral change
c. Subject matter experts and stakeholders that develop the risk management plan
d. Divergence and convergence of complexity symptoms

183. After acceptance of the project deliverables and transfer of ownership, what follow-up actions are prudent for both the project team and stakeholder?

a. Tailoring plans
b. Transfer of organizational process assets
c. Control auditing and agreement closure
d. Divestiture of any capital assets gained during the project

184. Following the approval of the charter, the business case, and the analysis of enterprise environmental factors, how does the project manager consolidate and communicate the preliminary body of work to stakeholders comprehensively?

a. Compile the information into a project management plan.
b. Facilitate a virtual meeting to read the information to stakeholders.
c. Develop a project launch keynote address for review by stakeholders.
d. Reference the project communications plan, and follow the lessons learned.

185. As the project activities progress, issues are added and resolved, whereas some issues are held for later timeframes. Persons and timeframes are assigned for each issue. Which list BEST describes essential data points to collect and communicate for each issue?

a. Responsible person(s), scope statement, and cost analysis
b. Prioritization ranking, stakeholders facing impact, and description of the issue
c. Project champion name, quality assurance team contact information, and corrective action steps
d. Due date, quantitative risk analysis, and procurement efficiency

186. How is the risk management measurement of reserve analysis BEST defined?

a. Technical performance benchmarks compared to actual performance
b. Labor resource flexibility available to support project delays
c. Ratio of actual resource allocations to the remaining risk in the project
d. Inventory of extra materials and unused labor to be adjusted in accounting

187. Which of the following are the primary outputs of the control procurement process in procurement management?

a. Final payments, reworked defective deliverables, and statement of work
b. Lessons learned, enterprise environmental factors, and prequalification records
c. Closed agreements, work performance information, and organizational process asset updates
d. Request for quotation, procurement schedules, and financial billing setup before purchases can be made

188. The project team identifies several dozen risks during the preliminary phases of the project. The team performs quantitative analysis on the identified risks. What key parameters are used to build prioritization of the risks?

a. Severity and likelihood
b. Stakeholder impact and detectability
c. Cost and duration
d. Resource allocation and liability cost

189. You are developing a stakeholder management plan and determine that the level of interest for each of your potential stakeholders is uncertain. What primary facets of stakeholder interest must be considered?

a. The stakeholder engagement plan
b. Relative organizational power and reputation
c. Subject matter expertise, financial literacy, and rights
d. Decision impact, ownership, and contribution

190. What is the sequence of project activities representing the shortest duration to complete the project and the longest continuous set of work called?

a. Crashing
b. Float time
c. Work breakdown structure
d. Critical path

191. What is the primary difference between the waterfall and iterative approaches to project life cycle management?

a. The iterative approach does not involve a work breakdown structure as with the waterfall method.
b. Waterfalls decide on resources much earlier than iterative approaches.
c. Waterfall methods are highly adaptable.
d. The iterative approach adds functionality incrementally to a rigid timeframe.

192. What are common types of project deliverables?

a. Service, product, and stakeholder analysis
b. Service, product, information, and combinations
c. Product, information, and stakeholder
d. Services, lessons learned, information, and return on investment

193. During the execution of fast-moving project activities and periodic reviews of project performance, the project manager abruptly resigns, leaving the organization to backfill the key role with a new project manager unfamiliar with the progress. What key data points in the issues log will help the new project manager assess the current situation of corrections needed?

a. Past data is irrelevant, and issues are subjective; begin a new issues log.
b. Interview all persons assigned to issues who logged activities during the project.
c. Review current issue status, relative prioritization, and planned efforts to correct the problems.
d. Summarize data of issues that affected the perform integrated change control board.

194. During weekly performance communication meetings for a multisite construction project, the team members report to the project manager that four different quality activities occurred in the prior week: (1) a third-party audit of compliance to standards, (2) destructive testing of the steel framework, (3) rework of drywall due to poor workmanship, and (4) government fines issued due to structural hazards found in a previously completed structure in the project. Which of the activities represent a cost of internal failure?

a. Rework due to poor workmanship
b. Government fines for hazards
c. Destructive testing for adherence to standards
d. Independent auditing to standards

195. When performing a stakeholder analysis and assessing the stake each group or individual holds in the project's success, the project team must consider the following:

I. Moral or legal rights of certain stakeholders
II. Interest in project decisions made
III. Demographic data and market performance
IV. Contributions made including financial, resources, or information

a. I and III only
b. II and IV only
c. II, III, and IV only
d. I, II, and IV only

196. As the senior project manager at your consulting firm, your team commonly executes similar projects successfully for multiple clients. As the senior project manager, you have responsibility for the lessons learned register. What is the best classification and use of this register for future projects?

a. External Environmental Factor—an influential element that drives project and organizational strategy
b. Change Management Plan—the process to adjust project baselines
c. Organizational Process Asset—a tool used to overcome challenges and issues found in prior projects
d. Issues Log—a record documenting project nonconformance and corrective actions

197. As your first project management experience enters the closeout phase, what tools or resources will you evaluate to strengthen the likelihood that future project performance will be improved?

a. Relocation to a different project management organization
b. Issues log, lessons learned register, and final project reports
c. Continuous skills development in engineering principles
d. Researching how to create blame-free working relationships

198. The project manager for a construction project recently resigned and was replaced by a new project manager. The new manager observed several inconsistencies with the performance metrics and reporting approaches compared to internal standards. The new project manager changed the data collection, analysis, and reporting methods shortly after finding the issues. Within 24 hours, several stakeholders began withholding further financial support for future project phases due to the change in performance reporting. What mistake did the new project manager likely make?

a. Stakeholders are not permitted to support new project managers.
b. Financial baselines were exceeded coincidently.
c. Change management lapsed and altered the decision-making of key stakeholders.
d. The project manager did not track the issues in the issues log prior to implementing the changes.

199. A custom automotive manufacturer is performing a rapid turnaround work order for a client. The job is part of a larger project to build out a fleet of autonomous mail delivery vehicles. During the rush work order, multiple assembly phases in the production process contributed to quality defects, a missed project deadline, and a project cost overrun to rework the defects. Assembly and project employees described a lack of awareness of the customer's specifications for the defective parts. How BEST could the project manager have prevented such quality errors?

a. Assign a trained team to sort out defective finished goods from acceptable and absorb the cost overruns.
b. Use quality management to capture, monitor, and control customer requirements before executing project tasks.
c. Employ a human resources management plan to retain quality engineers on the project team.
d. Use project quality management planning to add in a waste cost factor into the project plans.

200. During project activity work to compile and publish a global research study, the project manager receives notice that multiple printed sections of the work were translated incorrectly for distribution in Japan. It is not clear to the project manager how the printing team and the translation team did not prevent the error. Which quality tool is the BEST choice for the project manager trying to resolve the issue?

a. 5 Why analysis
b. Risk-based process hazard analysis
c. Plan-do-check-act cycles
d. Statistical process control

Answer Key and Explanations

1. C: Effective problem-solving begins with identifying or defining the problem to be solved. Measurements and analysis of the state of the problem and any possible solutions gives validity to how the team is solving the problem. After implementing a valid solution, there must be a control or sustaining force to prevent recurrence of the former failed state. These concepts are like the DMAIC process of six sigma.

2. B: Capturing project knowledge and lessons learned alone is not enough. If the information sits in a database or manual and no project managers or stakeholders review and learn from the lessons, they are useless. Organizations want project managers, or organizational leaders, to coach each other and adopt these changes. It is important to take advantage of these lessons by internal or external communication and change. The other choices on this list are beneficial to any project organization but don't alone provide the connection between knowledge and creating impact.

3. B: Stakeholders expend resources with the expectation that a viable project will provide some benefit in return. The expenditures come in the form of money, labor, material resources, or information. The cost-benefit analysis addressing these resources provides stakeholders with the ability to make key decisions.

4. A: The purpose of the lessons learned register is to capture key learnings (problems, risks, opportunities, threats, etc.) into a central database to analyze and improve future project planning and execution. It is used for positive outcomes not punitive outcomes.

5. A: A precursor step is to create the schedule management plan. Thereafter the schedule creation follows the process of define activities, sequence activities, estimate activity durations, develop the schedule, and finally control the schedule.

6. B: Reporting of variances can be accomplished using measures of variance prescribed in the schedule management plan. Variances are based on the acceptable accuracy performance and any occurrences where an allowed variation is exceeded. Level of accuracy refers to approved ranges in activity durations. Control thresholds distinguish acceptable variance from unacceptable conditions.

7. C: The project team can use the supplier's information to absorb the decline in supplier capability by adjusting project baselines. The team can drop the supplier (or diminish the resource quantities obtained from that supplier by using an alternate supply source. Last, the project team can audit and support the supplier to find improvement and capacity opportunities. The wrong choice would be to use defective parts and relax critical-to-quality measures. This choice will most negatively affect the deliverable.

8. D: An effective quality management plan begins with defining the customer and stakeholder measures of quality or specifications. A requirements traceability matrix summarizes these criteria well. A voice of the customer analysis translates requirements to features and key quality indicators.

9. C: Activity durations are estimated in the schedule management planning phase. To plan and allocate resources effectively, there must be a level of accuracy calculated, for example, for each activity and for the plan overall. These estimates guide the team to plan for the actual execution of project work.

10. A: Examples of expert judgement supporting the phase or project closeout process include regulatory review by government and organizational lawyers reviewing formal contracts for fulfillment.

11. C: Baselines are defined reference points set throughout the project life cycle for cost, scope, and time. Performance can be monitored against these baselines at various stages in the life cycle. Baselines are rigid to maintain a measurement standard for leadership and stakeholders. Variance and needs for adjustment to these baselines must go through a change management process. These tools would be expanded appropriately when dealing with several projects in a portfolio.

12. C: The five Cs of written communication are best practices used to make communications more effective, including: correct grammar, control idea flow, clear purpose, concise, and coherent flow. Coherent flow refers to the art of logically sequencing and flowing information and topics to the audience bookended by introductory and summary elements.

13. C: The RACI matrix and acronym describes who is responsible for project resources, the persons who are accountable to certain tasks or activities, the persons who may need to be consulted to complete an activity, and persons who must be informed of the results of an action or outcome.

14. C: For issues that are significant and/or are repeated, whether or not such issues get resolved, it is important that the project manager consider expanding the lessons learned register. This could apply to a portfolio/program or the parent organization itself. The register serves to help future project teams avoid past mistakes and issues solved or encountered in the past.

15. D: Data collected in the project work phase includes work performance, change requests, open issues, and identified risks. These are compiled onto forecast documents or registers within the project management process of the organization.

16. B: The cost estimation plan feeds into the budget process. The budget process of a project often also includes contingency resources such as staffing, parts, or discretionary money for deviations from plan. This transition from estimation to actual planned allocation creates more concrete requirements in the budget regarding resources needed.

17. C: In larger projects, the project management plan is crafted prior to the first team meeting so that members can have clear direction on responsibilities, scope, and success measures. Activities such as reviewing lessons learned from previous projects should be completed as a closeout task from the prior project.

18. D: Self-organizing teams share the characteristics of trustworthiness, adaptability, team-focus, and commitment to a team vision. Not all members of self-organizing teams necessarily have advanced engineering training. Advanced engineering training cannot be considered a characteristic of self-organizing teams. A self-organizing team likely exists without advanced engineers.

19. A: It is important that decisions are documented and that project sub-plans are adjusted accordingly to meet the expectations of the risk response chosen. This may include changes to the budgets, work activities, schedules, resources, and quality systems existing before the response was decided.

20. C: The sender of project communications is responsible to ensure clarity and correct delivery. Recipients must take responsibility for receiving the communication, interpreting the information and acknowledgement of understanding.

21. C: The scope management process ensures that the project activities include the necessary steps to achieve the project deliverables. Scope provides clarity regarding what is relevant and sufficient to achieving deliverables. This includes alignment to customer requirements. To clearly communicate the task elements needed to achieve scope, a work breakdown structure is a concluding piece of the scope plan.

22. C: Any changes to project baselines or to key planning documents like the budget will be routed through the perform integrated change control (PICC) team. Changes to these types of documents must be reviewed critically, and any changes must be communicated to the right stakeholders. Changes can have significant impacts on performance, monitoring, and future project deliverables.

23. D: Process analysis refers to the assessment of processes and any opportunities to implement improvements that lower waste, increase efficiency, and increase customer satisfaction. This type of analysis is specifically targeting those types of opportunities. Traditional root cause analysis is used in a wider range of situations.

24. D: Project quality management plans indicate the significant and allowable levels of defect and, often waste, in the project activities. There are often natural process variations that may create defect or waste. Not all such variations are cause for documenting a formal issue for the project team to solve. If defects or waste are significant, the issue should be documented on the issue log for corrective action.

25. A: The acceptance details of the deliverables are documented within the scope management plan. These deliverable details help shape the project scope. Key specifications of the deliverables are contained within the quality and/or requirements sub-plans. The scope statement also reinforces the acceptance criteria for deliverables. There is no such deliverables management plan in the project management body of knowledge.

26. A: The categories of lessons mentioned in the question indicate that it is possible to group the lessons by the 6 Ms common to root cause analysis tools like the fishbone diagram. By sorting the lessons into categories, including measurement, methods, machinery, materials, (hu)man elements, and environment, you can focus on smaller groups of knowledge and gain understanding faster. You might then be able to use tools such as multi-voting and designed experiments to capitalize on these lessons after categorizing.

27. B: The dilemmas listed include ineffective communication schedule, poor team interaction, and poor data retrieval. A system to manage and retrieve project information and a platform for communication and team member collaboration would represent the best improvements.

28. C: The documents most commonly reviewed and archived at the closeout phase are grouped into reports, standards, and registers. Registers group include the risk register, issues log, change log, and lessons learned register. The standards grouping includes requirements documentation and the basis of estimates. The reports group includes project communications, quality reports, and the risk report.

29. D: Upon deciding to accept a proposed change, the project manager will have planned any resources needed for implementation to be ready to integrate into the project smoothly. Where stakeholders will be affected by the change, notifications are made to various degrees. After the change is implemented, the project manager is wise to monitor the intended effect of the change is meeting expectations. All of the above are true.

30. C: The linkage between the scheduled project milestones and the project quality, deliverable, and performance criteria is the requirements traceability list. This list often includes work breakdown information but also includes other valuable information such as validated specifications, objectives, and scope details.

31. D: The lessons learned register can serve as an organizational process asset when used as historical knowledge and means to influence project success. Lessons learned are also a form of documentation of project knowledge. Third, the lessons register is a key source of information controlled within any information management systems like a PMIS. Enterprise environmental factors, however, are internal or external influences that can positively or negatively affect the outcomes of the project plan. Lessons learned registers do not directly fall within this category.

32. C: Engagement is analyzed with two common techniques: mind mapping and engagement assessment matrix. The latter lists all project stakeholders and classifies each based on levels of engagement (unaware, resistant, neutral, supportive, and leading). The matrix marks where each stakeholder falls currently by denoting "C" and where the project team wants to strategically improve engagement levels and by denoting a "D" elsewhere on the continuum for desired state. The largest gaps between current engagement and desired engagement are prioritized.

33. D: Cost-reimbursable contracts define terms in which the buyer makes payments to the seller as the costs are incurred. High procurement variance is an ideal situation for cost-reimbursable due to the variation in resource timing. Fixed price is suited for low variance procurement needs, whereas time and material contracts blend both approaches.

34. D: Large groups of stakeholders are best served with pull communication methods where members of the large group can retrieve communication and data as needed. Generally speaking, high-impact and key stakeholders are better suited also receiving push communications regarding performance. These push forms can include reports, key-performance indicator scorecards, emails, and virtual presentations.

35. A: Earned value analysis uses the WBS, scope, schedule, and budget information compared to work performance data to give a progress report to predict expected completion time and cost performance. The analysis compares the plan to the actual performance to give a forecasted outcome.

36. A: Project or phase closeout serves to get the final project tasks completed before providing the customer with a final acceptable deliverable. It also serves as a time to craft and issue a final project report. Choices C and D may be considered good secondary purposes of the closeout process but not the main purpose.

37. B: Voice-of-the-customer events allow the project team to collect and analyze customer needs and customer views on quality and performance. Project teams can translate those expectations into the critical-to-quality parameters and how those further translate into operations performance metrics. The lean six sigma answer was too vague.

38. D: Availability is the key word here referring to the day-to-day scheduling of labor and resources. Resource calendars are tools to manage resource availability. The resource breakdown schedule (RBS) is not an ideal answer because the RBS simply maps out the resources needed at different activities. The RBS does not reflect day-to-day utilization.

39. A: Of the five common neutralization strategies to consider, mitigation serves to lessen the impact or likelihood of the risk. By adjusting resource utilization, adding redundancy, and getting an early preventive start before the peak risk impact happens, the team uses a mitigation strategy.

40. B: Stakeholders expect to have their specifications and needs met during the project. They also generally desire a degree of communication and attention by the project management team and organization. The project manager has responsibility for the stakeholder engagement plan including reassessing the plan when weaknesses are found. In this situation, after reassessment, the project manager must fix the team's attentiveness to the stakeholders' expectations and resolve their complaints.

41. C: The three elements to the PMI talent triangle are leadership, strategic/business management, and technical project management.

42. A: The histogram divides sequential data from a data set into bins or buckets of fixed ranges. These bins show the quantity of data values that fall within the range of each bin. The result is a bar graph showing how the data is distributed across the bins. The histogram helps visualize process behavior and cause and effect.

43. C: Virtual teams with minimal supervision must have clear deliverables and milestones. They also must have periodic monitoring and reporting of progress toward these milestones and deliverables. Communication among the virtual team ensures that changes, progress, and issues are discussed to avoid failure of the process. Depending on the level of trust and expertise in the virtual team, team leaders decide how much working hours monitoring is performed, if at all. Consultants and subject matter experts are not necessarily needed in virtual teams.

44. B: Multiple deliverable criteria may be of concern to the buyer. The seller is primarily looking to turn a profitable sale within their capabilities and provide suitable service and quality to the buyer. These are the primary objectives in the project buyer–seller relationship.

45. A: The impact bubble diagram combines three parameters into a visualization of the relative severity and priority of each of the several risks the project team faces. The x and y axes of the graph plot two of the three parameters, whereas the diameter of each plotted data point represents the third parameter, such as impact.

46. D: Request for proposal (RFP) invites multiple vendors to present how their products or services solve a problem for the buyer. This is the best answer. RFI is a basic fact-finding request, whereas RFQ is a more detailed financial and scope deliverable. Statement of work is issued by the buyer to describe the scope of what vendors must achieve to win the bid.

47. B: Commonly used techniques for gathering these key risk details include brainstorming, interviewing, and checklists. The checklists serve as basic quality tools to collect multiple types of risk data from a process or service. Life cycle assessment is not a common tool for risk data identification.

48. D: Stakeholders are expecting to be informed of key performance indicators as the project progresses. This form of accountability placed on the project team and manager reinforces adherence to the project plan, and taking preventive and corrective actions to keep the project on track toward deliverables.

49. A: To effectively eliminate and prevent nonconformances in the issues log, the team must implement corrective and preventive actions. The right corrective and preventive actions are best determined using root cause analysis tools and related process analysis tools.

50. C: The descriptions of benchmarking, interviews, and brainstorming were all described in the question as actions the team took to develop the quality plan and satisfy the stakeholder concerns. Mind mapping, a process of organizing elements or concepts into a visual map to show relationships and categorization, was not described.

51. C: Prompt lists within the risk management plan provide recognizable features of the manifestation of certain risks in the project performance data. Project managers aware of these prompts can quickly identify when a risk is affecting the project and can lead adjustments or corrective actions as needed to keep performance on track.

52. C: Interconnections and interrelationships among stakeholders can enhance the project plan and/or organizational strategy. The best tools to explore the stakeholders include power/interest grid, stakeholder cube, salience models, and the directions of influence model. These each are ideal analysis tools.

53. C: Configuration is a term connected with outcomes such as the deliverable(s) or their features. Change management is project process oriented such as changing baseline financials or schedules.

54. A: The project manager must have a degree of control over the procured resources for project activity execution. Control is defined as the measurement of how well utilization aligns with the resource plan and schedule. The project team is able to make adjustments and corrections to ensure utilization aligns with expectations.

55. A: The answers can be narrowed down to two development choices. Phase-gate development is the best answer; development using this tool is predicated on a known or stable scope. Agile development is a related tool but involves an evolving scope as progressive iterations are completed.

56. A: Tailoring is the varied use of inputs, tools, techniques, and resources to effectively manage the achievement of deliverables. For projects where unforeseen issues or roadblocks may occur, tailoring aids in ensuring the project progress can be agile when needed. A hybrid tailored management approach—where customer requirements can be developed and delivered in the continuing project as they become known—would allow the project team to progress in a flexible, agile way.

57. C: Key success factors are commonly added to the project charter and often include traditional measures of cost, quality, scope, and time. In this scenario, customer satisfaction, schedule adherence, and quality are key factors explicitly mentioned by the stakeholders.

58. A: The most effective approach to solving the uncertainty problem is to build expertise among the team members. Work instructions describe a specific process in more explicit terms, whereas error proofing prevents someone from mistakenly bypassing the right procedures.

59. B: Supplementary techniques to the five Cs include active listening, skill enhancement, cultural intelligence, and stakeholder expectation management.

60. D: The project is expected to meet customer and stakeholder requirements. The project management team must define the relevant deliverables that meet these requirements. Defined project goals that align to the customer requirements and set deliverables is a means by which team performance achieves relevance.

61. A: The stakeholder management process primarily involves understanding and meeting the expectations of stakeholders. The plan is best suited with prioritizing the stakeholders based on how much their stake or expectations affect the project.

62. A: After each phase or project is completed, compiled lessons learned are valuable for improving future iterations of the organization's project management function.

63. A: The perform integrated change control (PICC) group ensures that changes to the project plans are valid and well integrated into the existing project. This work of the PICC is performed within the context of the direct and manage project work element of the overall project management plan.

64. A: The team must survey the customer base and determine what critical-to-quality parameters exist and how to link those to the production operation. A critical-to-quality house process translates the voice of the customer to operating parameters. This tool is best suited to align customers with operations.

65. C: The matrix defines the current state and the desired state for all key stakeholders to the project. In this example, an unaware quality function must be aligned to the customer expectations for recapturing market share. Furthermore, resistant vendors and labor must be improved to at least supportive functions. The neutral maintenance force is not a threat.

66. B: Cost, schedule, quality, and scope measurements are generally common interests for the project management organization and for stakeholders. These are key performance measures for most projects.

67. C: Agile project life cycles are adaptive to unforeseen risks and events (both positive and negative). The agile project team adapts work, resources, scope, and plans to keep the deliverables and metrics on track. Agile is also used in a feedback method as the project deliverable(s) are being continuously developed during the project work.

68. C: The resource management plan and stakeholder engagement plan are both part of the overall project management plan and detail communications needs for personnel resources and project stakeholders.

69. C: Three key types of documents or elements that are commonly updated at closeout include lessons learned register, organizational process assets, and any operational support documents. Projects often discover new methods, lessons, and process improvements for the benefit of future projects. An element that is not likely updated would be the baselines for all future projects. Baselines are typically created or evaluated for each individual project.

70. C: Tracking and analyzing cost of quality data is important and can be useful to an organization but it is not considered an essential facet of project quality management. Designing quality into products and services; driving improvement using quality tools; and performing preventive and control functions are all considered essential facets to project quality management.

71. A: When project activities or work are being completed, the project manager must be continuously monitoring the status of schedule (or task) completion and progress toward deliverables. To do so, work performance data must be captured and effectively analyzed to gain valuable information for decision-making. The remaining choices include responsibilities that are generally secondary functions to the project manager's primary duties.

72. C: Before considering vendors or providers where resources could be procured, the project leaders must have a rough idea of what budget exists for these resources. Funding approval is obtained earlier in the project near the time of charter and business case development and does not directly bear on procurement decision phases.

73. D: The best answer is to enter into formal performance agreements or contracts with the labor provider. Metrics for performance must align with project performance indicators and align with objectives.

74. C: The scope statement includes the acceptance criteria, key features, parameters, or requirements that must be met in each deliverable before they can be considered acceptable. The scope statement, as a part of the larger scope management plan, is where you can find this information.

75. A: Tailoring is the process through which the project manager and the parent organization analyze the proposed project and determine the needed inputs, tools, techniques, and phases likely needed to complete the project effectively. Devising a tailored approach to a project builds confidence in stakeholders that the project will be successful.

76. C: Internal communication of problems within the project and, more importantly, the actions being performed to resolve the problems are valuable to key leaders of the project. Awareness helps the leadership act in a broader scope to ensure the issues do not derail the project plans.

77. C: Earned value analysis (EVA) specifically involves tracking expected vendor schedule and cost performance against actual performance. Any variances are highlighted, and vendors responsible for the variances are held accountable for solutions. Trend analysis, claims administration, and auditing may all be subsequent tactics used after EVA is performed.

78. A: Baselines are approved standards reflecting key project elements—such as schedule, cost, quality, and scope—that stakeholders and project teams monitor to compare planned performance to actual performance during project execution. Project management information systems (PMIS) reports may also give this type of information; however, PMIS reports are not dedicated solely to the critical performance evaluation as are baselines.

79. A: Recommended skills beneficial to enhancing project communications include active listening, skill enhancement, and cultural intelligence. Other listed choices are not included in the recommended techniques in the project management professional body of knowledge.

80. D: An accurate issue log without outstanding action items gives the project manager and the organization data for improving future projects. Issues and their corrective actions can translate into lessons learned, offer insight into potential project risks, and may strengthen the organizational process assets (such as communication tools, organizational behaviors, and human resource standards).

81. A: The impact matrix plots probability of occurrence against relative impact. A unit-less relative risk value is derived from the product of the probability and the impact. Negative impacts are considered threats, whereas positive impacts are considered opportunities. Any combination of probability and negative impact implies a threat to the project. Any combination of probability and positive impact implies an opportunity to the project. The schedule risk of high negative impact and low probability is a weak threat. The cost risk of moderate positive impact and high probability is a moderate opportunity.

82. D: Project deliverables are either intermittent within the project or solely at the completion of all activities. Stakeholders expect to be aware of the project plan, scope, and charter depending on their level of investment into the project. The completed result of the activities is naturally a key deliverable as well. A deliverable such as the charter will describe key performance indicators such as performance to budget and schedule baselines.

83. C: The perform integrated change control (PICC) process is defined using a written change management plan. Baselines such as those for scope, cost, and schedule provide input data against which to reference the proposed change. Project documents such as the requirements traceability matrix are also used as inputs to the change process. Sub-plans such as the human resource management plan are not necessarily used in all change reviews.

84. D: Configuration management tools apply to adjustments to key features, specifications, or attributes to the deliverable(s) or outputs of the project. Change management tools apply to adjustments of the procedures, plans, baselines, or supporting documentation of the project. Team A focuses on configuration, whereas Team B focuses on change management.

85. C: Variation and reliability are quality terms. Variation is the degree of spread seen about a mean. Higher variation generally indicates lower quality. Reliability is also a measure of performance quality, such as mean time between failures. Choosing procurement sources based on quality performance aligns with customer expectations.

86. C: Engaging stakeholders using mind mapping most commonly visualizes (or plots) the cross-connections between stakeholders to tease out common concerns or interests. Using these common details, project management can increase engagement across the majority of the identified stakeholders.

87. A: Resilience is defined as preparation to absorb or overcome known risks to the project. Tools and techniques such as risk identification, analysis, and probability assessments may support the creation of a risk resilience strategy.

88. D: Integrated risk management solves the shared risk problem within an organization covering multiple projects, portfolios, and programs. The shared organizational resources that these rely on to function should have an integrated risk management plan to shield all from disruptions to shared tools, systems, and technologies.

89. D: Raw data from the execution work must be transformed into some type of useful information. From there, the information can be applied to performance reporting and metrics communication tools.

90. B: Cost of quality accounting places quality costs into four categories: prevention, appraisal, internal failure, and external failure. The most expensive and damaging costs are external failures, whereas the most proactive and valuable costs are prevention. To maximize output quality, costs are tilted toward higher preventive expenses. A tilt will drive down the internal and external failure costs.

91. C: Project management is highlighted by clear communication, process and subject matter knowledge, reliable tracking and preventive tools, and the human/financial resources to achieve the deliverables.

92. D: Stakeholders should be asked early in the planning process what performance indicators are most important to them and what communication delivery method meets their preferences. Compiling these details early and building communication systems to meet those expectations is essential to an effective stakeholder management plan and communications management plan.

93. B: The work breakdown structure gives granular explanation of the activities needed to achieve the scope. The quality management plan describes how to meet customer expectations for project performance and deliverable attributes. The constraint matrix is a risk-based document that advises planning efforts. Only the requirements traceability matrix—a tool to match customer requirements to each planned deliverable—is best suited.

94. B: Essential responsibilities of the project manager during integration include being able to block distractions from the team. This allows the team to focus on the project deliverables, plans, charter, and objectives.

95. B: Awareness of the physical and process-oriented inputs supports the development of a strong project management plan. Organizational process assets (OPA) are the norms and procedures used by the organization in support of projects. Examples include procedures, tailoring policies, and how reporting/information sharing is achieved. Enterprise environmental factors are broader organizational systems and tools used to support projects and other organizational tasks. Examples include internal culture, governance, and the nuts and bolts of the telecommunications infrastructure.

96. B: The standard project charter has several key elements that provide team members and stakeholders the necessary information needed to align to the project. The purpose statement, key stakeholder list, scope, and defined objective are examples of those key elements. The other options listed are not reflective of key charter elements.

97. C: The use of multi-voting allows the project team and other organizational stakeholders to derive a decision from a knowledgeable, representative group. This approach avoids or minimizes conflict between internal parties or stakeholders while arriving at a suitable conclusion. Stronger outcomes are achieved in this situation using multi-voting.

98. A: The impact bubble diagram plots two of the three parameters on separate axes. Each bubble plotted on the chart represents a risk; the diameter of each plotted bubble represents the third parameter, usually severity.

99. D: Project changes will affect the decision-making of stakeholders. Evaluating and communicating those proposed changes will help stakeholders avoid making bad decisions against their original interests in the project. Regulatory agencies may sometimes require management of change record keeping but not always.

100. D: Monitoring performance against stakeholder requirements implies that those performance results must be communicated to relevant stakeholders. The communications management plan, and specifically the subsection detailing the communications monitoring process, will describe to the project team how to communicate results during and at the end of the project.

101. C: Fully destructive testing provides 100% assurance of the quality performance of the vendor output but no goods remain for use in the project after the test! Statistical sampling and performance testing against specifications are cost-effective ways to gain assurance of the whole lot from the vendor. Evaluation before using the materials in the project helps avoid higher costs of failure and project delays.

102. B: Two of the most common analysis tools used by the PICC are alternatives analysis and cost-benefit analysis. Alternatives analysis weights all competing options to derive the ideal choice. Cost-benefit analysis addresses the alternatives by weighing the project benefit to the resource expense needed.

103. C: The charter approval acknowledges that the project aligns with financial, strategic, and business case initiatives. The charter authorizes work to begin on a project and is a sign of successful integration by the project manager. The determination of the full project schedule may occur before or after the charter approval. A completed schedule is not a prerequisite to the charter.

104. B: The objective of the lessons learned register is to build positive outcomes for future projects by minimizing the impact of past failures (or capitalizing on opportunities observed in the past). This benefit can happen between projects chronologically or between phases within a project. Databases of lessons learned are kept within an organization but may also be available through trade or industry organizations to help all organizations collectively.

105. D: Specifically, a cost control variance threshold would alert the project leadership and stakeholders to an unacceptable decline in project cost performance.

106. D: The project charter is a key alignment document. The project team, champions, and importantly the stakeholders receive consistent information regarding the project scope and how it will be executed. The charter is a precursor to the project management plan, where deep analysis on risks and resources occurs.

107. B: The work breakdown structure (WBS) is a scope management tool to divide the project into smaller and more understandable, more manageable components. The WBS deconstructs the entire scope of the project and bridges the team to align scope with schedule, budget, and work activities. The monitor and control project work phase executes on the defined work activities, but that phase is not where the WBS is developed.

108. A: The phase in which a project kick-off (or launch) meeting is held depends upon the project size. Smaller projects can hold a kick-off meeting earlier in the planning phases because generally fewer persons are supporting the project and more interaction is possible in an agile manner. Larger projects generally have larger support teams and require more dedicated planning activities prior to communicating the official start. Implementation phases involve larger project kick-off meetings. Resource attainment does not necessarily correlate to when project launch meetings are held.

109. D: Rolling wave schedule planning focuses higher attention on near-term project activities and a lighter attention on longer outlook activities forthcoming. The wave is repeated in this way as the project progresses. Technique pairing must include a tool to breakdown coming work into at-hand activities (decomposition), whereas longer-term work is kept in bulk status awaiting attention (work packaging).

110. B: An effective communication management plan ensures that information is securely and reliably distributed to the right people and organizations, at the right times, with relevant knowledge for decision-making. The content, methods of delivery, and accuracy must be controlled so that trust may be maintained in the communications and in the project leadership.

111. D: To provide value to the actual performance data, the project manager must report how that data compares to forecasts and baselines. Schedule forecasts on attainment and cost forecasts (against planned budget) give meaning to the work data.

112. C: Gathering all final evidence of procurement performance among all vendors (or service providers) helps inform the organization ahead of future projects. The lessons learned register and the collective negotiating tactics used in future project procurement processes are the beneficiaries of these final documents.

113. A: Project procurement is established through contracts and agreements between supplier and buyer. These contracts and agreements detail the terms of service, output specifications, and related financial conditions between both parties.

114. C: Configuration refers to features and attributes of the tangible or intangible deliverable(s) created by the project. Change refers to the adjustment of project process related components such as baselines, schedules, plans, and budgets. The distinct and separate use of these words is important in project management. A verification audit serves as a configuration tool to give assurance that the project is achieving the deliverables according to the expected quality standards.

115. B: Many points of advice are included in the procurement management plan to support the project team's ability to monitor performance. Here, the choice of procurement timetables relative to the project plans and schedule is the only correct choice. Key metrics may be used to monitor performance by vendors. The procurement management plan would also tend to include coordinator advice on how such requirements will align with the project plan.

116. B: Although the skills to perform project closeout are valuable, closeout management is not a formal project management knowledge area.

117. A: High-functioning teams are characterized by high levels of trust, productivity, collaboration, and decision-making skills. New hires with these characteristics would likely assimilate well into the team.

118. A: Resilience is the art of adding resource buffers into the project to soften any negative impact when unknown risks occur and threaten the project deliverables and objectives.

119. D: Extremely low levels of defect risk imply that a quality-based contract is paramount to this procurement strategy. Sole source contracts may achieve this outcome but are not necessarily focused on highest quality. Sole source could be advantageous by gaining leverage over the vendor to achieve quality, but that is not guaranteed. Low-cost may also achieve this, but generally one sacrifices quality when choosing low-cost options. A fixed budget contract is common where the project team selects a vendor based on financial constraints. Again, this may not ensure the contract is strong in quality-based details.

120. C: A process that is not clearly understood can be visualized with a flow diagram. The flow diagram shows the step-by-step flow of raw materials or information in order through the process and gives clarity to stakeholders.

121. B: The risk management plan includes quantifiable data on how much each risk would likely affect the project. Where risks are associated with resources allocation, those quantifiable risk figures are described in financial and scheduling terms. Last, communicating the project teams' functional responsibilities to stakeholders supports improved stakeholder confidence and lower threat of risk.

122. C: Meeting facilitation involves the effective use of clear communication and meeting goals. Facilitation creates stronger buy-in and increased participation from members creating the charter.

123. D: Risk analysis in relative terms implies that being able to quantify and rank risks relative to others within the project allows prioritization. Risks can carry severity and likelihood, both elements determining the relative risk compared to others. Consultant support is a tempting answer but not specific enough to answer the question.

124. A: Project stakeholders have diverse "stakes" in any given project. Financial, business, reputational, and legal are common reasons. The stakeholder benefit analysis addresses these primary concerns using a benefits management plan to map out how unique stakeholder benefits will be achieved. The pro forma financial statements and business cases explain the most likely outcomes stakeholders can expect from the project.

125. D: The project management team monitors stakeholder engagement by focusing on relationships, performance, and strategy. Stakeholder relationships must be assessed often to ensure the baseline expectations are known. Project performance against the expectations provides a gauge of how those expectations are being met. Engagement strategies are fluid and must change when necessary.

126. B: The question implies that root cause analysis tools are needed to evaluate some project issues. The tornado diagram is the only choice that is not a root cause tool. Tornado diagrams are used in quantitative risk analysis.

127. C: Risks can be realized and captured in a risk register throughout the project life cycle. Early in the project process tends to be when most risks are identified; however, risks can become known during execution, during sub-plan development, and even while the closeout occurs. The best answer is that risks are identified throughout.

128. C: Of the four key skills needed for effective project communication, the nonverbal communication and presentation skills most accurately meet the described need. Nonverbal cues delivered face-to-face supplement a presentation and can exhibit more emotions and passion compared to dull memo of the performance. It is important that stakeholders receive feedback from their audience however that material is created by the audience or stakeholders and presented to the portfolio manager.

129. A: In agile project management approaches, adaptive project execution is critical. Agile project teams must be flexible to reallocate resources as knowledge is gained from the process.

130. D: Auditing serves to give an unbiased assessment, often independent, to stakeholders regarding quality performance. Stakeholders have an interest in receiving accurate assurances of quality performance. Data monitoring and defect evaluation are likely elements of a quality program, but these are generally performed by the project team or an operation and may not provide a strong, independent assessment to stakeholders.

131. C: The lessons learned register completed after each project is considered an organizational process asset and used for the benefit of future projects.

132. B: The best choices include SWOT, constraint, and root cause analysis techniques. SWOT addresses strengths, weaknesses, opportunities, and threats. Constraint analysis performs validation on the assumptions and constraints in the project planning. Root cause analysis derives the true reasons for failures or nonconformances.

133. A: Stakeholders have a vested interest in the success of the project. Stakeholders also have a vested interest in the ongoing performance of the phases and activities of the project as it works toward deliverables. Project teams monitor performance data against key performance benchmarks to be able to summarize progress to stakeholders. Clearly communicating performance levels to stakeholders is critical to keeping strong engagement.

134. D: The communications monitoring process within the communications management plan includes explanations of how information must be communicated across the organization and stakeholders. It also includes the requirements each stakeholder makes upon the project team regarding information sharing and communication. These road maps and specifications are the basis of the monitoring process.

135. A: Decomposition—the dissolution of scope and deliverable details into more manageable subcomponents—includes five key steps: division of deliverables into subsidiaries, deliverables analysis, work breakdown organization, tagging of work breakdown steps, and verification of decomposition effectiveness.

136. A: An effective cost management plan must factor in known risks, planned use of resources over time, and the relevant charter details like scope, deliverables, and performance metrics. These inputs are the driving information sources for creating the cost management plan.

137. D: The nominal group technique involves ranking brainstormed ideas by a larger group to determine which ideas gather the most motivation toward the scope development.

138. A: Lessons learned during project work generally arise when facing risks or issues. Capturing lessons learned requires evaluation and analysis. These risk-based or issue-based reflection points are times when the ability to meet business case objectives accurately are evaluated.

139. C: The five key components of the scope baseline include the work breakdown structure (WBS), the WBS dictionary, the project scope statement, the work package, and the planning package.

140. A: Because the project team is aware of the requirements needed to achieve the desired performance levels, their main objective is to find a capable firm able to meet the performance criteria. The team does not need to request information from prospective vendors; the project team should clearly know what the expectations are on any vendor. Rather, the project team should request and expect to receive request for proposal (RFP) documents first from any vendor they speak with. The team wants to know how a new vendor will specifically meet the expectations and solve the problem at hand. A secondary document would include the request for quotation. The statement of work may be an early document issued by the project team to prospective vendors.

141. B: The best answer describes a tool that enforces a planned improvement, execution, and evaluation process. The plan-do-check-act model in continuous improvement is the ideal basic choice; the model focuses on smaller/focused improvement initiatives. Agile and phase-gate tools are more appropriate as larger project management tools. 5 Why root cause is a tool to evaluate the true reasons for an issue or lesson learned. 5 Why analysis may or may not be necessary when making improvements based on lessons learned.

142. B: The context diagram is used to model the scope in the project. The diagram provides a visual representation of how customers use the deliverable and how the business systems create and deliver the product or service.

143. A: Essential criteria used to decide if a project is valid and worth beginning are centered on customer, financial, and strategic perspectives. Customer needs or demands must be likely satisfied before pursuing the project activities and investing money. The organization funding or performing the project also expects to obtain a return on its investment and achieve any broader business objectives. Without strong indications that these measures would be satisfactory, the project will not likely be considered or started.

144. D: Statistical process control (SPC) charts translate the quality parameters (most typically quantitative-based parameters) into production run rules. The tool charts and highlights any variation in a process that is not due to normal fluctuations. SPC charting in addition to strong preventive maintenance of the equipment ensures low variation in the outputs.

145. D: The neutralization strategy of "exploit" takes advantage of an observed opportunity to eliminate or reduce risk. The strategy is most commonly used on high-benefit opportunities and when there is a high likelihood of positive outcomes.

146. A: Systems thinking is defined as the ability to analyze how and organization's or project's goals, elements, and interconnectivity are enjoined and become affected as progress or change is made over the course of functioning.

147. B: Cost-reimbursable contracts align with the project needs in this example. The project needs flexibility with payments due to variation in project work. More specifically, the project team would benefit most from a cost-reimbursable plus incentive contract. A fixed-price contract would be wise if the project work variation was low.

148. D: Resilience is developed by strong planning when creating the risk management plan. How a project team allocates resources for known and unknown risks through financial, resource, and schedule buffers will allow the team to be resilient and absorb the impact these risks may have on the project deliverables.

149. B: The project team is expected to meet or exceed quality and deliverable expectations; reworking or resolving the early quality errors is the ideal expectation. Where the schedule must be extended by 14 days, formal approved adjustment to the schedule baseline can be achieved with stakeholders.

150. C: Risk neutralization when the impact becomes more than a project manager can handle most commonly leads to an escalation strategy in which organizational, program, or portfolio project managers take over the project management duties. These are more severe situations in which drastic change is needed. Transfer is not an ideal answer; transfer is the strategy of shifting certain intensive yet arguably mundane duties away from the project manager so he or she can focus on more important duties.

151. A: The business benefits management plan is a timetable explaining when the organization is expected to achieve the benefits expected from the project. This plan shows financial, milestone, deliverable, and intangible benefits to multiple stakeholders. This forward-looking projection can be compared during the project execution to gage performance to expectations.

152. C: The critical defects must be resolved before any further production is created. The project team is facing a nonconformance and must analyze the situation for the underlying root cause before they can effectively resolve the issue. The other choices also can be used to feed into corrective action processes but would not be the next best choice for the team. The root cause must be first determined. Alternatives analysis may be a valuable second tool to assess other paths forward in the project.

153. A: Your final report is expected to recap how well the project executed on quality, cost, schedule, and resource metrics. Also, the customer and/or stakeholders will need assurance that the approved scope was achieved. It is also beneficial to describe how known and unknown project risks were managed; this gives customers and stakeholders greater assurance of the reliability of the project results.

154. D: Projects can be divided into process groups based on the types of activities generally performed. Creating the scope, objectives and WBS will occur in the planning process group.

155. C: The relationship of start to finish (SF) reflects activity overlap, and the successor activity does not begin until the predecessor finishes.

156. D: Many interdependencies must be assessed by the program manager. These include all of the listed choices.

157. D: The perform integrated change control (PICC) forum serves as a time and place to assess and decide proposed changes to key parts of the project plan. This forum ensures the proposals are evaluated for how they will affect the project. It also serves to manage change and prevent miscommunications and errors in project outcomes.

158. A: A clear problem statement includes objective descriptors of the problem the team must overcome. Truth is gained through valid objective data; over-broad wording does not clearly state the true scale of the problem. The statement must align with the objectives listed in the charter and must avoid listing premature solutions. Customer-focused problem statements are common in continuous improvement projects such as lean and six sigma.

159. D: The work breakdown structure is the tool that facilitates deconstruction of the scope into smaller and more manageable activities.

160. D: Many approaches are available to perform corrective and preventive actions when facing issues in the project activity phases. Deference of these actions not wise because many issues will likely have a negative impact to the outcomes and performance of the project.

161. C: Changes made to project systems as the result of the perform integrated change control (PICC) process include updates to the project management plan or its sub-plans, formal approved change requests that prompt baseline, or document updates elsewhere in the project system.

162. C: A professional agreement among multiple parties that describes the rationale, scope, objectives, deliverables, and stakeholders for a project gives the project manager a tool to keep all involved parties committed to a common purpose. The charter, therefore, is a reference point for continued authority for the project manager.

163. B: Each stakeholder has different level of investment into the project. Each may require different data or information in communications, although many will want similar information as others. Mapping the different preferences and having a clear plan of execution on communication will best achieve those needs. The specific communication strategies for each stakeholder is added to the communications management plan.

164. B: Dormancy, urgency, and proximity represent risks focused on time. Dormancy means that there is a period between risk occurrence and risk detection. Urgency implies that it is a timeframe between risk occurrence and implementing a solution. Proximity refers to a timeframe between risk occurrence and impact to meeting project objectives. Other examples relate to ability to control risks and the social impact of the risks in the project.

165. D: The risk register serves as the location to compile threats, weaknesses, and opportunities observed from prior projects and during current projects. Risks can be either negative or positive in potential impact.

166. A: The risk breakdown structure and the PESTLE analysis are examples of prompt lists. Prompt lists are useful reference lists of known risk categories to the project team

167. B: At times of project professional and stakeholder disagreement, interpersonal skills such as conflict management, facilitation, and meeting management are generally the project manager's most effective tools.

168. C: The situation described in the question reflects on-demand scheduling. The progression of further activities depends on marketplace demands. When demand is low, activity stalls. When demand is high, activity spikes. Throughput capacity is essential to manage the ebb and flow of this model.

169. A: The three hierarchical breakdowns of resources among project activities are organizational, work, and resource. These account for the usage of persons and resources as well as the activities needed to complete the project.

170. A: Classification of the stakeholders in a register begins with documenting stakeholder vitals such as names and contact information. The register then must include relative power and influence assessments for each stakeholder to help in prioritization. The third component includes assessment information such as key requirements and project life cycle relevance for each stakeholder. These main components support effective stakeholder prioritization.

171. A: Common traits of persons demonstrating high emotional intelligence include: having a vision, empathy toward others, integrity, respect, systems thinking, and a focus on what matters most.

172. A: The described complaints from stakeholders explain that any additional use of resources does not shorten the activity duration. This implies that diminishing returns are present. As more resources are applied, their effectiveness in reducing activity duration or achieving results is lost. The project manager must revisit the strategy to overcome diminishing returns in the schedule management plan.

173. A: The most relevant choices of those provided are the external environmental factors and internal process assets. The other choices are not inherently relevant to the charter development.

174. D: Three critical elements to the team performance monitoring include net competencies by the entire team, assignment performance data, and team turnover rate. Measures of team solidarity may also be used. These measures best allow the project manager to evaluate and optimize human resources, behaviors, and skills in the project.

175. B: Dependency relationships are characterized by two dimensions. First, the dimension of proximity is reflected as either internal or external (or even some distribution between the two).

The second dimension reflects the degree of obligation of an activity—mandatory or optional. The permutations of these four classifications determines if or how the project team can exert control and correction over variances to the schedule. These factors determine activity dependencies, limitations to adjusting activities influences resource management, and schedule control.

176. A: The best choice is the resource estimation package—similar to a cost budget. This tool supports planning for quantity, type, and support needed at each scheduled activity. The basis for estimates analysis is a subelement of the estimation package and only outlines risks, ranges, and methods to reach the estimations. The resource breakdown structure reflects accurate and specific quantities and resources needed to complete each activity in its smallest actionable form.

177. A: The direct and manage project work process includes steps for executing the changes approved in the project integrated change control system. This is a process as defined in the project management professional body of knowledge.

178. D: The business case study is used to validate the economic feasibility of a project before the project is authorized or started. As the project planning phases move ahead, the business case validity keeps the project manager, team members, and stakeholders aligned to the benefits of the project. Elements of the business case are also seeded into the project charter and management plans in the project itself.

179. B: To ensure alignment of all team members, stakeholders, and organizational support, project work must not begin until the charter is fully approved.

180. C: The tailoring approach of stability is intended to address unstable scope requirements. Furthermore, stability approaches to tailoring are positive when it is yet unclear if a project will be an adaptive or agile design where scope is intended to change.

181. C: Triangular distribution equals the average of the most likely, the optimistic, and the pessimistic durations: $(10+7+16)/3 = 11$ days.

182. A: An effective project manager is able to blend the use of contextual (or business/market-related) skills with cognitive (or interpersonal) skills to overcome such complexity in the integration process.

183. C: The best answer in this question is to close the agreement between the parties and plan for future auditing to ensure the deliverable continues to meet expectations throughout its expected life. Similarly, a continuous improvement project would include a follow-up sustaining activity to ensure the improved state did not revert back to the original problems. Furthermore, a final report may be necessary from the project team to summarize the overall performance.

184. A: The project management plan serves as a summary road map for the preliminary project documents such as the charter and business case. Once compiled, the project manager or team is best able to communicate the vital details to the persons and organizations needed for project work.

185. B: Many types of data may be valuable to individual project teams when documenting on the issues log. Most importantly, the team should be capturing a clear description of the issue at hand. Also, the team will want to prioritize all issues on the log so that resources are used wisely, and the plan is kept on schedule and on budget. Last, where issues may impact stakeholders or customers, it is important to capture that information for each issue and communicate as needed to such stakeholders.

186. C: Reserve analysis is a risk management tool used to compute the ratio of resource reserves allocated for risk management compared to the amount of remaining risk at any given point in the activity execution.

187. C: The closure of the procurement control process implies that the agreement has ended between buyer and seller due to the completion of the contract or completion of the phase/project. Thus, a closed agreement indicates this end of the process. Final work performance information is delivered between parties, and the project organization likely updates any organizational process assets as a result of the completed agreement.

188. A: Quantitative risk analysis within the project management scope generally includes prioritizing the identified risks based on severity of impact and the likelihood of occurrence. The multiple of these two quantitative elements gives a risk scope that can prioritize which risks must be mitigated or controlled first.

189. D: Key to the stakeholder management plan is to capture the driving concerns of persons affected by the project outcome. These persons are affected by decisions made in the project and have an ownership in the project. Ownership may be financial or otherwise. Last, stakeholders often have something to contribute to the project whether that is financial, personnel, material resources, or information. These drivers are critical for consideration when creating the stakeholder plan.

190. D: The critical path represents the longest continuous set of activities from start to finish. This path is also the shortest duration needed to get the project completed, assuming other noncritical path activities get done in parallel as needed.

191. B: The main difference between these two approaches involves when resources are introduced. Waterfall life cycles are predictive with resources established early, whereas iterative cycles introduce resources at the appropriate time.

192. B: Deliverables represent tangible and intangible outputs of the project process that provide some benefit or satisfaction to the customer or stakeholder. Physical deliverables include a product or information. Intangible may include a provided or available service. Some deliverables can be a combination of two or more of these examples.

193. C: A replacement project manager is generally expected to continue the project progress from the former project manager. An accurately compiled issues list in the first portion of this project should have updated status (open/closed), a prioritization score, and details of performed or planned efforts to correct the issues. It is the responsibility of the project team to carry through with the relevant issues regardless of who is leading the project team.

194. A: Cost of quality accounting includes preventive costs, appraisal costs, internal failure costs, and external failure costs. The rework of drywall due to poor workmanship is an example of an internal failure cost. The parts and labor to repair the wall are incurred due to a quality failure. The government fines issued to a completed structure are external failure costs because failure identification often begins by a person or entity outside of the project organization.

195. D: Stakeholders have factors that hold importance to themselves regarding any project. The stakeholder analysis is a personal investigation into the factors that influence and drive the behavior of the project stakeholders. Outside factors such as demographics and marketplace performance are important to business case development but not significant to the stakeholder analysis.

196. C: Organizational process assets are tools that can be continuously used and improved by project teams in an organization. The lessons learned register, a type of asset, is a long-term history of learning from past projects used to help future project teams avoid similar issues.

197. B: At the close-out phase of the project, the ideal documents to review to strengthen future project performance include the issues log, lessons learned register, and the final project reports. These documents support improved skill in future projects.

198. C: The project manager failed to follow the change management process and alert key stakeholders of the proposed change before implementation. The stakeholders reflexively made financial decisions regarding the new reporting, regardless of the new accuracy of the reporting.

199. B: Designing quality into the process from the start using requirements capture, quality monitoring methods, and control tools would push efforts and costs toward prevention, not failure. A quality management system with these elements is ideal.

200. A: The project manager does not appear to understand what the true root cause of the mistake was. Discovering the root cause with a tool such as the 5 Why will lead the team to implement the right preventive measures. 5 Why analysis asks three to five rounds of why questions to dig into the underlying reasons for the problem. The other choices are quality tools but not applicable when discovering root causes.

How to Overcome Test Anxiety

Just the thought of taking a test is enough to make most people a little nervous. A test is an important event that can have a long-term impact on your future, so it's important to take it seriously and it's natural to feel anxious about performing well. But just because anxiety is normal, that doesn't mean that it's helpful in test taking, or that you should simply accept it as part of your life. Anxiety can have a variety of effects. These effects can be mild, like making you feel slightly nervous, or severe, like blocking your ability to focus or remember even a simple detail.

If you experience test anxiety—whether severe or mild—it's important to know how to beat it. To discover this, first you need to understand what causes test anxiety.

Causes of Test Anxiety

While we often think of anxiety as an uncontrollable emotional state, it can actually be caused by simple, practical things. One of the most common causes of test anxiety is that a person does not feel adequately prepared for their test. This feeling can be the result of many different issues such as poor study habits or lack of organization, but the most common culprit is time management. Starting to study too late, failing to organize your study time to cover all of the material, or being distracted while you study will mean that you're not well prepared for the test. This may lead to cramming the night before, which will cause you to be physically and mentally exhausted for the test. Poor time management also contributes to feelings of stress, fear, and hopelessness as you realize you are not well prepared but don't know what to do about it.

Other times, test anxiety is not related to your preparation for the test but comes from unresolved fear. This may be a past failure on a test, or poor performance on tests in general. It may come from comparing yourself to others who seem to be performing better or from the stress of living up to expectations. Anxiety may be driven by fears of the future—how failure on this test would affect your educational and career goals. These fears are often completely irrational, but they can still negatively impact your test performance.

Review Video: 3 Reasons You Have Test Anxiety
Visit mometrix.com/academy and enter code: 428468

Elements of Test Anxiety

As mentioned earlier, test anxiety is considered to be an emotional state, but it has physical and mental components as well. Sometimes you may not even realize that you are suffering from test anxiety until you notice the physical symptoms. These can include trembling hands, rapid heartbeat, sweating, nausea, and tense muscles. Extreme anxiety may lead to fainting or vomiting. Obviously, any of these symptoms can have a negative impact on testing. It is important to recognize them as soon as they begin to occur so that you can address the problem before it damages your performance.

Review Video: 3 Ways to Tell You Have Test Anxiety
Visit mometrix.com/academy and enter code: 927847

The mental components of test anxiety include trouble focusing and inability to remember learned information. During a test, your mind is on high alert, which can help you recall information and stay focused for an extended period of time. However, anxiety interferes with your mind's natural processes, causing you to blank out, even on the questions you know well. The strain of testing during anxiety makes it difficult to stay focused, especially on a test that may take several hours. Extreme anxiety can take a huge mental toll, making it difficult not only to recall test information but even to understand the test questions or pull your thoughts together.

Review Video: How Test Anxiety Affects Memory
Visit mometrix.com/academy and enter code: 609003

Effects of Test Anxiety

Test anxiety is like a disease—if left untreated, it will get progressively worse. Anxiety leads to poor performance, and this reinforces the feelings of fear and failure, which in turn lead to poor performances on subsequent tests. It can grow from a mild nervousness to a crippling condition. If allowed to progress, test anxiety can have a big impact on your schooling, and consequently on your future.

Test anxiety can spread to other parts of your life. Anxiety on tests can become anxiety in any stressful situation, and blanking on a test can turn into panicking in a job situation. But fortunately, you don't have to let anxiety rule your testing and determine your grades. There are a number of relatively simple steps you can take to move past anxiety and function normally on a test and in the rest of life.

Review Video: How Test Anxiety Impacts Your Grades
Visit mometrix.com/academy and enter code: 939819

Physical Steps for Beating Test Anxiety

While test anxiety is a serious problem, the good news is that it can be overcome. It doesn't have to control your ability to think and remember information. While it may take time, you can begin taking steps today to beat anxiety.

Just as your first hint that you may be struggling with anxiety comes from the physical symptoms, the first step to treating it is also physical. Rest is crucial for having a clear, strong mind. If you are tired, it is much easier to give in to anxiety. But if you establish good sleep habits, your body and mind will be ready to perform optimally, without the strain of exhaustion. Additionally, sleeping well helps you to retain information better, so you're more likely to recall the answers when you see the test questions.

Getting good sleep means more than going to bed on time. It's important to allow your brain time to relax. Take study breaks from time to time so it doesn't get overworked, and don't study right before bed. Take time to rest your mind before trying to rest your body, or you may find it difficult to fall asleep.

Review Video: **The Importance of Sleep for Your Brain**
Visit mometrix.com/academy and enter code: 319338

Along with sleep, other aspects of physical health are important in preparing for a test. Good nutrition is vital for good brain function. Sugary foods and drinks may give a burst of energy but this burst is followed by a crash, both physically and emotionally. Instead, fuel your body with protein and vitamin-rich foods.

Also, drink plenty of water. Dehydration can lead to headaches and exhaustion, especially if your brain is already under stress from the rigors of the test. Particularly if your test is a long one, drink water during the breaks. And if possible, take an energy-boosting snack to eat between sections.

Review Video: **How Diet Can Affect your Mood**
Visit mometrix.com/academy and enter code: 624317

Along with sleep and diet, a third important part of physical health is exercise. Maintaining a steady workout schedule is helpful, but even taking 5-minute study breaks to walk can help get your blood pumping faster and clear your head. Exercise also releases endorphins, which contribute to a positive feeling and can help combat test anxiety.

When you nurture your physical health, you are also contributing to your mental health. If your body is healthy, your mind is much more likely to be healthy as well. So take time to rest, nourish your body with healthy food and water, and get moving as much as possible. Taking these physical steps will make you stronger and more able to take the mental steps necessary to overcome test anxiety.

Review Video: **How to Stay Healthy and Prevent Test Anxiety**
Visit mometrix.com/academy and enter code: 877894

Mental Steps for Beating Test Anxiety

Working on the mental side of test anxiety can be more challenging, but as with the physical side, there are clear steps you can take to overcome it. As mentioned earlier, test anxiety often stems from lack of preparation, so the obvious solution is to prepare for the test. Effective studying may be the most important weapon you have for beating test anxiety, but you can and should employ several other mental tools to combat fear.

First, boost your confidence by reminding yourself of past success—tests or projects that you aced. If you're putting as much effort into preparing for this test as you did for those, there's no reason you should expect to fail here. Work hard to prepare; then trust your preparation.

Second, surround yourself with encouraging people. It can be helpful to find a study group, but be sure that the people you're around will encourage a positive attitude. If you spend time with others who are anxious or cynical, this will only contribute to your own anxiety. Look for others who are motivated to study hard from a desire to succeed, not from a fear of failure.

Third, reward yourself. A test is physically and mentally tiring, even without anxiety, and it can be helpful to have something to look forward to. Plan an activity following the test, regardless of the outcome, such as going to a movie or getting ice cream.

When you are taking the test, if you find yourself beginning to feel anxious, remind yourself that you know the material. Visualize successfully completing the test. Then take a few deep, relaxing breaths and return to it. Work through the questions carefully but with confidence, knowing that you are capable of succeeding.

Developing a healthy mental approach to test taking will also aid in other areas of life. Test anxiety affects more than just the actual test—it can be damaging to your mental health and even contribute to depression. It's important to beat test anxiety before it becomes a problem for more than testing.

Review Video: Test Anxiety and Depression
Visit mometrix.com/academy and enter code: 904704

Study Strategy

Being prepared for the test is necessary to combat anxiety, but what does being prepared look like? You may study for hours on end and still not feel prepared. What you need is a strategy for test prep. The next few pages outline our recommended steps to help you plan out and conquer the challenge of preparation.

Step 1: Scope Out the Test

Learn everything you can about the format (multiple choice, essay, etc.) and what will be on the test. Gather any study materials, course outlines, or sample exams that may be available. Not only will this help you to prepare, but knowing what to expect can help to alleviate test anxiety.

Step 2: Map Out the Material

Look through the textbook or study guide and make note of how many chapters or sections it has. Then divide these over the time you have. For example, if a book has 15 chapters and you have five days to study, you need to cover three chapters each day. Even better, if you have the time, leave an extra day at the end for overall review after you have gone through the material in depth.

If time is limited, you may need to prioritize the material. Look through it and make note of which sections you think you already have a good grasp on, and which need review. While you are studying, skim quickly through the familiar sections and take more time on the challenging parts. Write out your plan so you don't get lost as you go. Having a written plan also helps you feel more in control of the study, so anxiety is less likely to arise from feeling overwhelmed at the amount to cover.

Step 3: Gather Your Tools

Decide what study method works best for you. Do you prefer to highlight in the book as you study and then go back over the highlighted portions? Or do you type out notes of the important information? Or is it helpful to make flashcards that you can carry with you? Assemble the pens, index cards, highlighters, post-it notes, and any other materials you may need so you won't be distracted by getting up to find things while you study.

If you're having a hard time retaining the information or organizing your notes, experiment with different methods. For example, try color-coding by subject with colored pens, highlighters, or post-it notes. If you learn better by hearing, try recording yourself reading your notes so you can listen while in the car, working out, or simply sitting at your desk. Ask a friend to quiz you from your flashcards, or try teaching someone the material to solidify it in your mind.

Step 4: Create Your Environment

It's important to avoid distractions while you study. This includes both the obvious distractions like visitors and the subtle distractions like an uncomfortable chair (or a too-comfortable couch that makes you want to fall asleep). Set up the best study environment possible: good lighting and a comfortable work area. If background music helps you focus, you may want to turn it on, but otherwise keep the room quiet. If you are using a computer to take notes, be sure you don't have any other windows open, especially applications like social media, games, or anything else that could distract you. Silence your phone and turn off notifications. Be sure to keep water close by so you stay hydrated while you study (but avoid unhealthy drinks and snacks).

Also, take into account the best time of day to study. Are you freshest first thing in the morning? Try to set aside some time then to work through the material. Is your mind clearer in the afternoon or evening? Schedule your study session then. Another method is to study at the same time of day that you will take the test, so that your brain gets used to working on the material at that time and will be ready to focus at test time.

STEP 5: STUDY!

Once you have done all the study preparation, it's time to settle into the actual studying. Sit down, take a few moments to settle your mind so you can focus, and begin to follow your study plan. Don't give in to distractions or let yourself procrastinate. This is your time to prepare so you'll be ready to fearlessly approach the test. Make the most of the time and stay focused.

Of course, you don't want to burn out. If you study too long you may find that you're not retaining the information very well. Take regular study breaks. For example, taking five minutes out of every hour to walk briskly, breathing deeply and swinging your arms, can help your mind stay fresh.

As you get to the end of each chapter or section, it's a good idea to do a quick review. Remind yourself of what you learned and work on any difficult parts. When you feel that you've mastered the material, move on to the next part. At the end of your study session, briefly skim through your notes again.

But while review is helpful, cramming last minute is NOT. If at all possible, work ahead so that you won't need to fit all your study into the last day. Cramming overloads your brain with more information than it can process and retain, and your tired mind may struggle to recall even previously learned information when it is overwhelmed with last-minute study. Also, the urgent nature of cramming and the stress placed on your brain contribute to anxiety. You'll be more likely to go to the test feeling unprepared and having trouble thinking clearly.

So don't cram, and don't stay up late before the test, even just to review your notes at a leisurely pace. Your brain needs rest more than it needs to go over the information again. In fact, plan to finish your studies by noon or early afternoon the day before the test. Give your brain the rest of the day to relax or focus on other things, and get a good night's sleep. Then you will be fresh for the test and better able to recall what you've studied.

STEP 6: TAKE A PRACTICE TEST

Many courses offer sample tests, either online or in the study materials. This is an excellent resource to check whether you have mastered the material, as well as to prepare for the test format and environment.

Check the test format ahead of time: the number of questions, the type (multiple choice, free response, etc.), and the time limit. Then create a plan for working through them. For example, if you have 30 minutes to take a 60-question test, your limit is 30 seconds per question. Spend less time on the questions you know well so that you can take more time on the difficult ones.

If you have time to take several practice tests, take the first one open book, with no time limit. Work through the questions at your own pace and make sure you fully understand them. Gradually work up to taking a test under test conditions: sit at a desk with all study materials put away and set a timer. Pace yourself to make sure you finish the test with time to spare and go back to check your answers if you have time.

After each test, check your answers. On the questions you missed, be sure you understand why you missed them. Did you misread the question (tests can use tricky wording)? Did you forget the information? Or was it something you hadn't learned? Go back and study any shaky areas that the practice tests reveal.

Taking these tests not only helps with your grade, but also aids in combating test anxiety. If you're already used to the test conditions, you're less likely to worry about it, and working through tests until you're scoring well gives you a confidence boost. Go through the practice tests until you feel comfortable, and then you can go into the test knowing that you're ready for it.

Test Tips

On test day, you should be confident, knowing that you've prepared well and are ready to answer the questions. But aside from preparation, there are several test day strategies you can employ to maximize your performance.

First, as stated before, get a good night's sleep the night before the test (and for several nights before that, if possible). Go into the test with a fresh, alert mind rather than staying up late to study.

Try not to change too much about your normal routine on the day of the test. It's important to eat a nutritious breakfast, but if you normally don't eat breakfast at all, consider eating just a protein bar. If you're a coffee drinker, go ahead and have your normal coffee. Just make sure you time it so that the caffeine doesn't wear off right in the middle of your test. Avoid sugary beverages, and drink enough water to stay hydrated but not so much that you need a restroom break 10 minutes into the test. If your test isn't first thing in the morning, consider going for a walk or doing a light workout before the test to get your blood flowing.

Allow yourself enough time to get ready, and leave for the test with plenty of time to spare so you won't have the anxiety of scrambling to arrive in time. Another reason to be early is to select a good seat. It's helpful to sit away from doors and windows, which can be distracting. Find a good seat, get out your supplies, and settle your mind before the test begins.

When the test begins, start by going over the instructions carefully, even if you already know what to expect. Make sure you avoid any careless mistakes by following the directions.

Then begin working through the questions, pacing yourself as you've practiced. If you're not sure on an answer, don't spend too much time on it, and don't let it shake your confidence. Either skip it and come back later, or eliminate as many wrong answers as possible and guess among the remaining ones. Don't dwell on these questions as you continue—put them out of your mind and focus on what lies ahead.

Be sure to read all of the answer choices, even if you're sure the first one is the right answer. Sometimes you'll find a better one if you keep reading. But don't second-guess yourself if you do immediately know the answer. Your gut instinct is usually right. Don't let test anxiety rob you of the information you know.

If you have time at the end of the test (and if the test format allows), go back and review your answers. Be cautious about changing any, since your first instinct tends to be correct, but make sure you didn't misread any of the questions or accidentally mark the wrong answer choice. Look over any you skipped and make an educated guess.

At the end, leave the test feeling confident. You've done your best, so don't waste time worrying about your performance or wishing you could change anything. Instead, celebrate the successful completion of this test. And finally, use this test to learn how to deal with anxiety even better next time.

Review Video: 5 Tips to Beat Test Anxiety
Visit mometrix.com/academy and enter code: 570656

Important Qualification

Not all anxiety is created equal. If your test anxiety is causing major issues in your life beyond the classroom or testing center, or if you are experiencing troubling physical symptoms related to your anxiety, it may be a sign of a serious physiological or psychological condition. If this sounds like your situation, we strongly encourage you to seek professional help.

Thank You

We at Mometrix would like to extend our heartfelt thanks to you, our friend and patron, for allowing us to play a part in your journey. It is a privilege to serve people from all walks of life who are unified in their commitment to building the best future they can for themselves.

The preparation you devote to these important testing milestones may be the most valuable educational opportunity you have for making a real difference in your life. We encourage you to put your heart into it—that feeling of succeeding, overcoming, and yes, conquering will be well worth the hours you've invested.

We want to hear your story, your struggles and your successes, and if you see any opportunities for us to improve our materials so we can help others even more effectively in the future, please share that with us as well. **The team at Mometrix would be absolutely thrilled to hear from you!** So please, send us an email (support@mometrix.com) and let's stay in touch.

If you'd like some additional help, check out these other resources we offer for your exam:
http://mometrixflashcards.com/PMP

Additional Bonus Material

Due to our efforts to try to keep this book to a manageable length, we've created a link that will give you access to all of your additional bonus material.

Please visit https://www.mometrix.com/bonus948/pmp to access the information.

Made in the USA
Las Vegas, NV
11 February 2022